IBERIAN AND LATIN AMERICAN STUDIES

The Novels of José Saramago

IBERIAN AND LATIN AMERICAN STUDIES

The Novels of José Saramago

Echoes from the Past, Pathways into the Future

DAVID G. FRIER

UNIVERSITY OF WALES PRESS
CARDIFF
2007

British Library Cataloguing-in-Publication Data
A catalogue record for this book is available from the British Library.

ISBN 978-0-7083-2015-0

Typeset by Columns Design Ltd, Reading
Printed in Great Britain by Antony Rowe Ltd, Chippenham, Wiltshire

To Wendy,
Minha Companheira de Jangada

Permissions

The author gratefully acknowledges the permissions granted by Harcourt for reproduction of quotations from the English translations of *Baltasar and Blimunda*and *The Cave*worldwide and from other novels by José Saramago in North America only. He also acknowledges the permissions granted by Random House for reproduction of the same quotations from all novels by José Saramago (other than those from *Baltasar and Blimunda* and *The Cave*) in the UK, the Republic of Ireland and the British Commonwealth (with the exception of Canada). He would also like to thank José Saramago himself and Editorial Caminho in Lisbon for permission to reproduce quotations in Portuguese from the novels and other works of José Saramago, as well as Margaret Jull Costa for her consent to use excerpts from her translations of *All the Names, The Cave* and *The Double.* Finally, he gratefully acknowledges the permission given by Juan Sager for reproduction of quotations from the English translations prepared by Giovanni Pontiero of *Baltasar and Blimunda, The Year of the Death of Ricardo Reis, The Stone Raft, History of the Siege of Lisbon, The Gospel According to Jesus Christ* and *Blindness.*

The author and publisher gratefully acknowledge the permission granted by the following to reprint:

Extracts from *The Cave* and *Baltasar and Blimunda* by José Saramago, published by Harvill Press. Reprinted by permission of the Random House Group Ltd.

Excerpts from *The Year of the Death of Ricardo Reis* by José Saramago
Copyright © José Saramago
Editorial Caminho, SARL Lisbon, 1984, English translation by Giovanni Pontiero
Copyright © 1991 by Harcourt, Inc., reprinted by permission of Harcourt, Inc.

Contents

Series Editors' Foreword xi

Acknowledgements xiii

Abbreviations xv

Introduction 1

1. José Saramago, Nobel Laureate 1
2. A Voice Untamed 9
3. Portuguese History and Tradition 11
4. Literary, Political and Cultural Context of Saramago's Novels 16

Notes 24

Chapter One
Privilege and Exclusion: *Levantado do Chão* and *Memorial do Convento* **31**

1. Introduction 31
2. Social and Economic Relations 32
3. Domingos, João and António Mau-Tempo: The Extinction of a Name, or the Inexorable Rise of a Family? 44
4. The Suppression of Resistance 48
5. Alienation and Natural Processes 52
6. Hierarchies of Power 68

7. The Illusion of Permanence and the Potential for Change 78

Notes 90

Chapter Two
'Além da conversa das mulheres, são os sonhos que seguram o mundo na sua órbita': Centripetal and Centrifugal Forces 111

1. Introduction 111

2. 'No' News is Good News: *História do Cerco de Lisboa* and *O Evangelho Segundo Jesus Cristo* 113

3. From the Plough Buried in the Sand to the Hidden Flying-Machine: Opportunities for Escape 133

4. From Blimunda to the Doctor's Wife: Gramsci and the Transformation of Portugal 152

Notes 166

Conclusion: Death, the Ultimate Injustice; Love, the Ultimate Triumph 175

1. *As Intermitências da Morte*: Skeletons and Moths 175

2. Ricardo Reis and the Stasis of True Death 183

3. Oh Death, Where is thy Sting? 196

Notes 208

Bibliography 215

Index 227

Series Editors' Foreword

Over recent decades, the traditional 'languages and literatures' model in Spanish departments in universities in the United Kingdom has been superceded by a contextual, interdisciplinary and 'area studies' approach to the study of the culture, history, society and politics of the Hispanic and Lusophone worlds – categories which extend far beyond the confines of the Iberian Peninsula, not only to Latin America but also to Spanish-speaking and Lusophone Africa.

In response to these dynamic trends in research priorities and curriculum development, this series is designed to present both disciplinary and interdisciplinary research within the general field of Iberian and Latin American Studies, particularly studies which explore all aspects of **Cultural Production** (*inter alia* literature, film, music, dance, sport) in Spanish, Portuguese, Basque, Catalan, Galician and the indigenous languages of Latin America. The series also aims to publish research on the **History and Politics** of Hispanic and Lusophone worlds, both at the level of region and that of the nation-state, as well as on **Cultural Studies** which explore the shifting terrains of gender, sexual, racial and postcolonial identities in those same regions.

Acknowledgements

The preparation of this work was made possible in large part thanks to a Semester's study leave in 2000 funded by the Arts and Humanities Research Board, whose support for my work I gratefully acknowledge. I am also grateful for the matching semester's leave funded by the University of Leeds, which allowed me to set this project under way.

My ideas were stimulated greatly by the Quarter which I spent teaching a graduate seminar on Saramago's novels at UCLA in the Spring of 2000. I gratefully acknowledge the invitation received from Professor Randal Johnson to teach at UCLA, as well as the stimulating debate, insightful observations, and cheerful enthusiasm and goodwill displayed by the outstanding students who took this course. I also gratefully acknowledge the insights and fresh perspectives offered by many excellent students in Leeds over the years, especially by my current research student, Rhian Atkin.

In Leeds, I received constant support and encouragement from Professor Paul Garner and my closest colleagues in Portuguese, Stephanie Dennison, Lisa Shaw (now at the University of Liverpool), and Luís Varela, formerly *Leitor* of the Instituto Camões in Leeds.

Amongst other British colleagues, I would like to thank Mark Sabine (of the University of Nottingham) for allowing me to read a copy of his very insightful Ph.D. thesis, and to recognize the outstanding work of the late Giovanni Pontiero, Saramago's first English translator, who gave me great encouragement in my early forays into the mysterious but endlessly stimulating world of Saramago's fiction.

Others who have contributed to the completion of this work in a variety of ways include Ellen Sapega, Adriana Martins, Bob Potter, Larry Friedman, Maria Eduarda Vassallo-McGeoch, Mary-Lou Daniel, Anna Klobucka, and, of course, José Saramago himself. My apologies if I have inadvertently omitted any others who should be included in this list.

Finally, I would like to thank Sarah Lewis and her colleagues at the University of Wales Press for their hard work, patience and positive spirit in the preparation of this volume, and, last but not least, my wife Wendy, who has read my work and commented on it, given support and encouragement when these have been needed, and who has tolerated her husband's years of near-obsession with flying machines, stone rafts, and murky archives with endless good humour.

David Frier
Leeds
8 June 2006

Abbreviations

The following abbreviated titles have been used within the text to refer to Saramago's major works:

Ano = *O Ano da Morte de Ricardo Reis*

Baltasar = *Baltasar and Blimunda*

Cadernos = *Cadernos de Lanzarote: Diário*

Cave = *The Cave*

Caverna = *A Caverna*

Cegueira = *Ensaio sobre a Cegueira*

Conto = *O Conto da Ilha Desconhecida*

Double = *The Double*

Evangelho = *O Evangelho Segundo Jesus Cristo*

Gospel = *The Gospel According to Jesus Christ*

História = *História do Cerco de Lisboa*

History = *History of the Siege of Lisbon*

Homem = *O Homem Duplicado*

Intermitências = *As Intermitências da Morte*

Jangada = *A Jangada de Pedra*

Journey = *Journey to Portugal*

Levantado = *Levantado do Chão*

Livro = *Que Farei com Este Livro?*

Lucidez = *Ensaio sobre a Lucidez*

Manual = *Manual de Pintura e Caligrafia*

Memorial = *Memorial do Convento*

Names = *All the Names*

Objecto = *Objecto Quase*

Painting = *Manual of Painting and Calligraphy*

Raft = *The Stone Raft*

Todos = *Todos os Nomes*

Viagem = *Viagem a Portugal*

Year = *The Year of the Death of Ricardo Reis*

Reference to the text has been made primarily to the original in Portuguese. Where quotations are made from these works, English translations follow in parentheses, with an indication of the page numbers for the passage reproduced from the published translations (where there is no published translation, as is the case of *Levantado* and *Intermitências*, for example, I have supplied my own). I have also translated into English all quotations taken from secondary sources. Quotations from other literary authors, particularly Camões and Pessoa, are presented bilingually; again, where no published translation has been indicated, the English version is my own.

DGF
February 2006

Introduction

1. José Saramago, Nobel Laureate

On October 8 1998, the Nobel Prize in literature was awarded to the Portuguese novelist José Saramago. Even before this award, however, Saramago was a regular recipient of literary prizes in Portugal and further afield. These included two awards from the Portuguese PEN Club; the *Grande Prémio* of the Portuguese Writers' Association of 1992; the *Prémio Camões* of 1995 (awarded annually to an outstanding writer in Portuguese, in recognition of lifetime achievement); two awards for theatrical works; four literary awards from Italy; and the Foreign Fiction Award of the British newspaper *The Independent* for the best novel translated into English in 1993, *The Year of the Death of Ricardo Reis.*[1]

As recently as 1980, however (when Saramago was already in his late fifties), the future Nobel Laureate was virtually unknown even in his own country. This remarkable change in fortunes was due in part to chance circumstances and in part to the author's ability to work hard in developing a new and original voice in Portuguese fiction, which combines something of the neo-realists' reflection on the state of the nation with a self-critical awareness, largely absent during the dictatorship, that simple, programmatic solutions such as those propounded by underground resistance movements would be unlikely to heal fully the country's ills, as well as with a sensitivity to the fact that human well-being revolves around more personal and less clearly definable issues than political and economic structures in isolation. The single-mindedness with which he devoted himself to this task should be no surprise, however, as Saramago had already had to display this quality in order to break into the world of letters in the first place.

Indeed, the author could easily have been lost to literature altogether. His birth (in November 1922) and early childhood in poverty in rural Portugal would normally have led to an adult life of manual agricultural work (similar to that undertaken by his sympathetically portrayed João Mau-Tempo in his *Levantado*), and, even when his family moved to Lisbon, their low income and modest means required him to attend a vocational school rather than a more academic institution, so that there was no question of his going on to advanced formal study at university level. Although his first job was as a mechanic, however, the all-round education which he received gave him a taste for the life of letters which developed prodigiously in later life; and Saramago has since recalled that even as a youngster he read the poems of a writer named Ricardo Reis, who he believed at the time to be a real person (rather than a poetic device invented by Fernando Pessoa) and who later came instead to be adopted and adapted into one of his own most memorable fictional creations.[2]

His early writing consisted of an unremarkable novel entitled *Terra do Pecado* and another, *A Clarabóia* (of 1949), which has never been published. *Terra do Pecado* follows in the traditions of neo-realist fiction which dominated Portuguese prose in the middle decades of the twentieth century and has also been compared to *O Primo Basílio* by the nineteenth-century writer Eça de Queirós, as both novels incorporate a motif of blackmail of an apparently respectable woman by her maidservant. In his subsequent work (most notably in *Levantado*, but also in *Ano* and *Evangelho*), Saramago was to develop much more fruitfully the question of power relationships inherent in this early work.

After that, it was not until the 1960s that Saramago's name returned to the bookshelves with two volumes of poetry, *Provavelmente Alegria* (1966) and *Os Poemas Possíveis* (1970), which did not earn him any more than a passing mention in Lopes and Saraiva's *História de Literatura Portuguesa*.[3] The 1970s saw the journalist (as Saramago now was) produce *inter alia* a regular output of newspaper chronicles (later published in four books), a collection of short stories (*Objecto*, of 1978), and in 1977 his first major novel, *Manual*. Horácio Costa, the most reliable authority on Saramago's early literary endeavours, sees all of these works as containing the seeds of what was later to become the most prestigious novelistic output in recent Portuguese literary history: although there is evidence in texts such as *O Ano de 1993* of a search for a new style of expression, it is clear that many of the recurrent themes, leitmotifs and images of successful novels such as *Cegueira* and *Jangada* are already evident in this period.[4]

It is ironic that when success finally came to Saramago, it was indirectly the result of a dramatic historical upheaval similar to those which provide the starting point for many of his novels. Just as the Baltasar of *Memorial* finds major changes in his life being dictated to him by historical events, so in his middle age Saramago suddenly found himself out of work after being sacked from his job as editor of the Lisbon newspaper *Diário de Notícias* in 1975, amidst the ideological recriminations as Portugal rebounded from fascism to Marxism and then to market capitalism.

Lacking alternative employment, Saramago dedicated himself full-time to writing, spending several months in a rural community in the Alentejo region, thus returning to surroundings similar to those of his own family. The stories and experiences of popular struggle against the vested interests of property owners, a corrupt clergy and an insensitive state which he recorded in that region (well known as one of the traditional bedrocks of communist support and activism in Portugal) were to form the substance of the novel which first brought him major public recognition, *Levantado*, in 1980.

This novel also marked the adoption of a style of writing based on an avowedly oral technique which adopts only periods and commas as punctuation,[5] but also making use of this eccentric manner of sentence formation in order to seamlessly blend in with the basic plot endless instances of narratorial commentary on the events recounted (sometimes humorous in tone), anachronistic comments, narrative perspectives which shift between internal focalization on individual characters and sometimes rambling commentary on events which take place both within the fiction and in other contexts, theoretical alternative plot developments, and frequent reference to the important distinction in discourse between signifier and signified, that is between the reality of the Alentejo in which Saramago lived for a number of months and the fragile web of words which gives it some illusion of reality to us as readers. As Saramago himself writes in his comments on the dust jacket of the novel:

> E o meu sonho foi o de poder dizer deste livro, quando o terminasse: 'Isto é o Alentejo'. Dos sonhos, porém, acordamos todos, e agora eis-me não diante do sonho realizado, mas da concreta e possível forma do sonho. Por isso me limitarei a escrever: 'Isto é um livro sobre o Alentejo'.[6]

> [And it was my dream to be able to say of this book when I completed it 'This is the Alentejo'. However we all awake from our dreams, so that what I now find myself facing is not that dream come true, but the only concrete form which that dream could possibly take. Thus it is that all I will say is 'This is a book about the Alentejo'.]

Saramago's recognition here of language and discourse as the medium which both reveals and, simultaneously and inevitably, obscures the reality of the Alentejo is, in fact, used to great effect in this and other novels, and it appears that this was, to some extent at least, a conscious decision taken on the basis of his experience of living in the Alentejo and mixing with a population with limited formal education. This is revealed in discussions with Reis about the origins of an oral style designed to give a degree of apparent autonomy to the narrative and the characters within it:

> I ended up sitting down to write the book, I knew what I wanted to say, but I wasn't satisfied with it, there was some kind of block about writing the book; but I began to write it, I got to page twenty-something, and suddenly . . . I found that I was writing in the manner that I use now.[7]

These comments are expanded on (and contradicted in one point of detail) in another passage reproduced by Fernandes, where Saramago writes:

> Suddenly (and this is the wonderful part) I was already at the twentieth section of the book and not very happy with it, when I realized how it could be written. I realized I would only be able to write it if I did it as if I were telling it. This is not done by putting so-called oral language into writing, because that is impossible, but by introducing into my writing a mechanism of apparent spontaneity, apparent digression and apparent disorganisation in the discourse. I say 'apparent' since I am only too well aware of the work it gave me to ensure that it turned out like that.[8]

It is noticeable that the writer places considerable emphasis on the word 'apparent' here: sophisticated intellectual city-dwellers (even an autodidact such as Saramago) cannot easily unlearn all the tricks of language with which they are familiar.

For if, on the one hand, the seamless mingling of successive voices in one continual flow of language creates some confusion as to the correct attribution in a given context of any particular words to specific characters, or even to the ever-shifting figure of the narrator,[9] this aspect of his work also permits the confluence of voices growing up from the soil of the Alentejo in a way which was not generally countenanced by the educated, left-leaning city elite who wrote of the problems of rural Portugal in the 1940s and 1950s from the top-down perspective of classical neo-realism.

It is instructive to compare and contrast genuine spontaneous rustic language with Saramago's more polished attempts to imitate this voice. Seixo reproduces as a sample of the original rustic style which the novelist sought to imitate a copy of a letter which he received from one of his contacts in the region after he returned to Lisbon from the Alentejo, and there are certainly clear similarities between the smooth flow of this text and some passages from his novels. Firstly, the following is the letter from João Domingos Serra:

> Exmo Senhor Saramago,
>
> o escritor; Meu caro amigo è com toda a Sinseriedade que lhe agradeço o seu convite a participar, na, ida, a, Lisboa, assistir à festa fòclorica e, tambem, na prezensa, do meu muito amigo, mas á càsos que mandam mais que as leis e, entao me acontéce agora a mim pois a doença arrebatou-me para pior e, então foi-me impossivel cumprir ésta promèssa a que eu estáva indeciso queira-me desculpar com paciencia, mas em todo caso nao quèro faltar de todo, pois aì vai a minha filha mais vèlha para subestituir o meu lugar e pronta a responder às preguntas que lhes queira fazer a meu respeito, sêja nos conflitos mais agudos ou, nos mais normais da minha vida e, dos meus 10 filhos e minha esposa, o, Senhor sàbe, muito oubrigádo por tudo, receba um grande abraço e, à sua esposa, deste vosso muito amigo João Domingos Serra conresponde por mim a minha filha mais vèlha, Maria Perpètua Oliveira Serra.
>
> Adeus muito oubrigàdo
>
> J.D.S.[10]

> [Dear Mr. Saramago,
>
> To the writer: My dear friend, it is with total sincerity that I thank you for your invitation to go to Lisbon and take part in the folklore festival, and in your presence as my good friend, but sometimes circumstances force your hand more than the law, and so it is with me, since my health has got a lot worse, so it has turned out impossible for me to keep this promise although I thought hard about it, please put up with me and forgive me, and I won't be

> totally missing, since I'm sending my eldest daughter in my place, and she will answer any questions you want to ask about me, whether about the bitterest conflicts or the most banal things in my life, about my ten children and my wife. So, Sir, thank you so much for everything, have my best wishes, you and your wife, from me, João Domingos Serra, it's my youngest daughter Maria Perpètua Oliveira Serra who is writing this for me.
>
> Goodbye, and thank you very much,
>
> J.D.S.]

Compare this text with the seemingly effortless language of a passage such as the following one from *Ano*, which mixes varying registers, subject matters and voices in a continuous torrent of language:

> Fiados de Deus e Nossa Senhora desde Afonso Henriques à Grande Guerra, esta é a frase que persegue Ricardo Reis depois que voltou de Fátima, não se lembra se a terá lido em jornal ou em livro, se a ouviu em homilia ou discurso, se estaria na propaganda do Bovril, a forma fascina-o tanto quanto o sentido, é um dizer eloquente, estudado para mover os sentimentos e afervorar os corações, receita de sermão, além de ser, por sua expressão sentenciosa, prova irrefutável de que somos um povo eleito, outros houve no passado, outros haverá no futuro, mas nenhum por tanto tempo, oitocentos anos de fiança ininterrupta, de intimidade com as potências celestes, é verdade que chegámos atrasados à construção do quinto império, passou-nos adiante Mussolini, porém não nos escapará o sexto, ou o sétimo, é tudo uma questão de paciência, e essa temo-la nós, de nossa natural natureza. (*Ano*, p. 321)
>
> [Trusting in God and Our Blessed Lady from the time of Afonso Henriques to the Great War. This is the phrase that has haunted Ricardo Reis since his return from Fátima. He cannot recall whether he read it in a newspaper or a book, or whether he heard it in a sermon or speech, it may even have been in the advertisement for Bovril. The words fascinate him, the expression is eloquent and calculated to rouse passions and kindle hearts, for it proves that we are a chosen people. There have been other peoples in the past and there will be other peoples in the future, but there are none that have endured as long, eight hundred years of steadfast loyalty, of constant intimacy with the heavenly powers. It is true that we were slow in creating the fifth empire, that Mussolini forged ahead of us, but the sixth empire will not elude

> us, nor the seventh, all we need is patience, and patience is in our nature.] (*Year,* p. 277)

This passage, of course, displays considerable erudition, with references to religious devotion, Portuguese and international history, contemporary politics, and obscure passages of the Old Testament.[11] Yet its actual phrasing and construction are often popular in tone: the so-called 'theme-rheme' form of sentence construction is adopted twice ('Fiados de Deus e Nossa Senhora desde Afonso Henriques à Grande Guerra, esta é a frase . . . ' and 'é tudo uma questão de paciência, e essa temo-la nós'); it exploits popular alliterative phrasing ('de nossa natural natureza'); and, while the sentence itself is an extremely long one, its construction is based on a succession of parallel elements, with the subordinate clauses never extending more than one level below that of the principal clause, so that the impression of linguistic complexity initially given by the passage is not, in fact, borne out by a syntactic analysis. Regarding the specific question of punctuation, the sentence looks long to those trained in reading the more complex rules of normal practice, but, once observed from the perspective of treating periods and commas merely as markers of pauses in delivery, the passage is soon broken down into much shorter and more easily manageable 'sentences', in the same way as may also be said of the letter from João Domingos Serra.

However, any rewriting of Saramago's distinctive style in more conventional language (attempted, with unfortunate consequences, by the first published English translation of *Memorial*) effectively destroys the fluency and rhythm of the original, even if it preserves the literal meaning of the words.[12] In this sense it is valid to recognize Saramago's own claim that all that he writes is designed to be heard:

> All the characteristics of my current narrative technique (I would prefer to say my style) derive from one basic principle, according to which everything that is *said* is intended to be *heard*. By this I mean that I see myself as an oral narrator when I write, and that I write those words to be read as if they were being heard. Oral narrators do not use punctuation, they speak as if they were composing music, and they use the same materials as musicians: sounds and pauses, high notes and low notes, others shorter or longer.[13]

There is undoubtedly much in the passage reproduced from *Ano* above which is attributable to popular forms. However, it is clear that this is a passage written by an author familiar with rhetorical effects, such as the creation of emphasis through repetition of the same idea in different forms ('estudado para mover os sentimentos e afervorar os corações') and the importance of implicit parallels ('outros houve no passado, outros haverá no futuro'). The passage also slyly moves from opening with a relatively innocent word ('Fiados') to introduce a cognate ('fiança') with much more (economically) specific overtones later in the passage (in apparent justification of the fiscal prudence of the Salazar regime) before an ironic closure which reflects on the supposedly eternal patience which Salazar encouraged in the 'povo de brandos costumes' ('people of gentle ways') over which he ruled.[14] Yet only a close examination of this passage reveals the meticulous nature of its composition and discloses the studied linearity within the labyrinthine complexity apparent on the surface. Picchio correctly identifies narrative technique as contributing to the very content of the novels:

> When Saramago puts in a comma and a capital letter, we are into another sentence, into the reply of another speaker, who nonetheless does not speak directly with their own voice, which is treated by the narrator in a dramatic Brechtian fashion; instead they speak through a 'recording', allowing the author to savour every word and phrase used (proverbs, sayings, expressions of multiple significance). And so it is the author's interpretation that is delivered to the readers. This is why I write of meaning created jointly by form and content. And that is also why I insist on talking of his style as ideological.[15]

Levantado is directed towards this mode of expression, and in this work, once again, verbal dexterity is combined with rhetorical flourishes to produce a prose style which is engaging, varied and persuasive, but which, very importantly, also acknowledges the voice of those who have traditionally been left unheard.

The success of Saramago's dream of writing in a convincing and original manner, in both content and style, led the novelist to develop the same formula in the later works which made his name. Yet if it had not been for the conjunction of events in the author's personal life and Portuguese political history in 1975, the dream of which he writes would have remained the secret heritage of small peasant groups in the Alentejo, and not only

Portugal, but the world would have been denied one of its most outspoken and memorable literary voices of the last twenty years.

2. A Voice Untamed

Saramago is renowned for his prominence in discussions of current affairs and politics, and not only in Portugal. One of the clearest cases of his willingness to make a stand in this way is in relation to the question of the Landless Peasant Movement in Brazil.[16] He has also made use of his status in order to draw attention to questions which might otherwise go untouched, such as the fate of the indigenous people of Chiapas: when Saramago travelled to Mexico in March 1998, he was explicitly warned by the Mexican government not to talk about matters other than culture.[17] Nonetheless, just over a week later, the Mexican newspaper *La Jornada* reported him as declaring 'If I may be permitted to intrude, I believe that the Indians of Chiapas will not be able to find any safe haven in Mexico'.[18] More recently, he incurred some notoriety thanks to provocative statements made during a visit to the Occupied Territories, comparing the actions of Israel there to those of the Nazis against the Jews in World War Two. It was hardly surprising that such remarks led to widespread protest in Israel and the withdrawal of his works from bookshops in that country; the writer was, however, unrepentant over the comments made.[19]

The expression of such outspoken views should not, however, be dismissed as mere attention-seeking, as the views aired arise from the same profound sense of conviction which has led to the writer's well-known affiliation to the Portuguese Communist Party and which inspire the powerful moral voice to be found in *Levantado*, *Memorial*, *Ano* and *Cegueira*. While *Evangelho* was almost certain to provoke controversy, particularly in Portugal, where the Roman Catholic Church retains a prominent role in public life, even this work derives its force from an essentially moral outlook: that no religion or other belief system is worthy of the sacrifice of any human life. It could even be argued that the very nature of the controversy unleashed by this work provided a retrospective justification for its composition, for, instead of simply maintaining a dignified silence towards this work (which, in spite of the undoubted forcefulness of its expression, the conviction of its characterization and the beauty and elegance of its language, says nothing new in purely theological terms) some representatives of conservative opinion overreacted, with the then Portuguese Sub-Secretary for Culture, António Sousa Lara, picking 25 April, the very anniversary of a revolution which dismantled the alliance between Church and State, as the date to declare that the government would not put forward for a European literary award a work which in his view had insulted the religious traditions of the Portuguese people.[20]

Saramago is a committed member of the Portuguese Communist Party, and he has repeatedly stressed his loyalty to the ideals of the movement,[21] but he hardly fits into the stereotypes still widely held in the West about a label tarnished by associations with the Cold War and Stalinism. The writer has gone on record as distancing himself from the excesses practised in the name of the proletariat in the former Soviet Union and elsewhere,[22] and on occasions the critical views which he has expressed on humanitarian grounds have been directed against those with whom he might be expected to share some ideological affinity: thus, in April 2003 he declared his disgust at the decision by Fidel Castro's government in Cuba to execute three hijackers in the name of state security.[23]

This stance is compatible with Saramago's claim to be a writer who happens to be a communist and not vice versa;[24] and he has made it abundantly clear that he does not view the writing of fiction in itself to be capable of bringing about the Revolution.[25] His writing is a means of expressing himself, of bringing to his readers the thoughts, feelings, and the honest misgivings of a man who happens to hold certain political views; but it is clear from what he writes on the subject that this act of writing would in itself be equally expressive, were his political views diametrically opposed to those which he does in fact hold.

Nonetheless, class consciousness and an awareness of the iniquities of modern capitalism are never far below the surface in his works, and Portuguese history is often reflected on in a manner which subverts traditional conceptions of historical truth, national identity, class and gender. This is so even with works set before the contemporary period, as the narrator's digressive style permits him to indulge in sly anachronistic allusions which are intended to be noted by the contemporary reader.

One can understand, therefore, why Saramago should be such a controversial figure. Portugal in many ways remains a socially conservative country, even thirty years after the Revolution of the Carnations, and hierarchies and established privilege are more easily removed from statute books than they are from human minds. Even in terms of legislation and socio-economic structure, one could argue strongly that to those of a left-wing persuasion Portugal has regressed rather than progressed since the heady days of April 1974,[26] and Saramago has been amongst those who have repeatedly raised their voices against the country's apparently meek acceptance of its place in the new economic and social order which has now taken hold in his country (most prominently, of course, through *Jangada* and *Caverna*). His past record and his status, both nationally and internationally, ensure that this is one voice which will not be afraid of speaking its mind; one may disagree with his opinions, but attempts to silence or marginalize him would lead only to the same social disease as lay at the heart of the old Soviet Union itself.

3. Portuguese History and Tradition

The history of Portugal has been a chequered one, sharing much in common with its traditionally more prominent neighbour, Spain: the experience of overseas expansion in the Renaissance and early modern periods; the subsequent maintenance of Empire, masking a decline in world power and real economic strength; a strong tradition of official loyalty to the more conservative ideals of the Roman Catholic Church, persisting from the time of the Inquisition through to the right-wing dictatorships of the twentieth century; and, finally, the establishment of democracy in the mid-1970s, leading to subsequent full integration into the European Union and the international capitalist economy.

Some of these points need to be expanded on, and not all of them are true in exactly the same way of Portugal as they are of its larger neighbour. The sense of awareness of history is a recurrent feature of Saramago's novels, and, while his novels of the 1980s in particular engage in a constant interrogation of established Portuguese assumptions concerning the nation's past, it is also important to understand what this received knowledge consists of. Indeed, given the strength of Portuguese preoccupation with national identity (the 'superfluous vertebra' in the body of national identity, of which Eduardo Lourenço writes regarding the state of Portugal[27]), it would be impossible to address questions of Portugal's past and future without first understanding how this nation, rightly or wrongly, has traditionally seen itself.

Firstly, regarding the period of European expansion in the fifteenth and sixteenth centuries, there has been a tendency to view the Portuguese as being by and large explorers rather than conquerors. While in recent years there has been a rejection of the term 'discovery' regarding the Spanish involvement in the Americas, in Portugal the same word has been used in connection not with the places reached by the Portuguese explorers but with the sea routes and navigational techniques required to reach them, and this spirit of adventure has been largely prized by Portuguese writers through the centuries, from Camões' *Os Lusíadas* to Pessoa's *Mensagem* and beyond, with the motif of the spirit of the age of discovery still recurring (even if only in a highly ironic form) in contemporary novels such as Lídia Jorge's *A Costa dos Murmúrios* and António Lobo Antunes' *As Naus* (both of 1988). This adventurous temperament, perceived to be so inherent in the Portuguese sense of identity, becomes a frequent motif in Saramago's fiction too, but with him it is less ironic in tone than it is with the other two contemporary authors mentioned. It should be noted, however, that this apparent lack of irony on Saramago's part is largely due to what will be demonstrated to be an imaginative transformation of the spirit of discovery rather than a direct reflection on Portuguese relations with the non-European other (certain passages of *História*, for example, demonstrate clearly that this writer is not prepared to accept at face value Lusotropicalist myth-making regarding the essential benevolence of Portuguese contact with the non-Christian world[28]).

In spite of the frequent foreign assumption that they are just like their Spanish neighbours, the Portuguese therefore feel themselves to be more pluralistic in outlook, and there is a correspondingly lesser stigma attached to the memory of Empire than is the case in Spain, as Eduardo Lourenço suggests, writing several years after the Revolution:

> Above all, there was a strange but consistent durability to the prime delusion of conventional colonial mythology, as it had been promoted by Salazar's regime. As the April Revolution was a

> perfect home-grown revolution, it did not take place with the conscious intention of *bringing a definitive end to the image of Portugal as the classical imperial power*, instead, within itself, it aimed to find an equally typical *Portuguese solution* to the problem of Decolonization.[29]

Such ideas have no doubt helped to contribute to the extraordinary Portuguese phenomenon of Sebastianism, the belief that the young king D. Sebastião, lost at the battle of Alcácer-Quibir in North Africa in 1578, will return out of the mist to lead his country back to greatness. Seen objectively, Sebastianic beliefs can be said to have done much through the ages to keep the people of Portugal passive (the twentieth-century dictator Salazar, for example, explicitly compared himself to the figure of *O Encoberto*, or 'The Hidden One'), and the military adventure in which the monarch died was, of course, a foolhardy one, but there is no denying the forcefulness of this image in the Portuguese psyche, which could be said to have done much to legitimize the Portuguese presence in Africa in the popular mind. The negative legacy of Sebastianism, both in the form of a sustained faith in the literal truth of prophetic statements and in its encouragement of passive expectation of messianic resolution to existing crises might, however, be seen to explain both Sousa Lara's extraordinary reaction to the success of *Evangelho* and Saramago's own motivation for writing the work in the first place, as a rejection of a static, rather than a dynamic, understanding of the notion of truth (presented in this case in the specific form of the understanding of the Word of God).[30]

The Portuguese rightly take some pride in their maritime heritage, including the discovery of the trade route to India (an expedition led by Vasco da Gama, 1497–8) and the first circumnavigation of the globe (under Fernão de Magalhães in 1519); during this period Portugal also played a significant part in the development of the modern sciences of cartography and shipbuilding. Although Portugal's hegemony of the seas did not last for long (once larger European powers became aware of the potential riches to be had) the Empire did endure until after the 1974 Revolution. This Empire (whose commercial exploitation is reflected in satirical terms by Saramago in his *Memorial*) allowed Portugal to retain a position of wealth and cultural prestige far beyond its natural means into the nineteenth century, thus masking an economy and a nation in steady decline, relying on slavery and the pillage of Brazilian treasures to remain economically viable.

Portugal's continued status as a colonial master also made it possible to present the nation as having a divinely-ordained 'civilizing' mission overseas, a notion which continued to be exploited for rhetorical purposes well into the twentieth century, as Salazar's regime attempted to justify its dependence on Africa (in both economic terms and those of status in the world) to an increasingly cynical public, at home and overseas. Even if Salazar had not found the Church a useful ally in terms of popular control (as is reflected most prominently in domestic terms by Saramago in *Levantado*), then, this fact in itself would have required the dictator to project precisely the kind of simplistic, reductionist image of the Catholic nation of Portugal as ordained by God for a special destiny which is implicit in the popular version of the three secrets of Fátima (which stress, *inter alia*, the need to combat communism and materialism in Europe). To do so, however, denies the very kind of multiculturalist outlook which was also used to justify the Portuguese overseas endeavour in the first place. Nonetheless, the regime's espousal of the Church disguised other traditions, including the important Arabic heritage which, despite the hostile rhetoric directed towards it in the period of Reconquest, has left an unmistakeable mark on the nature of modern Portugal (as is implicitly recognized in *História*), and, in cultural terms, the irreverent anti-clerical tradition which runs from the medieval Galician-Portuguese 'Cantigas' through Gil Vicente, to Eça de Queirós, and, in our own day, Jorge de Sena, Saramago himself, and many others.

It is this genuinely pluralist vision of modern society, including the nation of Portugal itself, which informs much of Saramago's work. The importance of a plurality of voices (most famously discussed, of course, by Bakhtin in connection with the writing of Dostoevsky[31]) is one of the key aspects of Saramago's writing, in terms of content and as regards the very process of writing itself; in addition, however, the novelist is at pains to introduce a wide cross-section of society in his novels, with women, in particular, adopting a more prominent role than that traditionally ascribed to them in the past. This growth in the prominence of women is not simply a reflection of social trends evident in the West in the past hundred years, for even in novels set firmly in the past, such as *Memorial*, female characters, such as the remarkable Blimunda, come to challenge the assumption that the shape of human history has been determined exclusively by men. Indeed, at a symbolic level, it will be propounded that women's own feminine qualities perhaps have the greatest power to transform modern life for the better, even if Saramago is very far from proposing that these qualities should coexist with the maintenance of the exclusively domestic roles normally assigned to women.

Aside from the period of Discovery and Empire, the other historical reality to which Saramago alludes in most of his novels is the one in which he grew up himself, that of Salazar's *Estado Novo* (New State) dictatorship, established in 1926 and abolished only with the peaceful Revolution of the Carnations in 1974. This regime, often labelled 'fascist' (although, in a strict analysis, not all the basic characteristics of fascist ideology were present to any significant degree[32]) had as its leader a conservative economist from Coimbra (perhaps comparable in some degree to the Dr Sampaio of *Ano*) in António de Oliveira Salazar. In terms of social policy, Salazar's aim was to create a virtuous but static Portugal, expressing the eternal 'truths' of a stability based on notions of God and the family, a process which also involved a degree of connivance from socially conservative elements of the Roman Catholic Church, who were equally anxious to combat what was feared as the sweeping wave of communism in Europe. None of this idealism, however, could excuse the brutality and intolerance of the regime, which suppressed free speech, freedom of the press, and intellectual life, and thus led many academics, writers and artists to seek exile abroad, and which developed one of the most unscrupulous and sinister secret police forces in the world, the PVDE (The 'Police for Vigilance and Defence of the State', later renamed the PIDE), who, in one of Saramago's most celebrated novels, call in for questioning even the innocuous (and himself conservative) Ricardo Reis.

The experience of life under the New State was one of the shaping influences of most of Saramago's life (he was already fifty-one when the Revolution took place), and resentment of what Salazar did to Portugal and generations of Portuguese is a key cornerstone of his fictional production, along with his insistence that both Portugal and other countries must be ever vigilant for a return to a similar state of 'austera, apagada e vil tristeza' ('avarice and philistinism,/ Heartlessness and degrading pessimism') feared by Portugal's national poet Camões as he contemplated a nation already displaying signs of decline in the 1570s.[33] We must bear this context in mind in viewing some of his more recent novels, such as *Caverna*, *Homem*, and *Lucidez*, which, although they do not make any specific reference to Portugal and they are clearly set in contemporary Western multi-party democracies, raise the awful spectre of a loss of identity comparable to that which so depresses Ricardo Reis initially on his return to Lisbon in late 1935, in *Ano*.

4. Literary, Political and Cultural Context of Saramago's Novels

Saramago emerged as a writer from the neo-realist movement which dominated Portuguese literary activity from about the 1930s to the 1960s. This movement had as one of its main sources of inspiration the need for a reaction to the dictatorship and was heavily influenced by the movement of the same name in Brazil, as exemplified by writers like Lins do Rego, Amado, Graciliano Ramos, and Raquel de Queiroz. The major figures of this movement in Portugal included Vitorino Nemésio, Fernando Namora, and, perhaps the most important model for Saramago, Alves Redol (whose major works such as *Gaibéus*, of 1940, and *Barranco de Cegos*, of 1962, mix the predominantly realist tone with a substantial element of invention). These works tended to depict in particular the hardships and neglect of rural Portugal, almost always from a socialist perspective, which led to many works being heavily censored or banned altogether. Saramago's own *Terra do Pecado* of 1945 fits into this pattern, but it also displays a marked influence from Eça de Queirós and nineteenth-century naturalist thought in its depiction of ordinary people as merely responding to conditioning from their environment, both natural and societal.

Yet this grim depiction of rural life became repetitive, and it also contained within it an essential paradox: if the ideological grounds for rejecting the dictatorship lay in proclaiming the fundamental humanity of each individual, then the restrictive, determinist vision of society which it depicted as the *de facto* reality of contemporary life essentially turned ordinary men and women into merely functioning units in the machinery of state. This is particularly evident in the frequent exploitation of imagery by writers of this generation which presented human beings as animals or insects, or, more dehumanizing still, as equivalent to machinery, which is the case, for example, in the short story 'Estrada 43' by Cardoso Pires.[34]

By the 1960s, some writers were beginning to move away from what had become a rather predictable formula and to seek new forms of expression which would seek an outlet for the deepest human feelings rather than to simply restate an already well-rehearsed depiction of hardship and misery. Thus, some writers, such as Jorge de Sena and the dramatist Sttau Monteiro, sought to seek more universal truths underlying the sad realities of the dictatorship in important works such as *O Físico Prodigioso* of 1966 and *Felizmente Há Luar!* of 1961, both essentially aiming to reanimate a vision of Portugal dehumanized as much by the sad, static representation of its plight as by the dictatorship itself. This is part of what Cardoso Pires hints at when he writes in his Preface to *Jogos de Azar* that the 'age of the astronauts' requires a more imaginative approach to fiction than the solutions which had been adopted up to that time.[35] As Sabine suggests,[36] it was time to consign to the dustbin of literary history the former over-idealistic and over-simplistic notion that attempts at purely mimetic and didactic fiction could create an unquestionable 'truth' for the reader.

During the three decades that separate *Terra do Pecado* from the earliest of his mature novels, Saramago too saw the unsuitability, both aesthetic and ideological, of the neo-realist school for the period after the Revolution. In spite of his own meagre literary output prior to the publication of his first novel of recent times, *Manual* in 1977, Saramago had not been idle, having spent many years as a literary and academic translator, which permitted him to observe the latest intellectual currents in many countries. However, when he found himself unemployed in the mid-1970s, the need to find a new, characteristic mode of expression became an urgent one. Two of the key works in this respect are *Manual* itself, and the 1980 drama *Que Farei Com Este Livro?*, the latter being published in the same year as his first major literary success, *Levantado. Manual* is important in its depiction of an artist making two (interrelated) moves towards maturity: one away from the static reflection of reality (expressed through faithfulness to visible detail but in a manner which is essentially dull and incapable of revealing any deeper truth) to the dynamic medium of recording thoughts and impressions (here through words) while simultaneously broadening his perspective away from his own immediate reality in order to embrace all of Portuguese society, a process completed with the Revolution of 1974 at the end of the novel. The success of the newly-confident writer is eventually rewarded not only by the fall of the regime but also by the rewards of his love with M., a much more meaningful experience than the casual, semi-committed relationship in which he is involved at the beginning of the text. Here, to take up a tradition inherited from Camões and one which was to become part of Saramago's own compositional habits (evident in *Jangada, História, Caverna, Homem* and also, through the respective protagonists' reluctance to accept it, in a negative form in *Ano* and *Evangelho*), we find the protagonist rewarded by the offer of love for his endeavours in unrelated fields. The engagement with the other implicit here is more than just a convenient plot motif repeated to bring a suitable aesthetic ending to lengthy novels: for, as Sabine hints, these novels also offer the prospect of celebration of victories won through a plurality of engagement, rather than through any notion of the imposition of one person's truth on a communal experience: 'Dialogue resolves "dúvida" by creating what Antonio Gramsci terms a revolutionary hegemony'.[37]

The Camonian echoes of these endings, with Portugal itself becoming the equivalent of the Island of Love of Cantos IX and X of *Os Lusíadas*,[38] are reflected also in *Livro*, which brings to life the figure of Camões, a familiar point of reference in Saramago's later fiction. Indeed, this is merely the first instance in Saramago's writing of his tendency to resurrect other writers from historical death into the life of contemporary discourse: Fernando Pessoa and Ricardo Reis in *Ano*, Bartolomeu Lourenço de Gusmão in *Memorial*, and, most daringly, the word of God in *Evangelho*. This is not to mention the myriad sly references to previous writings (from literary and other sources) which may be traced in his writing, principally in the blatantly intertextual *Ano*, but also in many other works, thus permitting the author to expand the imaginative force of his writing, and also to cleverly co-opt writers, dead and alive, to his own world vision.

Returning to this drama, however, Camões' importance is seen to lie in two conflicting views of him: one synchronic (the vision of the impoverished and as yet unrecognized poet trying desperately to hawk his work to a court and to publishers, with eyes for purely short-term needs) and the other diachronic (our knowledge of what both he and his work would become, the most revered writer and the most iconic work of Portuguese literature respectively). It is precisely this dual perspective which enables the drama to work at a conceptual level: the awareness of events subsequent to those depicted on stage on the part of the reader, who nonetheless remains attentive to the progression of events in the past, is later exploited to great effect in more important works such as *Memorial*. Here we see Camões attempting to find a buyer for a work which others (most notably the Salazar regime) later would be only too happy to exploit for their own ends, as is illustrated by the closing words of the drama, where the frustrated poet holds out a copy of his mighty work to the audience and asks them provocatively 'Que fareis com este livro?' ('What will you do with this book?').[39]

In spite of this sense of failure, however, *Os Lusíadas* is not purely the work of exaltation of Portuguese virtues which it appears to be, but also both a warning to the new young king, D. Sebastião, to maintain the standards of achievement set by his predecessors and a consideration of the nature of love: physical and romantic love, love for one's country, and love for others in general. It is the spirit of the Discoveries, the spirit which led Vasco da Gama to make the first contact with other continents which matters, not the petty self-seeking of his descendants in Saramago's play, and, most tellingly, the warning made to the young king through this work is as applicable to modern Portugal as it was in Camões' own day: the country must ask itself constantly whether its dealings with the outside world and within its own borders are motivated by love or by the 'vã cobiça' ('empty acquisitiveness') against which the Old Man of Restelo warns the Portuguese fleet as it sets out on its great voyage in Canto IV of the poem. If Saramago speaks with the voice of Camões, then, however ironic the act of quotation may be, to some extent he acquires the authority of the epic poet for his own statements, an authority over *Os Lusíadas* which had, of course, been usurped less openly by others in positions of political power during Saramago's own lifetime.

This emulation of the spirit of the Discoveries is a theme also taken up by the twentieth-century poet Fernando Pessoa, in the one work published in his lifetime, *Mensagem*, which is also seen to have been simultaneously exalted and distorted by the regime in *Ano* (*Ano*, pp. 35–6). It is, however, Pessoa's experiments in heteronymy, or the projection of alternative selves into his writing, which are the most telling influence in this novel, as we may see in the conception of the figures of Reis, Lídia and Marcenda, as well as in the recreation of their creator, Fernando Pessoa himself. The exploitation by Saramago of the figure of Ricardo Reis, in fact, leads directly into a meditation on how and why Portugal and most of Europe drifted into domination by fascism in the 1930s, as has been widely documented by Cerdeira da Silva and many other commentators since the publication of her excellent monograph on Saramago in 1989.

One may still wonder why it is that it is only after the Revolution that Saramago turns to consider the period of the dictatorship. Furthermore, we will frequently find Saramago asking what might otherwise seem the unthinkable question: did the Revolution succeed? In the sense that Portugal is now widely recognized as forming part of the democratic family of nations and that the brutality and widespread poverty and backwardness of the New State have become things of the past, one would think that the answer to this question would have to be an unambiguous 'yes', as the writer himself declares in contrasting past dreams with present ambitions, but he does also have his reservations:

> Everything that we used to want and which is now in place turned out in the end only to be the minimum necessary: freedom of thought, freedom to create political parties, not having to go about in fear of the political police. All of those things which once seemed our over-riding needs turned out to be no more than the bare minimum, the very least to which we have a right.[40]

Saramago is not alone, however, amongst the major literary (and other) figures of Portugal today in wondering on whose behalf the changes were undertaken which have made Portugal the country it is today; similar conclusions might be reached from works such as *O Cais das Merendas*, of 1982, by Lídia Jorge, and *A Floresta em Bremerhaven*, of 1975 by Olga Gonçalves, while Pereira Nunes quotes the Portuguese politician Francisco Salgado Zenha as regarding Portugal as a less than democratic nation in 1985, that is on the very eve of the country's accession to the European Union, an event which was supposed to provide definitive confirmation of its fully-fledged democratic credentials.[41]

Saramago's own best-known incursion into political controversy was the publication in 1986 of *Jangada*, a work questioning the prevailing mood of apparently unqualified satisfaction in Portugal and Spain that the Iberian nations had been admitted into Europe at a political and economic level, a process which the novelist appears to have regarded as consisting rather too much of one-way traffic from Brussels to Iberia rather than an ongoing dialogue between northern Europe and its new partners of the type envisaged by Raimundo Silva in the twelfth century towards the end of *História* (see *História*, pp. 340–2). Instead, in articles published a few years later, Saramago put forward the view that Portugal and Spain can and should be seen as both European and transcontinental.[42] The events of *Jangada* and other novels demonstrate that no real revolution can ever truly be considered to be over, for if it were so, then, once more, the political class would have achieved hegemony over the very people in whose name they claim to operate, and little would have changed in terms of real representation since the days of the dictatorship, as the writer declared in a recent interview with Reis:

> It is this which leads me to ask: in the end, who is Europe there for? The strange thing is that, even as they widened our concept of the unit of which we are citizens by turning us into European citizens, they have succeeded in reducing to virtually zero the effective participatory capacity which allows each one of us to say that we are citizens.[43]

Such considerations, although they are capable of universal application, are particularly pertinent in the case of Portugal, which has been unable to come to terms fully with the internal contradiction of the replacement of a civilian-run dictatorship by a parliamentary democracy through the intervention of a military coup, as Eduardo Lourenço points out:

> With no transition, the people of Portugal moved from their awareness of living in a semi-totalitarian or even fully totalitarian state to full awareness of participating in a revolution, without even asking any questions about the very complex and subtle conversion of the Armed Forces, which had been faithful to the former regime, into a dramatically forward-thinking movement [. . .] The

> April Revolution was accepted and celebrated as simply removing worn-out scenery in a way which would not change our tranquil and delightful life by the shores of the ocean and would not change the image which the Portuguese had of themselves. Or if it did change, it would be *for the better.* From being citizens of a repressive state, without any of the civil rights which are normal in Europe, we would turn ourselves miraculously into totally normal citizens of Europe and the democratic world.[44]

In other words, since democracy was bestowed upon Portugal and was not won by the nation in the way that happened in eastern Europe in 1989, for example, little has changed in the Portuguese mentality,[45] and the temptation to continue believing in false messiahs (as exposed by Saramago in works such as *Evangelho* and *Ano*) is as alive today as it was before the Revolution. Hence the irony that Saramago (whose work was denied official approval by a previous government for its supposedly blasphemous tone) engages in acerbic criticism of comments with a strong biblical echo made by António Guterres regarding the introduction of the European single currency:

> Truly, I do not know what to think. I read and re-read the declaration made by the Prime Minister at the meeting in Madrid, where they were discussing the name to give to the future single European currency; I stare wide-eyed at the words in disbelief, but his words don't move around, they just sit there, each one in its place, and, once put together, they make perfect sense: 'Regarding the Euro, when Jesus Christ decided to found his Church, he gave Peter the responsibility for its future by telling him that he was his rock and that he would found it on him. You are the Euro, and on this Euro we will build our Europe'. [. . .] I am left here wondering what the hell António Guterres thinks that his Jesus was doing in this world.[46]

Saramago's concluding reference to Jesus here is presumably intended to indicate that if there was a blasphemer in Portugal, it was not the novelist (who, with biblical authority behind him, depicts Jesus overturning the tables of the money changers in the temple; see *Evangelho*, pp. 425–6), but the prime minister, who sought to turn a spiritual and religious visionary into a dull economist, concerned only with the health of the continent's balance sheet. Instead of capitulation to such vaguely defined and (to their critics) fundamentally unaccountable (if not actually antidemocratic) bodies as the International Monetary Fund, then, Saramago seeks a society where each of us will be genuinely able to call to account those who act in our names: 'What is really needed [. . .] is the capacity of the citizen to become involved in all aspects of public life [. . .] I believe that all citizens should feel as fully committed to this task as the politicians say that they are'.[47]

Messianic belief in any kind of externally-imposed solution is therefore no substitute for hard work to improve one's own lot, and the same mood is also conveyed, through the metaphor of travel, in two quotations from Saramago's *Viagem* of 1981, one at the opening of the text, and the other at its end: 'O viajante viajou no seu país. Isto significa que viajou por dentro de si mesmo, pela cultura que o formou e está formando . . . Nenhuma viagem é definitiva' ('The traveller has travelled inside his own country. That means that he has travelled within himself, within the culture which shaped him and continues to do so [. . .] No journey is ever complete', *Viagem* pp. 13–14).[48]

And then, in similar vein:

> O fim duma viagem é apenas o começo doutra. É preciso ver o que não foi visto, ver outra vez o que se viu já, ver na Primavera o que se vira no Verão, ver de dia o que se viu de noite, com sol onde primeiramente a chuva caía, ver a seara verde, o fruto maduro, a pedra que mudou de lugar, a sombra que aqui não estava. É preciso voltar aos passos que foram dados, para os repetir, e para traçar caminhos novos ao lado deles. É preciso recomeçar a viagem. Sempre. O viajante volta já. (*Viagem*, p. 387)

> [The end of one journey is simply the start of another. You have to see what you missed the first time, see again what you already saw, see in springtime what you saw in summer, in daylight what you saw at night, see the sun shining where you saw the rain falling, see the crops growing, the fruit ripen, the stone which has moved, the shadow that was not there before. You have to go back to the footsteps already taken, to go over them again or add fresh ones alongside them. You have to start the journey anew. Always. The traveller sets out once more.] (*Journey*, p. 443)

However, it is important to note in the first of these excerpts that it is not only the outside world which the writer sees as constantly changing here, but also himself as observer of that reality. As Saramago remarks in an interview with the Spanish journalist Juan Arias: 'What has changed? It is as if there were two of us: one who changes and another one who observes the change. The one who changes is not unaware that he is changing, but he does not know in what ways he is transformed. And the observer does not know either, precisely because he is on the outside.'[49] In other words, although our understanding of the world depends on our ability to objectify it (that is, to render it static and comprehensible), the reality is that it (and we ourselves, as a part of the world) are constantly evolving and that we must be aware of this in order to fully comprehend both ourselves and the world in which we live. Each of the major novels by Saramago is therefore an entry into a new world as well as a re-exploration of an apparently familiar one, and the experience of exploring these worlds will alter our perceptions of ourselves, of Portuguese and universal history, and of what the world is like today. It is therefore a journey into the future as well as the past, a future rich in possibilities, as is acknowledged by the epigraph to *Jangada*, taken from Alejo Carpentier's *Concierto Barroco*: 'Todo futuro es fabuloso' ('The future is entirely fabulous').[50]

Saramago's novels depict many instances of oppression and exploitation, yet they are no litany of woes. In the present study we shall see that even the bleakest of his writings (*Cegueira* and *Evangelho*) can still hold out some hope for the future.[51] In an interview given in 1995, the author says that the light in which he views the world is not one of optimism but one of simple hope.[52] This note of hope is not only a vital component of his social vision: it is also the fuel which allows the *Passarola* to fly in *Memorial* and the mysterious force which restores sight to the blind in *Cegueira*. In Saramago's world, the age of miracles is far from over, and the present work will conclude with an examination of how, in spite of all of the more negative aspects of human existence in the past and the present, and in spite of the author's belief that there is no life after death, lasting value and meaningful fulfilment are open to all of us, regardless of the political system in which we live.

NOTES

1 The criteria for this prize took into account both the quality of the novel itself and that of the English translation, so that Saramago's

translator, Giovanni Pontiero, was recognized equally with the author himself in the award.

2 See Saramago's interview with Ivone Pereira, p. 218.

3 See Saraiva and Lopes, p. 1089.

4 See, for example, Costa, *José Saramago: O Período Formativo,* and Arnaut, *Post-Modernismo,* pp. 174–5.

5 In an interview with Reis, Saramago describes his use of punctuation as being like traffic signs by the roadside, which are not essential for driving and without which the driver (in this case, the reader) will pay greater attention to the road itself; see Reis, *Diálogos,* pp. 101–2.

6 Sabine points out (p. 37 and p. 37, n. 2) that these remarks very pointedly echo those of the important Neo-Realist writer Alves Redol, who described his *Gaibéus* of 1940 as 'a human documentary set in the Ribatejo'. Both Cerdeira da Silva and Viçoso have explored the specific relationship between Saramago and Redol in greater depth; see Cerdeira da Silva, 'Saramago e Redol', and Viçoso, '*Levantado do Chão* e o Romance Neo-realista', respectively.

7 Quoted in Reis, *Diálogos,* p. 42; later in the same work (pp. 102–3) Saramago goes on to explain precisely what he means by this new manner of writing, in a passage primarily focusing on his use of punctuation.

8 Interview with Millôr Fernandes, in *Jornal do Brasil* ('Suplemento Idéias') (11 October 1986), 12–13 (p. 13), reproduced by Fernandes, p. 43.

9 The ideal desired here is compared at one moment in *Jangada* to the effect of multiple voices heard in an opera, even with a recognition that the discursive form of literature does not allow for simultaneous representation of different voices: '[Q]uem está bem são os cantores de opera, cada um com a sua parte nos concertantes, três quarto cinco seis entre tenores baixos sopranos e barítonos, todos a cantar palavras diferentes, [. . .] já o leitor não é assim, quer tudo explicado, sílaba por sílaba e uma após outra, como aqui se mostram' ('The people who come off best are the opera-singers, each with his or her own part to sing, three, four, five, six between tenors, basses, sopranos and baritones, all singing different words, [. . .] but the reader is not like this, he wants everything explained, syllable by syllable and one after the other; as they are shown here'; *Jangada,* p. 14, and *Raft,* p. 5). Even with this ideal expressed here, however, Saramago would presumably not wish the parallel with opera outlined to be an exact one, as this would require the musicality and oral qualities of his prose to drown out the content. The real point, surely, is the desire (unrealizable in practical terms) that the coherence of a rectilinear presentation (required in order to make sense of events in a written presentation) could be married to the simultaneity and independence of individual speech acts.

10 Reproduced in Seixo (ed.), between pp. 242 and 243. I have preserved the spelling, punctuation and accentuation of the letter in the transcription given above. The letter 'h' appears to have been written

and then erased in the original immediately before the definite article *a* in the phrase 'a minha filha mais vèlha', towards the end of the text.

11 The Fifth Empire is the enduring Kingdom of God prophesied by Daniel to King Nebuchadnezzar (Daniel 2:31–45), an idea subsequently adopted by notable Portuguese writers such as the eighteenth-century Jesuit Padre António Vieira to proclaim their vision of how the earthly Portuguese empire should be administered in accordance with divine purposes. This rhetoric was then exploited by the Salazar dictatorship in justification of Portugal's African policies in the twentieth century.

12 Thankfully the original translated text prepared by Giovanni Pontiero was restored for the 1998 edition of *Baltasar*; the previous translation was published by Pan Books of London in 1989.

13 *Cadernos – II*, p. 49 (entry for 15 February 1994). The italics are Saramago's.

14 The reliability of this clichéd notion of a nation of 'brandos costumes' is a highly debatable one, not least because of the heavy-handedness with which Salazar's own security forces imposed his will; the suitability of this term to describe the Portuguese is denied outright by the cover of João Santos Lopes' book about the Colonial War *Às Vezes Neva em Abril* (Lisbon: Dom Quixote, 1998): 'That notion that the Portuguese are a people of gentle ways has been encouraged widely. We are not a people of gentle ways'; quoted in Pereira Nunes, p. 57).

15 Picchio, p. 137.

16 On the question of the landless movement in Brazil, see the preface which Saramago contributed to the book of photographs by the photojournalist Sebastião Salgado, *Terra*. This piece also appears (in Portuguese) in *Cadernos – IV*, pp. 181–8 (entry for 28 September 1996).

17 *Público*, 11 March 1998.

18 *La Jornada*, 20 March 1998.

19 The intellectual basis for Saramago's accusations was made in a much less inflammatory manner through an article published in April 2002, 'De las piedras de David a los tanques de Goliat', where he accuses the Israeli authorities of having been seduced by the sophisticated and powerful weaponry made available to them by the West. In another article published shortly before this, Saramago explicitly criticized the inhumanity of both Palestinian violence against Israelis and Israeli brutality towards Palestinians; see his article 'La explanada del absurdo', in *El País* of 24 March 2002. In the context of a highly polarized and heated debate, however, it is hardly surprising that he should incur some unpopularity and distortion of his words when he airs controversial views.

20 See the remarks attributed to Sousa Lara in the *Diário de Notícias* newspaper of 30 April 1992 (reproduced in Grossegesse, 'José Saramago: *O Evangelho Segundo Jesus Cristo*', p. 123). Significantly, even

after Saramago was awarded the Nobel Prize, Sousa Lara was unrepentant, accusing the author of owing his success largely to a talent for marketing his own image, although he conceded that even right-wing newspapers had supported Saramago during their dispute; see *Público*, 9 October 1998.

21 See, for example, comments made in Baptista Bastos, pp. 44 and 48–9.

22 See comments made during the discussion held at the Frankfurt Book Fair in October 1998 on 'On Being a Communist Writer Today', where Saramago explicitly excludes both Stalin and Boris Yeltsin from his own conception of communism, stressing instead the need for a spiritual dimension to drive any socialist movement. He also makes similar comments in Baptista-Bastos, pp. 44–5.

23 See Saramago, 'Cheguei até aqui'.

24 See the comments made at the Frankfurt Book Fair on 7 October 1998, reported in *Público*, 8 October 1998, as well as in Baptista-Bastos, pp. 42–3.

25 See Saramago's article 'Sobre literatura, compromiso y transformación social'.

26 In this connection Grossegesse writes of the apparently successful revolutionary conclusion to *Levantado*: 'In describing this final moment in its chaotic joy, which is nonetheless loaded with utopian overtones, the writer extends to the reader an invitation to recommence here and now a revolution which has been led astray when it was on the verge of fulfilling the expectations of a new Portuguese society marked by justice and camaraderie' (Grossegesse, 'Messianismo Telúrico', p. 209). By the time when the novel was published, the immediate revolutionary fever of 1974 had subsided, and already some of the social and economic changes made by the Revolution were being reversed, to Saramago's chagrin. For a brief account of the changes which took place between April 1974 and November 1975, see Birmingham, pp. 186–93. For Saramago's comments on the actions of successive Portuguese governments, see his 'Herculano e o 25 de Abril', originally published in *O Diário* in 1985 and reprinted in his *Folhas Políticas*, pp. 146–9, where he castigates politicians, the European Union and an increasingly prosperous Portuguese middle class for betraying the real aims of the 1974 Revolution, while also reiterating the potential of ordinary Portuguese citizens to transform the nation in a positive sense. At the end of this piece Saramago himself recognizes his own error in 1985 in having attributed the original remarks upon which he reflects to Herculano instead of Garrett (*Folhas Políticas*, p. 149).

27 Eduardo Lourenço, p. 11.

28 See, for example, *História*, pp. 61, 186–7, 195–6.

29 Eduardo Lourenço, p. 44 (the italics are Lourenço's).

30 For further discussion of this point, see my own 'José Saramago's *O Evangelho Segundo Jesus Cristo*', at pp. 380–2.

31 See 'Dostoeveky's Polyphonic Novel and its Treatment in Critical Literature', in Bakhtin, pp. 5–46.

32 For fuller discussion of this question, see Birmingham, pp. 163–4. Pereira Nunes quotes Manuel Vilaverde Cabral as remarking that Portuguese historians of the 1970s were reluctant to use the term 'fascist' for Salazar's regime, thus effectively lessening the negative impression of the dictatorship for those who did not live through it. She attributes the quotation to his 'O Fascismo Português numa Perspectiva Comparada', in *O Fascismo em Portugal: Actas do Colóquio Realizado na Faculdade de Letras de Lisboa em Março de 1980* (Lisbon: A Regra do Jogo, 1982), 19–30, at pp. 19–20; see Pereira Nunes, pp. 167–9, and Griffiths.

33 Camões, *Os Lusíadas*, Canto X, stanza 145 (see Camões, *Os Lusíadas*, p. 351, and *The Lusiads*, p. 226). For the implicit parallel to this danger of retrogression, see, for example, Saramago's expressions of concern in the 1990s about the danger of his country slipping into a process of 'desculpabilização do passado, o manso avançar das patas do fascismo' ('whitewashing of the past and stealthy insinuation of fascism') *Cadernos – II*, p. 113, entry for 10 May 1994.

34 This story can be found at Cardoso Pires, pp. 186–207; in the story in question, Cardoso Pires' apparent intention is to demonstrate the effective dehumanization of the workforce rather than to set it in stone. Saramago was also to use the device of comparison to insects, albeit more productively and imaginatively, in *Levantado* and *Memorial*, as will be discussed in Chapter One of the present work.

35 José Cardoso Pires, 'A Charrua entre os Corvos', in *Jogos de Azar*, pp. 7–11, at p. 9.

36 See Sabine, pp. 40–2.

37 Sabine, p. 57. Issues of a possible Gramscian framework for the ideological interpretation of Saramago's novels will be discussed in Chapter Two of the present work.

38 This motif is reproduced most literally, but also, perhaps, most imaginatively, in *Jangada*, where the Iberian Peninsula as a whole becomes an island and all the women of childbearing age on its soil suddenly and inexplicably find themselves pregnant.

39 For further discussion of this play and another dramatic work by Saramago, *A Segunda Vida de Francisco de Assis*, in the context of the author's concerns about the continuing relevance of Marxism in a country which had seemingly irrevocably adopted market capitalism, see Frier, 'In the Beginning Was the Word', especially pp. 223–7.

40 Baptista Bastos, p. 50.

41 Quoted in Pereira Nunes, p. 43.

42 See Saramago's 'A Península Ibérica entre a Europa e a América Latina', p. 11, and 'Europa sim, Europa não'. In the latter article, Saramago declares that he would be prepared to 'call the errant raft back from the ocean, having learned some lessons on its voyage, if Europe [. . .] would also publicly confess the errors, injustices and acts of contempt of which it is guilty'.

43 Reis, *Diálogos*, p. 147.

44 Eduardo Lourenço, pp. 59–60. The italics are Lourenço's.

45 See Lourenço, p. 59.

46 *Cadernos – III*, pp. 218–19 (entry for 16 December 1995).
47 Baptista Bastos, p. 51.
48 The translation here is mine. The initial section of *Viagem*, entitled 'Apresentação', is replaced in the English version of this work by a new authorial preface specially written for this translation (*Journey*, pp. xi–xii).
49 Quoted in Arias, p. 31.
50 See Carpentier, p. 198. These words are spoken by the figure of the *indiano*, a Latin American in Venice disillusioned by the apparently tired and routine nature of European culture, leading him to declare a preference for the unstable realities of his own continent: 'Llaman *fabuloso* cuanto es remoto, irracional, situado en el ayer [. . .] No entienden que lo fabuloso está en el futuro. Todo futuro es fabuloso' ('They call everything *fabulous* that is remote, irrational, that belongs to yesterday [. . .] They don't understand that the fabulous is in the future. The future is entirely fabulous'). Both Carpentier's urgent search for Utopia in his writing and his rejection of the imposition of accepted norms derived from a European environment alien to his own upbringing make the analogy to *Jangada* extremely pertinent, as will be discussed in Chapter Two. The English translation of Carpentier's text is taken from *Baroque Concerto*, p. 111.
51 I except from these comments the novel *Lucidez*, published in 2004, which has an unremittingly negative conclusion, based largely on the author's frustration at the effective neutering of mass protests against the Iraq war and its aftermath in many countries in 2003 and 2004.
52 Quoted in 'Todos os pecados do mundo', p. 82.

Chapter One

Privilege and Exclusion: *Levantado do Chão* and *Memorial do Convento*

1. Introduction

While Saramago has never hesitated to denounce social or economic ills when he perceives them, these two novels of the early 1980s are probably his most clearly ideologically committed ones. The definition of the ideological status of the author's fiction is not as self-evident as one might have thought: Sabine argues that only *Levantado* of the author's major works of the 1980s may be seen as unproblematically Marxist in its interpretation and suggests, in his reading of the four later works which he studies (*Memorial, Ano, Jangada* and *História*), that they privilege Marxist ideologemes while simultaneously highlighting the susceptibility of the situations outlined to alternative readings.[1]

This is not to dispute the concern with politics and public affairs of works such as *Ano* (where the dangerous drift of Europe into fascism and war seems to slip past Ricardo Reis almost unobserved, until it is too late) and *Cegueira* (which engages the reader in an ever-deepening dismay at the seemingly inexhaustible potential of humans for inhumanity towards their fellows, before some relief from this negative tone is obtained in the final chapter of the novel), nor the negative critique of the symbiotic relationship between market capitalism and Western conceptions of democracy which the author sees as deeply flawed in *Caverna* and *Lucidez.* All of these works, however, are clearer in what they reject than in the advancement of any particular positive programme,[2] and while their broad sweep is consistent with Marxist principles, these could not be said to be the only possible positive programme to be constructed in response to the negative scenarios depicted in each case.

Certainly in *Jangada* and *História,* Sabine appears to be correct in identifying only a tenuous basis for specifically Marxist readings within the evidence supplied by the texts; I would, however, dispute his contention that the same could be said of *Memorial,* for even if, at a microtextual level, it may be possible to argue along the lines proposed by Sabine regarding individual aspects of socialist ideology within that work, its overarching narrative development seems to indicate an unambiguously leftist interpretation of Portuguese history and (as far as this can be surmised from a text set in the past) of contemporary Portugal too. It seems justifiable, therefore, to group this novel together with *Levantado,* since both invoke the classical Marxist concept of the alienation of labour in their analysis of the realities described, using these negatives as a clear indication of how Portugal might become a better society.

The functioning of both of these novels depends on a contrast between the conflicting categories of rich and poor. These are expanded into a number of other contrasts: power and powerlessness, extravagance and prudence, artificial and natural behaviour, static and dynamic characters, sterility and fertility, death and life. In each of these pairs, the latter term is favoured over the former. These various categories also become thematically interrelated over the length of each novel in itself and between these two novels and other, subsequent, ones.

2. Social and Economic Relations

In *Memorial,* there is a lengthy contrast between the two categories identified by Oliveira Filho in eighteenth-century Portugal as 'os de "pança repleta"' (those with 'great paunches', that is, the wealthy) and 'os de "barriga agarrada às costas"' (those with 'shrivelled bellies', in other words, the poor).[3] On the one hand, over two pages of text at the opening of the seventeenth chapter are used to indicate the immense wealth and luxury which the Crown has at its disposal (*Memorial,* pp. 227–9), a fact which amply illustrates the profligacy of the court, whose disastrous management of the economy is measured by Birmingham in terms of an ever-widening trade gap between Portugal and Britain, as finished products were imported at higher costs than could be obtained for the raw materials derived from the colonies.[4] It is worth noting, then, that, contrasting with this depiction of luxury, the next chapter opens with a lengthy passage outlining the humble conditions under which Bartolomeu labours at the building site of the convent, emphasizing his reliance on 'força bruta' (p. 239) ('brute force', *Baltasar*, p. 224):

> São trabalhos já ditos, que mais facilmente se recapitulam por serem de força bruta, porém, é causa da sua reiteração não consentir que esqueçamos o que, por tão comum e de tão mínima arte, se costuma olhar sem mais consideração que distraidamente vermos os nossos próprios dedos escrevendo, assim de um modo e outro ficando oculto aquele que faz sob aquilo que é feito . . . (p. 239)[5]
>
> [These labours, as we have already said, can be described more easily because they require brute force, however, by constantly coming back to them we are less likely to forget things that are so common, and call for so little skill, that they tend to be overlooked, it is rather like distractedly watching our own fingers write, so that in one sense or another the agent of the doing remains concealed beneath the thing which is being done.] (p. 224)

As this chapter progresses, it becomes evident, that, whereas the previous one stressed the king's idleness and solitary splendour amidst the pomp and wealth of his kingdom

> . . . este D. João, quinto já se sabe de seu nome na tabela dos reis, sentado numa cadeira de braços de pau-santo, para mais comodamente estar e assim com outro sossego atender ao guarda-livros que vai escriturando no rol os bens e as riquezas (p. 227)
>
> [. . . Dom João, the fifth sovereign with that name on the roster of kings, sitting in a chair with arms made from lignum vitae, where he can rest with greater comfort and pay closer attention to the accountant who is drawing up an inventory of the realm's possessions and riches] (p. 212),

here Bartolomeu is an active worker and capable of relating to others, in this case the hunchback José Pequeno, who helps him earn promotion (pp. 240–1): these two disabled men may therefore provide a total contrast to the elegance of the king, and their work may be characterized by 'mínima arte' (p. 239) ('little skill', p. 224), in contrast to the fine craftsmanship evident in the continuation of the earlier passage, but, unlike the monarch, they are at least employed productively and actively engaged in cooperation with others rather than attempting to impose their wills on others for their own gratification. The king's own constructive powers are engaged only in the model of St Peter's basilica in Rome kept in his bedchamber (pp. 12–13) and in such impractical gestures as his arbitrary decision to expand the project at Mafra from a convent for eighty monks to one for three hundred (pp. 281–4), a task which (as the text explicitly reminds us, p. 257) will actually be carried out by others and not by him. This contrast between the huge scale of the king's projects and the ludicrously infantile construction of which he is capable on his own dispels the air of majesty evoked around him by the ironically pompous tones of the opening words of the novel:

> D. João, quinto do seu nome na tabela real, irá esta noite ao quarto da sua mulher, D. Maria Ana Josefa, que chegou há mais de dois anos da Áustria para dar infantes à coroa portuguesa e até hoje ainda não emprenhou (p. 11)
>
> [Dom João, the fifth monarch so named on the royal list, will pay a visit this night to the bedchamber of the Queen, Dona Maria Ana Josefa, who arrived more than two years ago to provide heirs for the Portuguese throne, and so far has shown no signs of becoming pregnant] (p. 3).

Further evidence of the extravagance of the Crown may be found in the episode where the king's own accountant seeks to warn him that the construction of the convent at Mafra is going seriously over budget (pp. 283–4). The king averts this unpleasant glimpse of real-world economics by silencing the messenger, and the means which he chooses to do so are at least preferable to those adopted by King Herod in *Evangelho*, but only in that instead of executing the employee who knows his secret (see *Evangelho*, p. 104) he is in a position to be able to bribe him into silence by increasing his salary (which will, of course, only worsen the financial problems previously identified by the accountant).[6] In this way the king's extravagance becomes the equivalent of the myopia in the special edition of *The New York Times* mentioned in

Ano as being prepared every day for John D. Rockefeller's solitary pleasure, in order to shield from him a world of strikes, wars and international tensions (*Ano*, pp. 265–6). The most interesting aspect of this discussion, however, is the earthy (and highly unrealistic) language in which the conversation between the two characters is conducted:

> Se vossa majestade me perdoa o atrevimento, eu ousaria dizer que estamos pobres e sabemos, Mas, graças sejam dadas a Deus, o dinheiro não tem faltado, Pois não, e a minha experiência contabilística lembra-me todos os dias que o pior pobre é aquele a quem o dinheiro não falta, isso se passa em Portugal, que é um saco sem fundo, entra-lhe o dinheiro pela boca e sai-lhe pelo cu, com perdão de vossa majestade, Ah, ah, ah, riu o rei, essa tem muita graça, sim senhor, queres tu dizer na tua que a merda é dinheiro, Não, majestade, é o dinheiro que é merda, e eu estou em muito boa posição para o saber, de cócoras, que é como deve estar quem faz as contas do dinheiro dos outros. Este diálogo é falso, apócrifo, calunioso, e também profundamente imoral, não respeita o trono nem o altar, põe um rei e um tesoureiro a falar como arrieiros em taberna. (*Memorial*, p. 283)
>
> [If Your Majesty will permit me to speak frankly, I am of the opinion that we are facing bankruptcy and must be fully aware of our difficult situation. But, thanks be to God, there has never been any lack of money. That is true, but my experience as treasurer has taught me that the most persistent beggar is the one who has money to squander, just like Portugal, which is a bottomless coffer, the money goes in its mouth and comes out of its arse, if Your Majesty will pardon the expression. Ha ha ha, the King laughed, that's very funny, are you trying to tell me that shit is money, No, your Majesty, that money is shit, and I'm in a position to know, squatting down here like everyone else who finds himself looking after someone else's money. This dialogue is fictitious, apocryphal, and libellous, and also deeply immoral, it respects neither throne nor altar, It makes a king and his treasurer speak as if they were drovers conversing in a tavern.] (*Baltasar*, pp. 268–9)

The narrator here displays the same kind of verbal irreverence for the royal figure as he does in the opening paragraph of the novel (as has been discussed by numerous commentators, including Arnaut[7]), but the narration succeeds also in passing comment through this language on both the king's attitude towards money and on the relative positions of king and accountant. Firstly, the king's economic policy is clearly based on the 'trickle-down' theories favoured by modern monetarists, namely the belief that by satisfying his own needs, some benefit may accrue to others from his consumption. In reality, however, the king's cavalier approach to the problem demonstrates that any such benefit will be of purely incidental interest to him, while the accountant's warning that 'the most persistent beggar is the one who has money to squander' prefigures the words of the doctor's wife in the later novel *Cegueira* that 'Penso que não cegámos, penso que estamos cegos, [. . .] Cegos que, vendo, não vêem' (*Cegueira*, p. 310) ('I don't think we did go blind, I think we are blind, [. . .] Blind people who can see, but do not see', *Blindness*, p. 309), thus suggesting (by association with the horrors visualized in that work) that royal policies are leading the country irresponsibly towards fiscal disaster.

Secondly, however, the accountant's description of himself as squatting down refers not only to the physical position adopted when passing excrement but also both to his adoption of an inferior stance in front of the king and (implicitly) to his own embrace of the same economic practice when it is to his own benefit, even though he is well aware of the long-term dangers of the policies being pursued. The Rabelaisian tone of this passage is recalled again only some three pages later, when the narrator imagines that Baltasar, in another moment of unlikely, carnivalesque equality with the monarch, might pen a letter to his ruler, including the following passage about the supplies provided to the workers at Mafra:

> os trinta mil portugueses recomendam-se muito e agradecem, a saúde deles vai assim assim, no outro dia houve aí uma caganeira tão geral que Mafra fedia três léguas em redor, alguma coisa que comemos e nos assentou mal, eram os gorgulhos mais que a farinha, ou as varejeiras mais que a carne, mas teve graça, ver um ror de gente de rabo à vela, com a frescura que vinha do mar, muito aliviadora, e quando uns acabavam havia logo outros tantos, às vezes era tal a urgência que onde estavam ali davam de corpo. (*Memorial*, p. 287)

> [Thirty thousand Portuguese send you their greetings and thanks, their health is so-so, the other day there were so many men with the runs that Mafra stank to high heaven for three leagues on all sides, we must have eaten something that didn't agree with us, weevils rather than flour, botflies rather than meat, but it was funny to

> watch all those chaps with their bottoms up in the air to catch the fresh breeze coming in from the sea, and no sooner had one bunch relieved themselves than another took their place, and sometimes they were so desperate that they squatted down on the spot.] (*Baltasar*, p. 273)

The accountant's statement has now come true: the scanty supplies which have trickled down to the workers have literally become excrement, and, whereas the accountant can at least live in a degree of relative comfort, Baltasar and others like him face life at the bottom of the heap. Equally noticeable is Baltasar's cheery and almost insolent attitude towards this state of affairs, amounting to a metaphorical smearing of human waste over the holy site so closely associated with the king's ambitions. As will be seen below, a similar motif is adopted in *Levantado* to indicate a more explicit rejection of the arbitrary 'authority' of state.

The Bakhtinian 'decrowning' of the king in this passage also indicates that his wealth is apparent more than real, and Portuguese readers will approach this passage well aware of both the material decline of the nation since the eighteenth century and the (related) deposition of the monarchy in 1910.[8] Although D. João was nicknamed 'O Magnânimo' ('The Generous') and displays considerable extravagance throughout the text in a court marked by luxury, the Crown is actually approaching bankruptcy:[9] despite the relative poverty of Baltasar's family, the king has been forced to buy land from Baltasar's father and other small landowners in the area where the convent is to be built (pp. 103–4), but it is soon insinuated (through a denial of doubt which only succeeds in raising that doubt) that the Crown will probably be in no position to pay off these debts: 'Tudo isto pertence ao mesmo dono, a el-rei, que se ainda não pagou, pagará, que lá de boas contas é ele, faça-se-lhe essa justiça' (p. 108) ('All these fields now belong to the same landowner, His Majesty the King, who has not yet paid for it but will no doubt pay, for, to do him justice, his credit is good', p. 100). The king, however, insouciant of these concerns, rewards those who support his megalomaniac building project by freely distributing gold to them (pp. 131–2), even though the project is clearly going over budget (pp. 136–7).

This leads into an ironic narratorial discourse on the blindness of authority in Portugal, according to which it is appropriate that one should 'honre [. . .] a gente de bem e de bens, não lhe exigindo que pague as dívidas contraídas' (p. 189) ('let people of rank and wealth be honoured, without demanding that they pay their debts', p. 176): what out of its context might be regarded as a maxim respecting the obligations imposed by social honour instead becomes a sly way of suggesting that those who lend money to this king can probably forget about ever seeing its return. This aside, placed alongside the revelation on the following page that the king has lost his lawsuit against the Duque de Aveiro, whose land had been expropriated by the Crown, indicates not only its material but also its spiritual and moral bankruptcy (p. 190). Nonetheless the economic madness continues: good agricultural land is neglected (p. 211), and whereas workers such as Francisco Marques obtain productive labour to solve problems of economic necessity (p. 233), the king's policies continue to adopt short-term solutions which will only exacerbate existing problems, as exemplified in the needless destruction of a kitchen garden at the convent site, sacrificed for the expansion of the convent (p. 285). A further reminder of the king's folly is given as valuable workers are forcibly led away to Mafra in chain gangs, through the words of an old man, who clearly recalls the Old Man of Restelo in Camões' *Os Lusíadas*: 'Ó glória de mandar, ó vã cobiça, ó rei infame, ó pátria sem justiça' (p. 293) ('Ah, empty ambition, senseless cupidity, infamous King, nation without justice', p. 278),[10] and the old man's final comment (the only part of this speech not derived from Camões) proves totally justified when he is struck over the head for his impudence and left for dead (p. 293). On this occasion, however, the Portuguese do not heed this warning, as is illustrated by the further extravagance of the journey of the royal court to the Spanish border for the marriage of Princess Maria Bárbara to a Spanish prince (pp. 300–3).

The wealth of the Crown comes primarily from Brazil (pp. 50 and 63), but also from the exploitation of local labour, as seen in the chain gangs which empty towns all over Portugal of their young men (pp. 292–3 and 312). There is no evidence anywhere in the text of any investment in order to stimulate economic growth in the future, a point which has also been made about the situation of Portugal under the historical D. João V:

> The central pillar of Portugal's eighteenth-century wealth and privilege was Brazilian gold discovered in the late 1690s [. . .] The

> old balance of payments problem was solved for nearly two generations and did not again present a serious crisis until the 1760s. The taxation of growing colonial trade meant that alternative sources of domestic revenue did not have to be approved by the cortes and parliament was not summoned again for more than a century once gold began to flow into Lisbon. John V was able to create an absolutist regime superficially similar to that of the much wealthier kingdom of France [. . .] With such wealth he could afford to neglect all the old structural problems of Portugal's domestic economy. Impoverished agriculture, inadequate transport and minimal industrial development were ignored so long as corn and cloth could be imported [. . .] Every problem in Portugal was temporarily solved by the king's gift of a little basket of gold coins bearing his effigy. The court of King John concentrated on pomp and ceremony while the English expatriates in Portugal turned their hands to commerce.[11]

In the context of the novel, this is seen to have an effect on the backbone of the Portuguese economy at the time (the rural economy), while the impoverishment of the land is represented by the sacrifice of the ordinary people involved in the project to build the convent. One notes here also Birmingham's comment that the easy cashflow from Brazil permitted the king to effectively suspend what democratic structures existed at the time and thus to impose his own will without question.

The sacrifices required of ordinary people in the novel to fulfil his wishes are not limited to the material, as this also involves repeated loss of life or injury to those who have devoted themselves to a project whose benefits they will never see: a young man who loses a foot (p. 246); three men killed in blasting (p. 286); the predicted death of Álvaro Diogo (p. 327), lost as a result of his devotion to his work, and the loss of Francisco Marques (p. 259), to be discussed in greater depth below.

This is all done to fuel the king's self-image, slyly indicated as illusory by the narrator's exploitation of Pessoa's description of the Infante Dom Henrique, which Saramago tells us was not actually written in connection with D. João only after we have read the paean of praise to wealth:

> Em seu trono entre o brilho das estrelas, com seu manto de noite e solidão, tem aos seus pés o mar novo e as mortas eras, o único imperador que tem, deveras, o globo mundo em sua mão, este tal

> foi o infante D. Henrique, consoante o louvará um poeta por ora ainda não nascido. (p. 227)[12]
>
> [Sitting on his throne amid the radiance of the stars, with his mantle of night and solitude, and with the new sea and dead eras at his feet, is the only emperor who truly holds the globe of the universe in his hand, these are the words with which the Infante Dom Henrique will be acclaimed one day by a poet who is not yet born.] (p. 212)

The king's own megalomania, which sees him take irresponsible decisions out of vanity, nonetheless has a deeper function here: for at three moments these ambitious plans contrast with the king's existential angst as he realizes that he is, after all, merely a common mortal (pp. 281, 289 and 290), and the novel closes without the completion of the convent, whose hollowness reflects the existential void lurking within all of the king's magnificent panoply of wealth (p. 328), as is pointed out by Óscar Lopes:

> But the mighty work of architecture is exposed as a clear expression and product of a specific form of absolute monarchy, of a specific society which on the outside is given to show, magnificence and megalomania but which is riddled inside with weaknesses, conflicts, hypocrisy, vice and decay, and which is based on a Pharaonic-type exploitation and coercion of the overwhelming majority.[13]

The Church (with the eccentric exception of Padre Bartolomeu Lourenço de Gusmão, who himself eventually flees the country in fear of the Inquisition; see p. 205) sides with royalty and privilege, but even so this is an alliance of convenience, exploited by the Church when this suits its purpose.[14] This is illustrated both in terms of the basic premise of the novel: in a tragic mode, as the collaboration between Church and state on the construction of the convent leads to the neglect of the country's broader interests and, ultimately, to the execution of Baltasar; and also in a comic mode, at the level of various subplots. In one of these, a young man, who had long desired to be admitted to the Franciscan order, finally achieves his ambition as a reward for finding some valuable silver stolen from a Franciscan church, but the very ease with which he finds the goods suggests that it was he who stole them in the first place:

> Regressaram as lâmpadas a Xabregas, e agora pense cada um de nós o que quiser. Terá sido o estudante, afinal tunante e bargante, que delineou o estratagema para poder entrar as portas e vestir o hábito franciscano como de facto veio a vestir, e por isso roubou e foi entregar, com muita esperança de que a bondade da intenção lhe perdoasse a fealdade do pecado no dia do juízo final. (p. 24)
>
> [The altar lamps were duly returned to Xabregas, and the reader may believe what he likes. Could it have been the student after all who was the culprit, devising this cunning strategy in order to force his way into the convent and don the habit of St Francis, as he did in the end, and could he have stolen and then returned the altar lamps in the hope that the worthiness of his intentions would absolve him from this wicked sin on the Day of Final Judgement.] (p. 16)

Similarly, when the Franciscan monk Frei António de S. José prophesies to the king that he will have an heir if he undertakes to build the order a convent which it has long desired (p. 25), the following narratorial comment, even as it denies abuse of influence by the Church, simultaneously suggests it to us:

> Vimos como em instância final saiu absolvido o estudante da suspeita do roubo das lâmpadas. Agora não se vá dizer que, por segredos de confissão divulgados, souberam os arrábidos que a rainha estava grávida antes mesmo que ela o participasse ao rei. Agora não se vá dizer que D. Maria Ana, por ser tão piedosa senhora, concordou calar-se o tempo bastante para aparecer com o chamariz da promessa o escolhido e virtuoso frei António. Agora não se vá dizer que el-rei contará as luas que decorrerem desde a noite do voto ao dia em que nascer o infante, e as achará completas. Não se diga mais do que ficou dito.[15] (p. 26)
>
> [We saw how the student was finally exonerated of blame in the episode of the stolen altar lamps. But it would be folly to suggest that because of secrets divulged in the confessional the friars knew of the Queen's pregnancy even before the Queen herself knew and could confide in the King. Just as it would be wrong to suggest that Dona Maria Ana, because she was such a pious lady, agreed to remain silent until the appearance of God's chosen messenger, the virtuous Friar Antony. Nor can anyone say the King will be counting the moons from the night the pledge was given until the child is born, and find the cycle complete. There is nothing to add to what has already been said.] (p. 18)

The sense of manipulation of events for effect here is completed by the wording of an earlier reference to the Franciscans: 'Com tais precedentes, sendo tão *favorecidos* os franciscanos de meios para alterarem, inverterem ou acelerarem a ordem natural das coisas, até a matriz renitente da rainha obedecerá à fulminante injunção do milagre' (p. 25) ('Given similar precedents, because the Franciscans are so *well endowed* with means to change, overturn, or hasten the natural order of things, even the recalcitrant womb of the Queen must respond to the solemn injunction of a miracle', p. 17).[16] This raises the possibility, through the sexual connotations of the word 'favorecidos', that the natural father of the child engendered may not be the king but Frei António himself, or at the very least another member of the order.[17]

The Church as an institution is quite clearly unsympathetic to the needs of its people, as is indicated by repeated incidents throughout the novel: the *autos-da-fé* where Baltasar and Blimunda meet in 1711 and then are separated permanently in 1739; the treatment of the death of Francisco Marques by the priest who delivers a sermon in which he claims that his workmates should envy him his martyrdom for the sake of the building of the convent (p. 263); the incident of the theft of the Franciscans' silverware (pp. 21–4), which is treated as a matter of greater urgency than the brutal murder and dismemberment of a woman's body (pp. 45–7); and, lastly, the attempted rape of Blimunda by a Dominican friar, whose weight on top of her body becomes more than a merely physical force, thus recalling the oppressive stone which crushes Francisco Marques to death earlier in the novel (p. 345).

In *Levantado,* the emphasis on material resources is a slightly different one, for there is none of the ostentatious luxury which may be seen in *Memorial.* The reasons for this are twofold: firstly, as a matter of simple realism, in spite of the privileged lives of the generations of landowners depicted here, this class of rural dictators-in-miniature did not enjoy anything approaching the same degree of wealth and luxury as did D. João V; and secondly, the constantly shifting narrative focus of the later novel is not developed in the same manner in *Levantado,* where events are unfolded to the reader much more from the perspective of the underdog. The landowning class therefore tends to appear only in caricature, under the guise of various names ending in the suffix *-berto,* which reflects their German ancestry, deriving as it does from a root signifying 'shining' or 'illustrious'.[18]

Nonetheless differences of class, power and privilege are clearly evident in this novel: whereas the rich may travel by tilbury (*Levantado,* p. 38), the ordinary man and woman are forced to walk long distances, or at best ride by horse or donkey (p. 15); Sara and Domingos' house does not even have a window (p. 22), while Lamberto sits in judgement from the luxury of a 'cadeirão hanseático' ('a grand Germanic chair', p. 34);[19] the poor struggle to pay their accounts for basic survival (pp. 82–4), but the aristocratic (and ironically named) D. Clemência is in a position to distribute food to them, even if she prefers to give them not meat but fat (p. 187). Any possibility of a charitable interpretation of this act is removed by her refusal to mix with the people whom she helps: not only does she lower food condescendingly to the people below (p. 188), but a reference on the previous page to roses growing out of a pile of wood invites a contrast with the Portuguese legend of Santa Isabel, the queen of D. Dinis, who gave help to the poor in a spirit of genuine charity.[20]

In *Levantado,* once again, the Church, represented here by the figure of Father Agamedes, sides with the rich rather than with the poor. This fact is most strikingly illustrated through a distortion of biblical text when the priest, who is clearly sharing a fine dinner with Norberto, asks for refreshment in the following terms: 'É a igreja grande consoladora nestas situações, sorve discreta o licor do cálice, por favor uma gota mais, *não o afasteis de mim*' ('The Church can be a great consolation in these situations, he said as he modestly sipped the drink from his chalice, another drop or two please, *do not let it pass from me*' p. 304).[21] The use of the specific word 'cálice' here, rather than the more basic 'copo', not only reinforces the ironic echoes of Christ's martyrdom, with which the priest refuses to identify,[22] but also suggests that the wine being enjoyed is in all probability a luxury wine such as Port or Madeira rather than the simple wine used at Passover. References in the text make it clear that this exchange takes place at the height of the election campaign of 1958, in which the opposition candidate General Humberto Delgado was almost certainly cheated of victory, before being executed in Spain, with the apparent connivance of the New State, some years later.[23] This small incident therefore sums up the desperate attempts to cling on to power on the part of the establishment at that time.

3. Domingos, João and António Mau-Tempo: The Extinction of a Name, or the Inexorable Rise of a Family?

A familiar narrative pattern is that of the late nineteenth- or early twentieth-century novel of the decline (and in some cases the ultimate extinction) of a once notable family. This subgenre includes such notable works as Thomas Mann's *Die Buddenbrooks*, Machado de Assis's *Dom Casmurro*, and, in Portugal, Eça's monumental *Os Maias*. Yet if there are losers, then there are also winners, and *Levantado* follows this pattern in that this novel depicts the changing fortunes of a family over several generations, culminating in the extinction of the Mau-Tempo ('Bad Weather') name with the birth of Maria Adelaide, who will bear the more combative (and less resigned) name Espada ('Sword'). Distinguishing this novel from its predecessors, however, is Saramago's sense of ideological and humanistic commitment, which leads him to depict not the gradual decline of the clan of the *-bertos*, but rather the inexorable rise of the humble Mau-Tempos. The eventual loss of their name is not a definitive loss of their legacy, whose continued survival is represented visually by the blue eyes shared by Maria Adelaide, João, and many of their ancestors before them, going back to the Germanic landowner who raped the girl by the spring centuries previously (p. 24).[24] The extinction of this family therefore happens in name only, and any preoccupation with that fact for its own sake is purely superficial, for the biological and cultural inheritance of the Mau-Tempos will continue to exist in Maria Adelaide and any children which she may bear.

Even if the family name is sacrificed, then, far greater gains are won for the community as a whole:[25] the depiction of the rise of the peasant class in this work revolves around the Mau-Tempos, but this is so only as a representative example of a wider reality and not as part of any suggestion that this family is inherently more important than others. When João's uncle Augusto Pintéu dies in an unfortunate accident, the reader is reminded that this misfortune is not singling out the Mau-Tempos in particular:

> Esta família Mau-Tempo parece escolhida pelo destino para negros casos, mas seria fruto de pouco entendimento assim supor. Afinal, até agora morreu apenas um, e se é em fome e misérias que

> estamos a pensar condoídos, qualquer outra família serviria. Ademais, nem de sangue é este tio. Casado com uma irmã de Sara da Conceição . . . (p. 64)
>
> [This Mau-Tempo family appears to have been singled out by Fate for bitter ends, but it would be poor understanding to believe this. After all, only one has died so far, and if we are going to think about hunger and misery, then any other family would do as well. Besides, this isn't a blood uncle: he married one of Sara da Conceição's sisters . . .]

The narrator here thus reminds the reader that what we are reading is the tale of a whole community and also gently scolds those who assume that all is as it seems at first sight. Thus the casual reader is reminded that deeper realities lie within the apparently transparent surface of this novel: the Mau-Tempos and their like are no less worthy of our attention and human interest than a supposedly great family such as the Buddenbrooks.

Nevertheless it is specifically through the efforts, sufferings and insights of the Mau-Tempos that the eventual coming of the Revolution is traced in this novel. This justifies Cerdeira da Silva in her claim that João Mau-Tempo is the central spine of the novel:[26] his suffering begins early as he has to become the main breadwinner for his family at the tender age of ten (p. 51); and he endures hardship and victimization before dying peacefully at home shortly before the 1974 Revolution. He is therefore like Moses, leading his people through the desert towards the Promised Land and living long enough to see it in the distance only to die before reaching it.[27] In spite of receiving only minimal education (p. 46), he and his son António, as well as various other characters representative of the people as a whole, are seen to learn as the novel progresses and to pass on the lessons which they have learnt to their own children (pp. 190–1), thus learning that 'tudo isto pode ser contado doutra maneira' ('all of this could be told in a different way', p. 14) and, equally importantly, that 'tudo isto pode ser feito doutra maneira' ('all of this could be done in a different way').

João's early experiences of work are harsh ones in an era when a strange combination of *machismo* and misapplied Christian rhetoric leads to many men accepting their own suffering almost as a badge of pride and being prepared to compensate for it only through the same non-solution of the bottle adopted earlier in the novel by João's father Domingos:

> Gabam-se os trabalhadores das pontadas que apanharam nos trabalhos da arroteia. Cada uma delas é medalha para vanglórias de taberna, entre o casco e o copo [. . .] E trabalha, mata-te a trabalhar, rebenta se for preciso [. . .] crucifica-te, estende o braço para a sangria, abre as veias e diz, Este é o meu sangue, bebei, esta é a minha carne, comei, esta é a minha vida, tomai-a, [. . .] façam-se em mim as vossas vontades. (pp. 73–4)
>
> [The workers boast about the wounds which they have suffered in the ploughing. Every one is a medal to be boasted about in the pub, on the way from the barrel back to the table [. . .] And work, work, kill yourself working, work till you burst if you have to, [. . .] crucify yourself, stretch out your arm so it may be bled, open your veins and say, This is my blood, drink of it, this is my flesh, eat, this is my life, take it, [. . .] may your wills be fulfilled in me.]

The heavily ironized allusions to Christ's Passion which were evident in the description of the collusion between Padre Agamedes and the landowners recur in this passage in a mood of genuine pathos. At this time João is prepared to accept back-breaking work which does not even give him a living wage (p. 76), but later, by the time of the outbreak of the Spanish Civil War, he is already reading clandestine political literature (p. 90). He has therefore realized that his own interests are vitally engaged in the workers' struggle to improve their lot, but even more significant at this point in the narrative is that he has learned the value of dissimulation, for he knows that it is more than his job is worth not to sign up to attend the anti-communist rally in Évora (p. 91).

João's development of a sense of strategy leads him to criticize Manuel Espada and the other workers who refuse to operate the threshing machine, not out of any ideological difference from them, but presumably because their instinctive refusal to cooperate is inviting trouble in return for no prospect of any significant gain: 'Por causa deles, diz João Mau-Tempo a Faustina, é que eu me deixei ir a Évora' ('It's because of them, João Mau-Tempo tells Faustina, that I allowed myself to be dragged off to Évora', p. 101). The futility of their actions is underlined when the troops come to look for the four recusants (with an implicit textual allusion to the biblical slaughter of the innocents, p. 103), as they are playing a pointless urination game (p. 102), a motif which will, however, take on greater significance later in the novel.

The punishment which the four youngsters receive is less severe than that suffered later in the text by Germano Vidigal or João, but it does demonstrate the spitefulness of the landowners, who blacklist them for a lengthy period (pp. 108–9). Nonetheless, in spite of João's misgivings about this action, it does not prove totally fruitless: firstly, it forces Manuel Espada into taking a job which will bring him into contact with António, whose sister Gracinda he will marry later in the text and with whom he will father the symbol of the revolution, Maria Adelaide; and secondly because it leads Father Agamedes to preach a hysterical sermon against communist agitators (pp. 119–21), which will in turn lead João to seek more authoritative teaching outside the Church:

> Ouve estes dizeres inflamados do padre Agamedes, compara-os em sua cabeça com o que conseguiu fixar da leitura de papéis que às escondidas lhe têm dado, faz o seu juízo de homem simples, e se dos papéis acredita alguma coisa, das palavras do padre não acredita em nenhuma. (p. 121)

> [He listens to these exaggerated speeches from Father Agamedes, he compares them in his head with what he has managed to establish from reading the leaflets which he has been given in secret, he reaches his judgement in his straightforward manner, and from then on he believes some things from such leaflets, but absolutely nothing from the priest.]

One notes in particular here the phrase 'compara-os em sua cabeça', which recalls the biblical description of Mary's reaction to the divine status of her son: 'But Mary kept all these things and pondered them in her heart'.[28] Here, however, the word 'coração' has been replaced by 'cabeça', thus placing João into the same group of characters as Father Bartolomeu Lourenço in *Memorial* who stress the importance of reason over simple faith. It is therefore noticeable that, later in the novel, when Father Agamedes preaches a second sermon similar in tone to this one, he does so to a congregation made up almost exclusively of old women (p. 181), while he will finally be silenced by António when he speaks up once too often at his sister's wedding (pp. 223–4).[29]

Future acts of defiance will be based on principles of solidarity and loyalty, as the workers cease to act like individuals and think of one another as comrades in a joint operation instead: António, in spite of initial misgivings about Manuel's reputation as a troublemaker (p. 123) soon realizes that he has a lot in common with him as he hears his stories of resistance (p. 124), just as later he will form a close friendship with his Spanish colleague in France (p. 288), while João, in repeated disputes, refuses to reveal the names of fellow collaborators to the police (pp. 156–8, 247–53) or even to Father Agamedes (pp. 160–1). The sense that something new and positive is afoot is strengthened by a comparison of the strikers to Christ's apostles (who, of course, also suffered persecution for their beliefs, p. 144), while later in the text secret political meetings will be held in the open air, just as was the case with the early Christians also (pp. 205–13), concluding with the believers fanning out to spread the word to others as widely as possible (p. 213).[30] This has its effect, with small locally-based actions, such as the proposed march for work on Montemor (pp. 308–9) in which one of the protestors, José Adelino dos Santos, is killed by the police (p. 314) but which Sigismundo correctly foresees as forming part of an eventual victory which even the dead will be able to celebrate (p. 308). Events such as these set people talking (as Blimunda also does in her subversive final journey around Portugal in the final chapter of the later novel; see *Memorial*, pp. 353–5), and through an inventive adaptation of the popular saying about the weather 'em Abril, águas mil' ('April, month of a thousand showers'), which is transformed into 'em Abril, falas mil' ('in April, month of a thousand dialogues', *Levantado*, p. 332) and 'palavras mil' ('a thousand words', p. 333), it is clear that the lid will finally be lifted on the centuries of oppression and silence and that the Mau-Tempo can now be transformed into a fairer forecast for the future.[31]

4. The Suppression of Resistance

One significant difference of emphasis between these two novels lies in the question of enforcement of authority, an issue which, for all the presence of the Inquisition in *Memorial*, remains more in the background in that novel than it does in *Levantado*. There are clear instances of the arbitrary and excessive use of power in the later novel, but these are generally not developed at length: the brutal punishment of the old man who criticizes the king (*Memorial*, p. 293); the enforced enslavement of men who are removed from the land to help build the convent (pp. 292–3); and the treatment of workers like animals or slaves once they are on the site at Mafra (p. 218). The explanation given by Cerdeira da Silva for the relative lack of repressive measures in evidence in this novel is probably a valid one, namely that repression is not necessary with a population so lacking in self-awareness as to simply internalize and accept unjust conditions:

> Power almost always acts on an ideological mechanism which turns repression into self-repression, turns the conscious person into an alienated one, so that a lot of the time there is no need for literal violence. Submission to the dominant order is something produced voluntarily by an ideological apparatus which is present, if invisible.[32]

It might also be suggested, however, that in *Memorial* the requirements of the plot are such that Baltasar, Blimunda and Padre Bartolomeu have to be allowed to build the *Passarola* safely away from the prying eyes of the Inquisition, while Sabine would also argue that the development of a Marcusian oasis of fulfilment in love and work is essential to provide a counterpoint to the more unpleasant realities of eighteenth-century Portuguese society.[33]

In *Levantado,* this issue takes on greater prominence as the people grow in awareness of their own circumstances. In one sense, this may seem a statement of the obvious, since this work depicts the gradual rise of the underclass to take charge of its own destiny with the 1974 Revolution. In another sense, however, this is a more radical statement, since the general assumption is that it was the intervention of the military and the negative influence of events in Africa which led to the downfall of the regime. However, Saramago's portrayal of the struggles of the people of Monte Lavre over three generations, and in particular his accounts of the deaths in captivity of the real-life characters Germano Vidigal and José Adelino dos Santos present a different perspective: that this was also the victory of the ordinary Portuguese man or woman over forces which were as much their enemy as they were that of the oppressed peoples of the African colonies. This is clearly demonstrated, for example, in brutal assaults on the ordinary workers, such as that by the Republican Guard, described in ironically colourful terms on p. 35 of the text.

A more farcical instance of the abuse of power lies in an incident where Adalberto orders the police captain Tacabo to take action against a shepherd who has brought his sheep on to his (Adalberto's) land, seemingly without his permission. It then transpires that the landowner did not recognize his own employee or his own sheep and the incident blows over in embarrassment for Tacabo, who had been forced to confront the man (p. 279). If the sheep had not been Adalberto's, however, then the arbitrary penalty which Tacabo wishes to impose (a fine of five escudos per sheep for a flock of six hundred) would surely have been enough to ruin the shepherd; and the threat is implicit in the passage of what might have happened if the man had not been in a position to pay up, as Tacabo is described as being 'senhor da lei e da carabina' ('in charge of the law and the gun').

Further instances abound of a variety of forms of brutality, intimidation and silencing of the mass of the people. One anonymous worker tells how he and his father were caught stealing food from the ground to overcome their hunger, and were then forced by the police to fight with one another in order to break their spirit (pp. 334–5), a fascistic exemplification of the familiar dictum 'Divide and rule'.[34] Several characters, including João (twice over), are taken into custody and treated with varying degrees of brutality and heartlessness. On the first occasion, João is held in Montemor,[35] but it is the second period of imprisonment which is more severe, as he is taken to Lisbon and held in Caxias prison for six months and then released without any real justification being given for his arrest or detention, or any information being provided to his family. In addition, when João is released from custody, on both occasions the authorities do so with a spitefulness which indicates that they still regard him as their enemy: the first time, he and his fellow prisoners are told to reimburse the state for the cost of their earlier transportation to their detention in Montemor (p. 163), while later the authorities deliberately release him from Caxias, near Lisbon, late on a cold and windy January night, in the sure knowledge that he has no shelter and no transport available to him to return home until the following day (pp. 260–2), and with the threat of renewed arrest for loitering hanging over him if he simply waits for daybreak in the street (p. 262).

However, the most sustained concentration on the issue of repression is to be found in the frightening treatment and eventual death of Germano Vidigal in prison (pp. 167–80), an episode which could be viewed as a representation in miniature of Portugal under Salazar, as it leads the attentive reader to recall the incarceration of António at Caxias which takes H. by surprise in the earlier novel *Manual* (*Manual*, p. 265) and looks forward to the sinister threat of the secret police surrounding even the innocuous Ricardo Reis upon his return to Lisbon in a later novel (*Ano*, pp. 171–2).

The events recounted here are shocking: Germano is interrogated, beaten and tortured in a number of ways, and when he eventually dies in captivity, the authorities do their best to cover up what has happened, claiming that he hanged himself while in prison. The actual torture scenes are seen through the eyes of the only surviving witnesses to them: the ants present at Germano's interrogation and torture (p. 169). While this inventive perspective on events reminds the reader that there were no human witnesses and in more general terms, no meaningful democratic structures which could have called the police to account for their actions, these ants represent more than a yearning for there to have been some kind of first-hand testimony to such injustices: they also provide a visual perspective on the abuses committed which is all the more striking for its unusual angle, and the ants themselves become a leitmotif used in both this novel and *Memorial* to represent the ordinary people, who are normally taken for granted in their purely functional roles within an economic structure designed to meet the needs of other groups. This anthropomorphization of the ants is, however, taken a stage further here than it is in works of the neo-realist period, where a comparison of humans to animals is made in order to indicate the degradation of the latter group. Here Saramago exploits this imagery in order to treat the ants as human (they are seen, for example, to be potentially capable of speech; p. 176) and thus, effectively, to rehumanize the mass of the workers who had been dehumanized by the very literary processes which were first adopted in order to demonstrate the workers' plight.

In this way the ants' eyeview perspective on Germano's torture and death reflects the fact that official silence over such abuses did not conceal the knowledge of their existence amongst the wider community. In a different context within this novel itself, for example, we see that, even if João is not subjected to physical torture or killed, he still has to endure captivity twice, both times merely for wishing to represent the needs of his people (pp. 148–63 and 231–65), experiences which he would surely have recounted to his friends and family afterwards in the spirit of the thousand dialogues of April. It will, therefore, be difficult to suppress the truth forever, as the narrator reminds us in taking a last look at the castle of Montemor, where Germano met his end:

> Dizem-se estas coisas por despedida, daqui de baixo vê-se o castelo, quem pudesse contar todas as histórias dele, as passadas e as que hão-de vir, erro grave seria julgarmos que por hoje se fazerem as guerras do lado de fora dos castelos, acabaram as acções em que são parte. (p. 179)
>
> [These things are said by way of farewell, from down here you can see the castle, if only we could tell all the stories relating to it, those from the past and those which are still to come, it would be a serious mistake to think just because today wars happen outside castles that there are no longer any events which take place there.]

At least later in the novel, when José Adelino dos Santos is killed, the doctor who inspects his body refuses to comply with the authorities' cover-up, insisting that the man is already dead even as the police go through the motions of appearing to try to save him (pp. 315–16). Absolute historical truth may be irrecuperable, as Sabine remarks,[36] but when available evidence points strongly in one direction, it is not surprising if that conclusion drives human responses to the presumptions made about past events; and, even if recent Portuguese history has been free of external wars, the quotation reproduced above appears to suggest that class warfare within the country continues to exist and to be represented by symbols of power such as the castle of Montemor.

5. Alienation and Natural Processes

In both novels there is a clear reflection of the core Marxist concept of the alienation of labour.[37] Ordinary people participate in a process which brings them only such meagre reward as their employers see fit to distribute to them. It is gratifying, however, that Saramago does not paint a purely manichaestic picture of society, placing the downtrodden but virtuous worker into a simplistic opposition to evil capitalists, but instead that his novels depict real characters interacting in a convincing way with a society based on complex, and sometimes contradictory, social and economic relations, whose central organizational pillar nonetheless is based on the exploitation of labour.

Almost all the ordinary workers in *Memorial* are seen to be exploited in one way or another. We first see Baltasar when he returns to Portugal after losing his left hand in the war of the Spanish succession, at the opening of the fourth chapter of the novel. The narrator makes it clear straight away that his loss fits directly into a pattern of alienated labour:

> Este que por desafrontada aparência, sacudir da espada e desaparelhadas vestes, ainda que descalço, parece soldado, é Baltasar Mateus, o Sete-Sóis. Foi mandado embora do exército por já não ter serventia nele, depois de lhe cortarem a mão esquerda pelo nó do pulso, estralhaçada por uma bala em frente de Jerez de los Caballeros [. . .] Sete-Sóis, mutilado, caminhava para Lisboa pela estrada real, credor de uma mão esquerda que ficara parte em Espanha e parte em Portugal, por artes de uma guerra em que se haveria de decidir quem viria a sentar-se no trono de Espanha, se um Carlos austríaco ou um Filipe francês, português nenhum. (*Memorial*, pp. 35–6)

> [This scruffy-looking fellow with his rattling sword and ill-assorted clothes, even though barefoot, has the air of a soldier, and his name is Baltasar Mateus, otherwise known as Sete-Sóis or Seven Suns. He was dismissed from the army where he was of no further use once his left hand was amputated at the wrist after being shattered by gunfire at Jerez de los Caballeros [. . .] Sete-Sóis, maimed and bedraggled, travelled the main highway to Lisbon, deprived of his left hand, part of which had remained in Spain and part in Portugal, and all because of a strategic war to decide who was to occupy the Spanish throne, an Austrian Charles or a French Philip, but no one Portuguese.] (*Baltasar*, pp. 26–7)

Baltasar's sacrifice has been made in the name of international power politics which are of no relevance to his life, but, once wounded, he has been left to his own devices, having ceased to be of any use to the same Crown which earlier demanded that he be prepared to lay down his life for its interests (an experience shared by António Mau-Tempo; see *Levantado*, pp. 197–8).

The impression of Baltasar's alienation from Portuguese society is only increased in Lisbon. The preparation for this disillusionment is achieved by an implicit comparison of the city to something like St. Augustine's City of God: Baltasar travels across the Tagus to Lisbon on a sunny day (*Memorial*, p. 39) with hints of a journey to paradise (p. 39), while it is emphasized that the city itself is placed up on a hill (p. 40). In reality, however, the reader has already witnessed the chaotic scenes of corruption and hypocrisy within the city in the previous three chapters of the novel, which reveal the reality of the life of court, clergy and commoner respectively: the potential Utopia witnessed from beyond the water turns out instead to be a dystopia, lesser only in the depths of nastiness plumbed than the anonymous city represented in the later *Cegueira*.

Even within this chapter itself, however, any lingering idealistic impressions of Lisbon are soon dispelled, firstly as the ferryman tells the passengers about the fifty English whores who have been on the loose in the city (p. 40),[38] and then as Baltasar's own experiences show him that he will find no more charity here than he has done elsewhere.[39] Before long, in fact, Baltasar wishes that he were still in the army, where he was at least provided for and could enjoy the support of others rather than being exposed to the every-man-for-himself environment of the capital: 'Na guerra há mais caridade' (p. 47) ('In war you find greater charity', p. 38).[40] As is noted by Lisboa in a more general context, then, the imagery of crossing the river here may indicate simply the definitive transition to a new stage in one's life.[41] The immediate novelty for Baltasar, therefore, is merely that he will now have to seek new forms of gainful employment.[42] This he does through a variety of manual jobs on the construction site at Mafra; on the other hand, however, his labour with Bartolomeu and Blimunda on the construction and maintenance of the *Passarola*, or flying machine, is work which he finds rewarding at a personal level, as Cerdeira da Silva explains: 'Amongst them there is no labour-contract between employer and employee, just a sharing of desires, and dreams held in common'.[43]

There can be no doubt that this contrast between Baltasar's level of participation in the two projects is intentional on the part of the novelist, as he reveals how his whole conception of the novel was changed radically as he became more aware of the expressive potential of the *Passarola*:

> My plan when I came up with the idea for *Memorial do Convento* was limited to the building of the convent, and it was only afterwards that I found out that at exactly the same time there was a priest

> who had the idea for making a flying machine. That changed things completely [. . .] From then on the novel had to be different, totally different. There was the whole contrast between things falling and things going up, heavy things and light things, things that want to fly and things that prevent flight; that whole relationship between freedom and authority, between invention and conventionality, took on another dimension which had not previously been in my plans and changed the nature of the novel completely.[44]

The sense of fulfilment achieved by Baltasar and Blimunda through their work on the *Passarola* is further demonstrated by their attempts to prevent Bartolomeu from destroying his own machine for fear of discovery by the Inquisition (p. 205) and their maintenance of it even after the priest's death. Their fulfilment reaches its climax in the maiden flight of the airship, which carries them over the convent at Mafra, leading it to look small in comparison to the heights which they have reached (p. 264). While it should be conceded that the *Passarola* also later leads Baltasar to his death, when he accidentally slips and releases it from its moorings (p. 335), it is important to remember that it gave him life as opposed to the mere functional existence which he would have had if his only occupation had been on the building site, which, of course, also costs several human lives.

The loss concentrated on with greatest pathos is that of Francisco Marques (p. 259), crushed under the giant stone brought to Mafra from Pêro Pinheiro for use at the convent. When the accident happens, the narrator explicitly points out that the worker was not fully involved in his task:

> Distraiu-se talvez Francisco Marques, ou enxugou com o antebraço o suor da testa, ou olhou cá do alto a sua vila de Cheleiros, enfim se lembrando da mulher, fugiu-lhe o calço da mão no preciso momento em que a plataforma deslizava, não se sabe como isto foi, apenas que o corpo está debaixo do carro, esmagado, passou-lhe a primeira roda por cima, mais de duas mil arrobas só a pedra, se ainda estamos lembrados. (p. 259)

> [Perhaps Francisco Marques was distracted or raised his arm to wipe the sweat from his forehead, or looked down on his native town of Cheleiros as he suddenly remembered his wife, but the wedge slipped from his hand at the same moment that the platform broke free, no one knew how but within seconds he was trapped under the cart and crushed to death, the first wheel passed

> over him, the stone alone, in case you have forgotten, weighs more than two thousand arrobas.] (p. 244)

There are various possible explanations for the character's alienation from the job in hand: the reference to the comforts of home, as opposed to life on the road; his enthusiasm for being able to spend the night with his wife and have sex with her (an intense and fulfilling experience, unlike the laborious drudgery of transporting the stone, p. 243); and, finally, the text twice stresses the intense heat in which the workers are being expected to their task (pp. 243 and 256), with the earth being compared in the second of these passages to a furnace and the sun to a spike in the ribs, thus suggesting that Francisco Marques is being sent to a form of hell for his impertinence in even thinking of achieving some degree of personal fulfilment.[45] This imagery, of course, contrasts with the words of the priest on the Sunday following his death, as he reassures his audience in pseudo-biblical language that the dead man will have gone to heaven for his demise in a sacred cause, just as once the Crusaders were similarly rewarded for their efforts to liberate Jerusalem (pp. 262–3).

In spite of these fine words, however, once they are placed in the context of the priest's desire that the project should continue and the need to encourage the workers in their efforts, it is his warnings about sin which are fixed more forcefully in the mind of the reader, especially when one considers what the 'official' Church position would have been on the sexual thoughts which may have been running through Francisco's mind at the moment of his demise. The later *História* will, of course, call into question the idealistic motives imputed to the Crusaders in their quest to 'liberate' soil regarded as belonging unquestionably to the Christian tradition, while the hypocrisy within the Church's appeals to the people for virtue here is exposed when it becomes evident that it benefits financially from the penances imposed for sinful behaviour (p. 155).

The experiences of other workers fit into similar patterns too: Julião Mau-Tempo (clearly an ancestor of the twentieth-century Mau-Tempos of Monte Lavre in *Levantado*) claims to have been lured to Mafra to work on the building site with false promises of plenty from his village priest to contrast with the poverty in his native Alentejo (pp. 235–6), and he, too, is distanced from the things which make his life meaningful:

> . . . afinal saiu-me tudo mentira, do paraíso não falo, que não sou desse tempo, mas de Mafra sim, se não consigo morrer de fome é porque gasto tudo quanto ganho, roto ando como andava, e, quanto a ser criado de el-rei, ainda espero não morrer sem ver a cara do meu amo, a não ser que me agonie de estar tanto tempo longe da família, um homem, se tem filhos, também se alimenta de ver a cara deles, bom era que se alimentassem eles de ver a nossa cara, é o destino, acabar-se a vida a olharmos uns para os outros, quem és tu, que vieste cá fazer, quem eu seja e o que faça, já perguntei e não tive resposta. (p. 236)
>
> [. . . well, I soon discovered that I had been misinformed, I can't vouch for paradise, because I wasn't around at the time of Adam, but I can speak for Mafra, and if I haven't died from hunger, it's because I spend everything I earn on food, I'm as shabbily dressed as I ever was, as for becoming one of the King's servants, I live in hope of seeing my sovereign's face before I finally pine away after all these years of separation from my family, when a man has children, he is often nourished just by looking at their faces, how reassuring it would be if our children could be nourished just by looking at our faces, we're fated to consume our lives looking at one another, Who are you, What are you doing here, Who I am and what I am doing here is a question I've often asked myself without receiving any answer.] (pp. 220–1)

In Julião's case, in spite of his awareness of the lies which have been told him and of the separation from his family which he is enduring for the sake of simple survival, he has still not achieved sufficient perspective to realize that he will not actually derive any benefit from being able to see the king's face. Nonetheless, in spite of his lack of learning and the traditional casting of members of his class as people effectively without a soul (a status reserved for the privileged and learned in this society), he asks questions of a type which Saramago's later (erudite) incarnation of Ricardo Reis seeks actively to avoid. In order for this full humanity of Julião's class to be recognized, however, it will be left to his descendants in another novel to create a society where privilege is abolished.

The final figure worthy of mention in the present context is João Elvas. To some extent, like Julião and Francisco Marques, he is a victim of the more powerful sectors of society: early on in the text, for example, we see the comic incident of a mendicant friar who steals from his begging-bowl (p. 61), an incident which illustrates that the Church not only does not do anything for its people but that it actually lives at their expense.[46] Similarly, when chain gangs are sent out to look for new workers to help at Mafra, no mercy is shown to João on the grounds of his age, and he is expected to work with 'pá e enxada' (p. 308) ('pick and shovel', p. 294) along with everyone else.[47]

Yet João Elvas is also privileged to receive tantalizing glimpses of a better life. When he accompanies the royal retinue to the Spanish border for the royal wedding, he is informed by a nobleman of the splendour of the provision for the bridal party (pp. 302–3 and 304–5). In spite of the undoubtedly kindly manner of this nobleman, it appears that he is still conscious enough of social differences to remind João how privileged he is to see the king in person (a reminder of Julião's earlier internalization of his own inferior status, mentioned above):

> . . . por muitos anos que ainda tenhas para viver nunca hás-de esquecer este momento de felicidade perfeita, quando viste D. João V passando no seu coche, estando tu de joelhos ao pé destas piteiras, guarda bem na memória estas imagens, ó privilegiado, e agora podes-te levantar, já passaram. (pp. 302–3)

> [. . . however long you may live, you will never forget this moment of perfect bliss, when you saw Dom João V go past in the royal coach while you knelt respectfully at the foot of those aloes, be sure to cherish these images in your mind, for you have been truly privileged, and now you may get up, since the royal party has passed and is well on its way.] (p. 289)[48]

This excerpt once again recalls the passage where the priest declares that Francisco Marques can already see the face of the Almighty (p. 263). The Almighty on earth, however, is the king, and by implication, these few seconds of privilege hardly make up for the miseries endured on earth. Nor does João's other brief glimpse of a better life (when he unknowingly hears from an open window the strains of Scarlatti's harpsichord music, p. 318) make up for the misery which is the lot of his class under the reign of D. João V.[49]

The functioning of the patterns of alienation is rather more complex in *Levantado*, where the emphasis is less on work and more on societal structures than in *Memorial*. Nonetheless it is clear that the workers exist for the sake of their work rather than vice versa, and that life remains difficult for them under the laws of capitalist economics: '. . . o dinheiro sobe, só para subir tem asas, não para descer. O lugar do dinheiro é um céu, um alto lugar onde os santos mudam de nome quando vem a ter de ser, mas o latifúndio não' (p. 13) ('. . . prices go up, they only have wings for ascent and not for descent. The home of money is a high heaven where the saints change their names when need be, but not the landowners'). In this passage, the sacred quality of capital (an assocation of ideas which is repeated later in the text; see p. 278) is explicitly associated with the high places intimately linked to the expression of power in this novel.[50] Even after the 1974 Revolution, in fact, the question is asked if all that much has changed:

> Enfim se está vendo quem mais força tem, diz Norberto a Clariberto, se lhes não dermos trabalho, é só deixar passar o tempo devagarinho e tornará o dia em que virão comer-nos à mão, são palavras de desprezo e rancor de quem por grande susto passara [. . .] mas isto é como a onda do mar, não a enfrentes com rijeza de corpo, pareceria coragem e é tonteira, baixa-te o mais que puderes, e ela passa sem quase dar por ti. (pp. 357–8)

> [Now we'll see who is more powerful, Norberto tells Clariberto, if we don't give them any work, all we'll have to do is let time just go by, and the day will come again when they will come to eat out of our hands, these are the bitter and scornful words of someone who has suffered a great shock [. . .] but this is like the waves of the sea, you shouldn't stand up to it with an upright body, which may seem courageous but is really stupid, get down as low as you can, and it will wash over you almost unnoticed.]

Once again, everything is seen to be designed in the interests of the rich and powerful: the roads, which are at first described as 'estradas reais' ('royal highways') may soon become 'nacionais' ('national highways') when the monarchy is overthrown (p. 12), but the same people find themselves at the top, with the workers once more at the bottom.

As in *Memorial*, the novel provides the reader with references to the major events of history as well as to the experience of the times on the part of the ordinary citizen; in this case, however, the echoes of real-world events are meticulously placed, even if they are referred to only in the vaguest of terms, as Sabine observes:

> The novel clearly indicates, however, that historical knowledge is power. It presents the workers' acquisition of power as directly

> proportional to their acquisition of historical and economic awareness through narrative reference to historical events of national/ international significance only as experienced, witnessed or apprehended by characters within the diegesis.[51]

The vagueness of these references reflects the perspective of those for whom Europe was a distant and almost imaginary world. When major events in history are alluded to, the focus of the narration shifts imperceptibly to a reflection of the news through the media, to which only the privileged have any access in this society:

> . . . o czar foi deposto, as potências estão preocupadas com o que se passa na Rússia, grande ofensiva na frente ocidental, a arma do futuro é a aviação, mas a infantaria é a rainha das batalhas, nada feito sem a barragem de artilharia, o domínio dos mares é indispensável, revolução na Rússia, bolchevismo. Adalberto lia o seu jornal, olhava pela janela inquieto o tempo enevoado, partilhou das indignações da gazeta, disse em voz alta, Isto passa. (p. 57)

> [. . . the czar has been overthrown, the world powers are worried about what is happening in Russia, a major offensive on the western front, aeroplanes are the weapons of the future, but foot-soldiers are the queens of battle, nothing can be done without heavy artillery, control of the seas is essential, revolution in Russia, Bolshevism. Adalberto read his newspaper, looked anxiously out the window at the misty weather, shared the indignation of the journal, and said aloud, This will all blow over.]

There are obvious precedents here for the figure of Ricardo Reis, who also receives his news of the world entirely from newspapers working to a particular agenda, and one notes here Adalberto's naïve faith that the Russian Revolution will not prove to be a significant event, even as he observes the mists in which he is presumably seeking to identify the figure of some D. Sebastião to save the nation (and more particularly his own interests) from following the dangerous example set by the toppling of the czar. His lack of concern also disguises the fact that the reference to the infantry as the 'queen of battle' implies the mass slaughter of young men on all sides in the trenches. For the ordinary workers (many of them illiterate), however, the news of the deposition of the Russian monarchy would have been shrouded in even more mists of uncertainty than those perceived by Adalberto.

This lack of awareness of the full circumstances surrounding their struggle has its effect on the workers. When João decides to go to seek work in Lisbon, his first view of the capital is similar to Baltasar's in *Memorial*, in that the city appears to offer a lot more seen from a distance than in reality: 'De cima destes sobreiros vê-se Lisboa, se está claro o dia, quem diria que é assim tão perto, afinal julgávamos que vivíamos no cabo do mundo, são erros de quem não sabe nem teve quem lhe ensinasse' (p. 77) ('From up on top of these cork-trees, you can see Lisbon on a clear day, who would have thought that it was so near, since we thought we lived in the middle of nowhere, these are the misconceptions of people who had nobody to teach them otherwise').

João soon finds out, however, that the streets of Lisbon are not paved with gold, and he has to return home in disappointment (p. 79). His wide-eyed innocence regarding the city, indicated through an ignorance of the symbolism of its monuments, represents his symbolic exclusion from the values of the nation to which he (nominally) belongs:

> E olha a Avenida da Liberdade, para que será este palito espetado no meio, isto são os restauradores, ah, não sabia, e em segredo comigo mesmo digo, E continuo a não saber, as vergonhas da ignorância são as que mais custam a confessar, porém coração ao largo, subiremos a Avenida da Liberdade. (pp. 77–8)

> [And he looks up the Avenida da Liberdade, what is that giant toothpick stuck up in the middle, that is Restauradores, ah, I didn't realize, and I quietly said to myself, I still don't understand, the shame of ignorance is the hardest one of all to admit, but let's pluck up our courage and go up the Avenida da Liberdade.]

This passage reflects ironically on the use of the name 'Avenida da Liberdade' in a society without either economic or political freedom, but João is also clearly unaware that the monument which he irreverently compares to a giant toothpick symbolizes the restoration of sovereignty to the Portuguese people after an interlude of foreign domination; as long as his kind are unaware that they are citizens of this sovereign nation, the further-off will be the day when they actually come to be in charge of their own destinies. This minor incident therefore amounts to a reflection on the potentially deceptive exploitation of concepts such as 'freedom' in order to blind the public to artificially imposed constraints that tether them. Instead of such theoretical concerns, however, in the context described the people have no option but to remain focused on their own material survival on a day-to-day basis.

The workers are thus frequently pressurized into acting against their own interests: João see better prospects for himself in the army than in civilian life (p. 62), while António openly acknowledges the training which he received in the military (p. 224), but this requires him to put his life at risk and endure tough living conditions in the service of a country which has done little for him, as he refers to the poor quality of the food served up to the soldiers (p. 225).[52] António's own enlistment is clearly presented as a loss of freedom, as he wistfully goes off to the barracks while contemplating the alternative of a life as an outlaw like José Gato, a Robin Hood-type figure of local legend (p. 199), although, in fact, António's structured and ideologically informed resistance will prove more worthwhile than José's essentially self-seeking spirit of rebellion.[53]

Harsh conditions and personal sacrifice are also involved in civilian work, where on one occasion a group of young workers is made to race one another to their place of work. This is done to create rivalry within the group, which then leads the last in the race (in this case João) to want to reassert his virility by achieving more than the others in the job itself after being told sharply 'não és homem nem és nada' ('You aren't a man, you aren't anything at all', pp. 74–5).[54] Essentially, this is simply a means of pressuring the employees to maximize the return given to their employers. This exploitation of them as a resource rather than as people in their own right is illustrated more clearly still in the only job which João is able to obtain after his release from prison, where the workers are given medical treatment when required but only in order to rush them back to work sooner than they really should, leading the narrator to compare the job to a death camp and the workers to rubbish being dumped on tips: 'tu tens alta, tu também, e tu, e tu, é assim que os médicos nos tratam, e torna a camioneta a despejar no monte a carga com a saúde a meio pau' (pp. 268–9) ('you can go, you too, and you, and you, that's how the doctors treat us, and the truck once again spills out on the mountainside its cargo of semi-healthy workers').

The workers, then, are treated merely as part of the process of production rather than as the end towards which the whole process is directed, and this contrast also raises a deeper sense of alienation running throughout the text of *Levantado* and based on a contrast between natural processes (with which the workers are intimately linked) and the artificial arrangements imposed on the land by the landowners. Repeatedly the landowners attempt to prevent the time-honoured use of the land's resources by refusing to collect the harvest or even by destroying it, which thus becomes a political weapon to force the workers into renewed submission to their feudal overlords: this occurs twice after strikes (pp. 38 and 139), and again during the general election campaign of 1958, where the landowners try to give a warning to the population about the issues at stake if General Humberto Delgado wins (p. 304).

By way of contrast with this disregard for natural cycles, at the popular level João and Faustina overcome suspicion from her family about their relationship and become united to one another through a spontaneous exchange of vows (p. 68), reminiscent of the pseudo-marriage ceremony undergone by Baltasar and Blimunda in *Memorial* (see *Memorial*, p. 56). João and Faustina then celebrate by making love and enjoying a simple meal of bread and *chouriço* (*Levantado*, p. 70), having earlier taken the risk of passing by the same spot where earlier in the novel Augusto Pintéu died crossing a flimsy bridge in a raging stream (pp. 64–5). They at least are not afraid to set foot on the bridge leading to their union and face the elemental forces of nature which drive them in such a natural way, the narrative carrying a hint of the successful outcome of their relationship, as João declares to Faustina the fidelity which his father failed to show to Sara da Conceição: 'João Mau-Tempo atou as duas pontas, Farei tudo por ti enquanto formos vivos, na saúde e na doença' (p. 68) ('João Mau-Tempo tied together the two loose threads, I will do everything for you as long as we are alive, in sickness and in health').[55]

In spite of the conspiracy theories of the authorities, frequently the resistance which comes from the workers is presented as being simply a gut reaction to unjust treatment, most clearly illustrated when Manuel Espada denies that his non-cooperation with the threshing machine was ideologically motivated and blames it instead on simple fear: 'Ninguém nos ensinou, não sabemos de ninguém, nem de greves, a máquina é que comia muito e os frascais eram muito grandes' (*Levantado*, p. 107) ('Nobody taught us, we don't know anything about anybody, or about any strikes, the machine was eating everything up, and the bales of hay were really big'). Later on, his daughter Maria Adelaide will be more aware of the circumstances surrounding her life ('Maria Adelaide não é menos do que os outros, está de nariz levantado, curiosa', p. 350) ('Maria Adelaide is no less interested than the others, she has her nose up in curiosity')[56] but there will still be an instinctive element in her celebration of the Revolution: 'Então desceu Maria Adelaide à fonte, nem sabe por que escolheu este lugar' (p. 356) ('And so Maria Adelaide went down to the spring, she is not quite sure why she chose this place'). Rebellion is thus seen to be at its most potent when it is driven by a sense of genuine moral outrage, rather than one of pure ideological dogma.

Meantime the forces of law and order are visualized in supernatural terms as dragons (pp. 251, 270, 314, 329 and 333), or they are implicitly dehumanized by their presence being noted through numbers rather than names or other individualizing features (p. 312). The workers themselves, however, are repeatedly identified with a variety of different types of animal life, most notably ants and dogs.[57] Other forms of animate life also are mentioned, however, including the proliferation of fish which exist in the 'mar interior' ('inland sea') of the estates (p. 319), thus belying the apparent unchangingness identified in its landscape in the opening chapter of the novel.

The association with ants becomes particularly significant, as the implicit parallel with efficient workers is in many ways an ideal one for ideologically committed authors to express their admiration for the quiet achievement of the unsung heroes of the soil, and, indeed, this imagery does recur on a number of occasions in *Memorial* as well as in *Levantado*.[58] The danger of this approach is that the same imagery could be used equally powerfully by those with a different ideology in order implicitly to reduce humans to the level of animals; this is effectively what Salazar implied, for example, when he declared that education was not a matter which needed to be taken too seriously for the majority of the population, and such thinking also lies behind Lamberto's comparison of his worker's requests for better conditions to the howling of hungry wolves (p. 34).[59] Thus, in both of these novels Saramago rejuvenates the animal-related imagery in order to reveal workers who are determined to improve their lot and make themselves fully human, even when others treat them as not having this status. So, in *Memorial*, the ants on the building-site at Mafra also have their counterparts in the form of the bedbugs which suck at the royal blood (*Memorial*, p. 16), threatening an eventual collapse of the wasteful monarchy, just as the marvellous short story 'Cadeira' in *Objecto* recounts the (literal and metaphorical) fall of Salazar from the perspective of the woodworm inside the chair where he suffered his debilitating stroke.[60] These bedbugs represent the power of the people, little by little, to make a positive transformation to even the most corrupt form of government.

The ants are seen to move up the evolutionary scale by coming to resemble dogs, clear progress on the initial situation of the workers in the novel who did not wash or shave during periods of labour, much to the convenience of the landowners who thus not only kept the workers in their place but also destroyed their self-respect in the process:

> é ponto de honra e de homem que durante todo o tempo do contrato se não lave nem cara nem mãos, nem a barba se corte [. . .] É preciso que este bicho da terra seja bicho mesmo, [. . .] que o sujo [. . .] seja o halo glorioso do trabalhador no latifúndio, é preciso que o homem esteja abaixo do animal, que esse, para se limpar, lambe-se, é preciso que o homem se degrade para que não se respeite a si próprio nem aos seus próximos. (*Levantado*, p. 73)

> [It is a point of honour, throughout the period of contracted labour, that men do not wash their hands or face or shave their beards [. . .] It is necessary that this creature of the earth should be just a creature, [. . .] that filth [. . .] should be the glorious halo of the estate-worker, it is necessary for man to be below the animals, which lick themselves clean, it is necessary for men to be degraded so that they do not respect themselves or their fellow-workers.][61]

This is a matter of pride and self-respect, then, and the dogs which these workers later become learn to bite back against the 'podengos' (or bulldogs), the paid lackeys of the landowners (pp. 90, 254 and 255).[62] For this reason the dog which barks when Domingos and Sara da Conceição first appear in the second chapter of the text is significant (p. 20); after the opening chapter, with its ideologically slanted representation of the immutability of the countryside, its bark represents the beginning of change and the real *incipit* of the story of *Levantado*, a novel which closes with a reference to the dog Constante once liberation has finally been achieved (p. 366). Similarly, in *Jangada* the loosening of Iberia's ties with the rest of Europe is marked by the mysterious recovery of the voices of the dogs of Cerbère (*Jangada*, p. 9), just as, in a negative mode, *Lucidez* closes with the silencing of the dog owned by the exemplary doctor's wife, who has become too dangerous for the authorities to permit her survival (see *Lucidez*, p. 329).[63]

The conflicting potential of the use of animal imagery for different ideological purposes is reflected in the representation of dogs in the novel, for, as with almost everything else which is a potential instrument of change, the landowners realize their power sooner than the people do: early on Lamberto picks a 'cão escolhido entre os cães para morder os cães' ('a dog chosen from amongst the dogs to bite the dogs', p. 72), that is, a foreman from amongst the ordinary people to do his enforcement for him in return for somewhat better conditions than those enjoyed by his comrades (contemptuously referred to as a 'canzoada' or a 'pack of mutts', p. 72). At this stage of the novel the workers are described (with some irony, of course) as being 'piores que animais' ('worse than animals', p. 79), while the debt which hounds the poor is represented as being like dogs snapping at their ankles (p. 82); but before long the poor are beginning to learn useful lessons from the animal kingdom, as António observes around his feet the ants which wait eagerly like dogs to snap up any crumbs he drops (p. 87).

Progress is slow and littered with setbacks: when António and João are forced to go to the political rally in Évora, the mood on the journey home is said to be subdued and João feels that they were treated like sheep (p. 95), while the narrator describes the workers as being like birds which are unable to walk, let alone fly (p. 96).[64] A significant comparison to *Memorial* could also be seen in the wish expressed by João that he could simply have flown away from the scene (p. 95).

From now on the dogs, and the ants which imitate dogs, as in the chapter describing the interrogation and death of Germano Vidigal (p. 169), in the description of springtime in the countryside (p. 193), or when the workers prepare to take an unauthorized day off to mark international workers' day on 1 May (p. 331), are largely seen to be firmly on the side of the workers:[65] dogs bark to alert the people when the police come to search for the four young men who refused to work on the threshing machine (p. 103), and even if the police insult the workers by referring to their natural conditions as being those of beasts (p. 156), the angels up in heaven, with their privileged perspective, can see that, even as the narrator compares the people to ants, there is unprecedented movement afoot in the large estates (p. 145). Later, when the policeman José Calmedo goes to arrest João, he too sees an ant with its head raised like a dog's (p. 233), which contributes to his decision to renounce his role with the forces of law and order and to side with his own class instead (p. 231). By the time of Humberto Delgado's election campaign in 1958, the dogs are now firmly on the side of the people and are said to be barking 'entre o Minho e o Algarve, entre a costa do mar e a raia do levante' ('from the Minho to the Algarve, from the seashore to the eastern border', p. 305), while Norberto, whose ancestors set the dogs on the people, is now forced to tell Father Agamedes that he does not want dogs barking behind him (p. 305). Immediately after this episode, in fact, Agamedes is shocked to discover that there are men waiting for him who are (metaphorically) growling at him like dogs, and he also fails to notice the ants, 'levantando como cães as cabeças, e por enquanto caladas, que será de nós se um dia se junta toda esta canzoada' ('raising their heads like dogs, silent for now, whatever will happen to us if some days this pack of mutts gets its act together', p. 306),[66] a prophecy which appears to be on the way to fulfilment a few pages later when an army of marching ants is said to be really dogs (p. 312), an impression reinforced with the recurrence of this imagery (pp. 325–6) in relation to the military uprising in Beja in the first days of 1962: 'É tempo de ladrar juntos e morder certos' ('The time has come to bark in chorus and bite in the right places', p. 326).[67]

This imagery reaches its culmination after the revolution when the workers are now free to demand a living wage, being able to claim that they have passed the stage of being dogs and deserve to be treated as humans (p. 360). The workers' struggle therefore is seen to be integrated with the continual growth of the natural world, and it is not only crops which are raised from the soil in *Levantado*, but also the workers, their awareness of themselves as worthy of a better life, and thus the Revolution itself, as Grossegesse recognizes:

> The false earthly Trinity of Landowners, Clergy and State Apparatus will pass, while the peasant workers break free to their New Jerusalem of a society free of exploitation; this utopia was

perceptible throughout the ages in an earthly version of the biblical good news, analogous to the cycle of sewing and reaping plants.[68]

Thus, the apparent immutability of the setting of this novel masks a continuing ferment of change, as gases are seen to bubble constantly under the apparently stagnant waters of the large estates:

> olhando nós este brejo que parece morto, só cegos de nascença ou por vontade própria não verão o frémito de água que do fundo vem subitamente à superfície, ora das tensões acumuladas no lodo, entre o fazer, desfazer e refazer químico, até ao rebentar do gás enfim liberto. (p. 125)
>
> [When we look at this marsh which is apparently dead, only those who were born blind or have chosen to be blind will be unable to see the bubbling of the water which suddenly comes up to the surface from the bottom, as the pressure builds up in the mud, as chemicals join up, separate, and mix with one another again, until the gases released burst free.][69]

Similarly, hidden within the bodies of the women of this novel is another unseen force, the children whom they bring forth and who will change their society for good, even if that transformation may still be some way into the future: 'No seu ventre houve um pequeno movimento. E outro ainda. Mas quando o marido entrou, não lhe disse nada. Tinham mais em que pensar' ('Inside her belly there was a small movement, and then another one. But when her husband came in, she did not say anything to him. They had other things to think about', p. 22). The movement within Sara da Conceição's womb here is intended to echo that which the novel as a whole indicates as existing within the apparently (but deceptively) static depiction of the Alentejo in the opening chapter of the work.

6. Hierarchies of Power

While at one level Saramago's novels depend on a stark opposition between polar opposites (primarily expressed through the categories of rich and poor, or powerful and powerless), in real life these are tendencies rather than absolutes, and a closer examination of the novels reveals that these contrasts are not as simple as they may at first seem. The author can be merciless in his ridicule of the negative figures whom he portrays, and it is for this reason that characters such as D. João V in *Memorial* or the various *-bertos* in *Levantado* are really caricatures rather than fully developed characters, but the novels can still present greater subtleties in practice.

It has already been noted that *Memorial* features a kindly nobleman (first introduced, nonetheless, as a figment of the reader's and the narrator's joint imaginations: 'mas a nós não nos custa nada imaginar que ao lado dele se foi sentar um fidalgo caridoso e amigo de bem-fazer'; *Memorial*, p. 302) ('but it costs us nothing to imagine that some kind nobleman sat down beside him, one of those charitable souls whom one sometimes encounters', *Baltasar*, p. 288), who describes to João Elvas (and thus also to the reader) the arrangements made for the wedding of the Portuguese princess Maria Bárbara to a Spanish prince. To some extent he simply functions as another inventive narrative device to help bring the (ultimately) irrecuperable past to a passably convincing depiction of eighteenth-century life. Nonetheless, his kindly nature does not extend to leading him to question why he moves in the circles that he does, while João cannot.

As Arnaut points out, there are two further characters in the novel who bridge the gap between aristocratic and plebeian circles: the historical figures of Padre Bartolomeu Lourenço de Gusmão and Domenico Scarlatti.[70] Scarlatti, as a distinguished foreign guest at court, has a degree of security enjoyed by few in the Portugal of his time, while Bartolomeu, although he is aware that his scientific experiments probably would not find favour with the Inquisition, enjoys the benefits of royal patronage for a time, allowing him to straddle the line between the privileged and those who have reasons to resent that privilege: 'não me faltam protecções' (p. 65) ('I am not without friends who can protect me', p. 54).[71] This role therefore both corresponds to and contrasts with that of Father Agamedes in *Levantado*, who also coexists with those on either side of the divide between rich and poor, but exclusively for the benefit of the former, as is pointed out forcefully by Cerdeira da Silva:

> But Father Agamedes is an observant instructor of the people, representing the voice of power to the poor, a type of diplomat who has access to both sides, even if his choice has already been made,

in favour of the comfortable table, the favours to be received, and the relationships which can be had with those in power.[72]

Nonetheless, even within the group of the rich and powerful, some are more powerful than others. In one sense the king appears all-powerful in *Memorial,* but his favourite pastime of building a model of St Peter's basilica in Rome inside his own chambers indicates that real power does not lie with him, an impression confirmed by the ease with which the Franciscan order succeeds in duping him into agreeing to build them the convent which they have coveted for so long (p. 26).

The queen leads a pampered lifestyle, but she is reduced to being merely a vessel for the king's sperm (p. 17), and, while the king can dream without inhibitions of his own sexual potency (leading to a megalomaniac dream where he sees the biblical rod of Jesse growing out of his own penis, p. 18), at the end of the first chapter the queen has to suppress her erotic dreams about the crown prince (p. 17).[73] Later in the novel, the queen declares herself to be 'Farta [. . .] de ser rainha' ('tired of being queen', p. 105) and regrets not being able to have any other role in life (p. 114), which leads Cerdeira da Silva to suggest that this is the moment where she ceases to be merely a caricature and becomes a character with whom the reader can feel some genuine sympathy.[74]

In this sense, then, the queen prefigures the content of Manuel Milho's story of another queen (not identified with D. João's) and a hermit exchanging views on what identity they can have other than the clichéd roles which their respective labels impose on them (pp. 254–5). This story, however, ends with no resolution of what happens to them after their last conversation (pp. 263–4). Certainly, one can understand the disappointment expressed by Manuel's companions at the lack of a satisfactory conclusion to this narrative, but there are a number of (not mutually exclusive) explanations which might be proposed for this fact: Berrini compares Milho's incomplete narration to the *Thousand and One Nights* (and Júlio points out that Manuel is one of the few workers who is seen to effect a successful escape from the building site at Mafra by refusing the exploitative terms of employment proposed, a fact which implicitly supports Berrini's parallel to an execution postponed[75]); equally, as Real points out,[76] the abrupt termination of this apparent 'happy ever after' formula could be seen simply as a recognition that, in the eighteenth century, any relationship between two such socially diverse individuals would be doomed from the start. This conclusion should also intimate to the reader, however, that there may come a day in the future when such solidarity across class divisions will be conceivable: the plausible improbability of the parallel friendship established between João Elvas and the unnamed nobleman within the main narrative itself and the lack of closure to the novel as a whole (in that Baltasar is killed but his will and the *Passarola* remain untouched by the Inquisition) should perhaps suggest that the story of class relations does not close on the last page of the text.

The queen is last seen in any significant sense when reminding her daughter of her secondary role in the marriage which she is about to contract with a Spanish prince whom she has never met (pp. 313–4). Thereafter, like the queen in Manuel's story, she simply disappears: history may have relegated her to a secondary role but, within the fictional context and for this brief moment, she achieves some personal fulfilment as a character in the novel (even if only in the negative role of passing on resigned worldly wisdom to her daughter), which thus 'recuperates' not only the lives of ordinary people, but also others belonging to other disadvantaged categories.

The princess herself is left in no illusions as to her status. When she is taken to the border for the royal wedding, she is disturbed to see chain-gangs of men being led away and is told that they are being taken to Mafra to work on the convent built to celebrate her conception (p. 312). In one sense, she has a life of privilege compared to these men, but this is a key moment in her life as she awakens to the realization that the only difference between her and them is that her cage is a gilded one: 'Afirmou-se melhor a princesa, não era sonho nem delírio, e turbou-se de tão lastimoso espectáculo de grilhetas, em véspera das suas bodas, quando tudo devia ser ledice e regozijo' (p. 312) ('The Princess took a closer look. She was neither dreaming nor delirious, the sad spectacle of fettered slaves troubled her on the eve of her nuptials, which should have been an occasion for universal gaiety and rejoicing', pp. 298–9).

One notes here not only the naivety with which the princess assumes that the whole country will be celebrating her impending marriage, but also the use of the archaism 'ledice' ('gaiety'), recalling the Inês de Castro episode of Camões's *Os Lusíadas*, the opening scene of Bernardim Ribeiro's *Menina e Moça*, and two scenes from Almeida Garrett's *Frei Luís de Sousa* (which makes intertextual use of both of the earlier passages).[77] The reader is thus invited to seek gloomy parallels with the fate of the tragic Galician princess; with the melancholic account of the wanderings of Ribeiro's lonely heroine; and finally also with the disaster which strikes the house of Manuel de Sousa in the nineteenth-century drama, thus reminding the reader once again of the long-term unsustainability of the extravagance displayed by the royal family here. This does not decrease the pathos of the young princess herself as she is bartered into cushioned slavery, but it does at least suggest that the projected downfall of the monarchy may bring some happier ending to follow the grim times depicted for the ordinary people here, as one may also deduce from the lesson which Maria Bárbara appears to learn from what she is told:

> A princesa já não pensa nos homens que viu na estrada. Agora mesmo se lembrou de que, afinal, nunca foi a Mafra, que estranha coisa, constrói-se um convento porque nasceu Maria Bárbara, cumpre-se o voto porque Maria Bárbara nasceu, e Maria Bárbara não viu, não sabe, não tocou com o dedinho rechonchudo a primeira pedra, nem a segunda, não serviu com as suas mãos o caldo dos pedreiros, [. . .] e agora vai Maria Bárbara para Espanha, o convento é para si como um sonho sonhado, uma névoa impalpável. (pp. 312–13)

> [The Princess is no longer thinking about the men she saw on the road. It has just occurred to her that she has never been to Mafra, how strange that a convent should be built because Maria Bárbara was born, yet Maria Bárbara has never seen, known, or touched with her plump little finger either the first or the second stone of its foundations, she has never served broth with her own hands to the workers, [. . .] and now Maria Bárbara is leaving for Spain, for her the convent is like some vision in a dream, an impalpable haze.] (p. 299)

She is as alienated as the workers themselves, and the references in the last sentence of this passage to a 'sonho sonhado' and to a 'névoa impalpável' put the construction of the convent into implicit parallels with King Solomon's *vanitas vanitarum* (through the archaic lexical repetition)[78] and also with the chimeric promise of the Sebastianic myth respectively. The princess's distance from the unpleasant realities of Portuguese life is tempered by two echoes of other novels in this passage: firstly, the possibility of her charitable act of serving soup to the workers contrasts vividly with the hypocritical distance imposed by D. Clemência on the recipients of her alms (*Levantado*, pp. 187–8), while the reference to the princess's lack of experience of the convent built in her name contrasts vividly with the insistence of the travellers in *Jangada* on going to see in person and touch the breach in the Pyrenees which has given them and their compatriots new opportunities and new perspectives on the world (*Jangada*, p. 268). Even if she is unsure how to respond to the pitiful realities around her, then, one at least senses that this character has the potential to be more sympathetic to the underprivileged than her father.

If D. João V himself never really passes the level of being a two-dimensional caricature, then, this should not be seen as any criticism of Saramago's creative powers, for the text is littered with lively and convincing figures such as Baltasar, Blimunda, Padre Bartolomeu, and the various workers who accompany the giant stone on its journey from Pêro Pinheiro to Mafra. The real reason why the king is not depicted in a more convincing manner (as what E. M. Forster would call a 'rounded' rather than a 'flat' character[79]) is that he himself prefers to remain in splendid isolation, more intent on preserving his status as an almost divine figure than on relating to others.[80] His insistence on his role as 'Senhor', or 'Lord' (a word whose use involves a clear ambivalence between earthly rulers and the reference to the Christian God[81]) permits him brief moments of self-doubt and admission of his own mortality, but significantly these are kept entirely to himself:

> D. João V está numa sala do torreão, virada ao rio. Mandou sair os camaristas, os secretários, os frades, uma cantarina da comédia, não quer ver ninguém. Tem desenhado na cara o medo de morrer, vergonha suprema em monarca tão poderoso. (*Memorial*, pp. 288–9)

> [D. João V is in a room in the tower that overlooks the river. He orders the footmen, secretaries, friars, and a singer from the Teatro da Comédia to withdraw, for he wishes to be alone. Written on his face is fear of death, the greatest humiliation of all for so mighty a monarch.] (*Baltasar*, p. 274)

Nonetheless, in spite of these moments of apparent vulnerability, his overriding wish remains purely one of luxurious self-gratification, as a few lines later it is revealed that the main existential frustration which he can imagine is never being able to see the completion of his construction at Mafra (p. 289).

In *Levantado*, meantime, the privileged classes are presented largely as caricature (the repeated use of the names terminating in *-berto* for all of the landowners inevitably contributes to some oversimplification), but this should not be seen as a lack of awareness of nuance. It is entirely a result of the conscious choice of favouring the perspective of the underprivileged, and, while the depiction of the peasant communities of the Alentejo is a largely sympathetic one, it does not draw back from depicting the hierarchies and social problems which exist within the ranks of the poor themselves.

The first of these becomes evident in the marriage of Domingos and Sara da Conceição, a marriage marred by Domingos's alcoholism and also by the marginal status of his wife in all meaningful decisions.[82] The reader's first impression of them is as they traverse a harsh landscape on a rainy night to enter a small town with their child on a donkey (pp. 15–7). The parallels with the Holy Family are self-evident (even allowing for Sabine's insistence that they are 'tongue-in-cheek'[83]), but when the husband enters an inn, it is not to seek shelter for himself and his family but to drink while the family waits outside.[84] The fact that they do so when Sara is presumably already aware of Domingos's alcohol problem is a reflection of her subservience towards him, and the parallel with the Holy Family therefore operates in a transformed guise, with Domingos, the husband and father, taking on the role played by indifferent fate in the biblical story. When Sara upbraids him for this behaviour, she has to symbolically trespass on the male space of the bar, which leads to his accusation that she has humiliated him as a man:

> Boas razões são as dela, mas Domingos Mau-Tempo não gostou de ser chamado pela mulher à frente de homens, o que é que vão pensar, e enquanto atravessa o largo vai ralhando, Se tornas a fazer isto, zango-me. (p. 21)
>
> [Her reasons are sound, but Domingos Mau-Tempo did not like being called out by his wife in front of other men, what will they

think, and as he goes across the square, he rants, If you do that again, I will get really angry].

Domingos's reaction to Sara here (as his subaltern) is, in fact, essentially the same in nature as the contempt shown by D. João to his subjects, or by the landowners in *Levantado* to Domingos's own class.

As the narrative progresses, it becomes clear that Sara almost certainly would have been well aware of her situation: her parents warn her against Domingos for his alcoholic tendencies (p. 23), but she forces the issue by becoming pregnant (p. 24). Although this forces her into a difficult marriage, it is an early sign in this novel of the willingness of women to take their lives into their own hands, a tendency which reaches its culmination in Sara's great-granddaughter Maria Adelaide, who embodies hope for the future at the end of the novel and whose birth brings the saga of her family full circle by once again parodying that of Christ (pp. 294–9) and is therefore compared to a miracle (p. 295).

Within Sara's own lifetime, however, gender relations are depressing: she often has to hunt for Domingos and bring him home from the bar, blind drunk and as helpless as a child (pp. 27–8); he beats her to overcome his frustrations in other areas of his life (p. 27)[85]; they are frequently forced to move from one community to another to escape the consequences of her husband's excesses, including a fight with Father Agamedes in the church (p. 31). Twice she moves away from him (pp. 40 and 47–8); on the first occasion he soon comes to find her, promising to turn over a new leaf (p. 41). When he then returns to his old ways (p. 43), she goes into hiding, and he responds by asserting his rights of property over her, invoking the same kind of patriarchal rhetoric which the couple rejected when they first came together: 'Eu sou o pai e o marido' ('I wear the trousers here', p. 48). Significantly, however, on this occasion she does not give into his entreaties and is supported in this by José Picanço, in whose house she has taken shelter (pp. 48–9). Not only does José explain clearly to Domingos why he will not hand over the woman and her children (p. 48), but he also symbolically draws a line in the sand to defend her: 'por isso Picanço toma o seu risco e traça-o também no chão' ('for this reason Picanço takes up his stick and he also makes a line in the ground with it', p. 49).

This action is significant not only within its own context, but also because it looks forward to the line in the soil made by Joana Carda in *Jangada* in order to separate her past unhappy marriage from her new life as an independent woman, capable of deciding her own destiny; in her time (an unspecified period but clearly in the relatively recent past) her autonomy may gain her respect (see *Jangada*, p. 148),[86] but decades earlier Sara da Conceição is remembered by the police simply as 'louca, com título de perigoso' ('crazy, with a reputation for being dangerous', *Levantado*, p. 241). Once again, therefore, the gradual process of ordinary people gaining control over their own lives is visible not only within the context of a single work but also within the totality of the author's production: the action which grudgingly gains Joana the respect of her new-found lover in the 1980s sees her fictional ancestor excluded from being taken seriously on the basis of patriarchal assumptions which it will take those intervening eighty years to overcome.

Later in the novel there are hints that a similar scenario could be played out again in the following generation, as Faustina's family are said to be unhappy with João's courting of her because of Domingos' past reputation (p. 67). Once again, they settle matters in their own favour by taking control of their own lives and eloping (pp. 69–70), and this time the relationship proves to be a fulfilling one which lasts until João's death, shortly before the 1974 revolution.[87] Nonetheless, social progress is slow, as male drunkenness is said to remain a problem within the community (p. 80), and, in terms of women's awareness of their situation, Faustina betrays her political naivety in declaring her faith that 'de certeza o governo não faz coisas mal feitas' ('I'm sure the government doesn't get anything wrong') as João and their son António are press-ganged into attending a rally in support of Franco's troops in Spain (p. 91). Even João, for all his growth in awareness over the length of the novel, is occasionally still prone to traditional assumptions, as he declares himself disappointed to have a granddaughter rather than a grandson at the birth of Maria Adelaide (p. 296).[88]

Other significant episodes in the reflection of hierarchies of power in the novel include the hunger strike which António organizes in the army (pp. 225–7) and the ethical decision taken by the policeman José Calmedo to leave the force after the part which he plays in the arrest of João, who has done him no harm (pp. 231–5). Both of these actions indicate a growing awareness of a social conscience on the part of at least some of the agents of power, who are no longer content to do their paymasters' bidding without question. Significantly also, when João is released from prison in Lisbon in the middle of the night, the person who comes to his aid is called Ricardo Reis: but, unlike his cold and isolationist namesake in a later novel, this is an ordinary man of the people, happily married and prepared to act for the good of his fellow human beings by displaying charity when it is needed (pp. 263–5), as Cerdeira da Silva recognizes:

> The good Samaritan is Ricardo Reis, definitely not Pessoa's heteronym or even the character from another novel, but another version of him, perhaps dreamt up by the author as having learned through the trials of life to love his Lydia properly and to make a lasting committment to the people.[89]

This sense of solidarity is an important element in the novel. The landowners succeed in keeping the ordinary people at their mercy largely through internal divisions within the workforce, but this policy cannot be successfully applied indefinitely: although the first significant strike reported in the novel runs into trouble when the local workers find themselves facing other workers, specially brought in from the north by the landowners to work for wages which the locals will not accept (p. 37), when another strike comes about later in the text (pp. 143–7), solidarity is maintained and a small victory is obtained. Equally, António's experiences as an emigrant worker in France (and, in particular, the sense of cross-border solidarity which he develops with his Spanish counterpart Miguel Hernández) allow him to develop new insights which will help to bring about meaningful change for him and others (pp. 288–9). Similarly, the motif of an adolescent game of aimless urination played by António and his fellow workers in their youth (p. 102) later becomes a more meaningful display of resistance as Sigismundo relieves himself against the wall of the police station and stimulates a powerful Rabelaisian image by trying to imagine the potential consequences of everyone else doing so at the same time as well (p. 309).[90]

7. The Illusion of Permanence and the Potential for Change

It is vital to the interests of the landowners in *Levantado* to keep the workers ignorant, as Sigisberto concedes:

> A grande e decisiva arma é a ignorância. É bom, dizia Sigisberto no seu jantar de aniversário, que eles nada saibam, nem ler, nem escrever, nem contar, nem pensar, que considerem e aceitem que o mundo não pode ser mudado, que este mundo é o único possível, tal como está, que só depois de morrer haverá paraíso. (p. 72)

> [The great and decisive weapon is that of ignorance. It is a good thing, says Sigisberto, at his birthday dinner, that they know nothing, reading, writing or arithmetic, never mind thinking, it is good that they believe and accept that the world cannot be changed, that this world is the only one possible, just as it is, and that it is only after death that there will be a paradise.]

Clearly in reality no landowner would be likely to make such a declaration as openly as this. In practice, however, the advantages of such a policy are clear, as outlined by Cerdeira da Silva:

> It is in the guaranteed preservation of this scenario, whose natural order is in itself the justification for its own permanence, that the system finds its steadiness. For this to happen it is necessary to keep the workers alienated from the means of production, from the process of production, and above all in a state of ignorance that situations like these can actually be changed. It is therefore clear that they must also be kept well away from all intellectual activities and that their bodies should be worn out by physical labour, a medieval prescription for curing madness: a tired body does not allow the mind to function much.[91]

The link which the critic makes to medieval medicine is entirely appropriate in view of the feudal relationships in existence in Monte Lavre. On a national scale, this is exactly the type of attitude which bedevilled the official treatment of the mass of the Portuguese population throughout the New State, demonstrated by the comments attributed to Salazar himself by Avelãs Nunes:

> The recognition of the value of illiteracy and the defence of an elitist, anti-democratic and ultraconservative idea of culture and society were explicitly asserted by Salazar himself in 1933, in reply to a question from António Ferro: 'I believe that it is more urgent

to set up large elites than to teach the people to read. The great problems of the nation must be solved, not by the people, but by the elites putting the masses into the right situations'.[92]

The more direct expression of this condescending attitude, as placed into the landowners' mouth by Saramago is backed up by sustained imagery relating to the natural environment. This is achieved through an initial (and superficial) vision of unchangingness, superseded by a more dynamic vision of the landscape and all within it as subject to constant change.

The static images are associated particularly with the landowners and their allies. The landowners always have names terminating in *-berto* (a fact which leads Cerdeira da Silva to suggest an ironic association with the figure of the 'encoberto', or 'hidden one', D. Sebastião[93]), but, more than this, the recitation of their names recalls the genealogy of Christ given in Luke's Gospel,[94] thus permitting the narrator to reflect ironically on the quasi-divine role played by this family in the novel:

> . . . de Lamberto nasceu Dagoberto, de Dagoberto nasceu Alberto, de Alberto nasceu Floriberto, e depois veio Norberto, Berto e Sigisberto, e Adalberto e Angilberto, Gilberto, Ansberto, Contraberto, que admiração é essa terem tão parecidos nomes, é o mesmo que dizer latifúndio e dono dele. (pp. 195–6)

> [And Dagoberto was born of Lamberto, and Alberto was born of Dagoberto, and Floriberto was born of Alberto, and then there came Norberto, Berto and Sigisberto, Adalberto and Angilberto, Gilberto, Ansberto, Contraberto, what a surprise that they all have such similar names, they amount to saying the estates and their owners.]

Similarly, the priest is always Father Agamedes and the policemen throughout the generations are represented by the comically rhyming names Cabo Tacabo, Tenente Contente and Sargento Armamento. This practice is clearly no accident, as the narrator reminds us explicitly (p. 219) that Agamedes is, in fact, various different priests sharing the same name over several generations, in the same way as García Márquez repeats names such as Úrsula and Aureliano Buendía in his depiction of Macondo in *Cien años de soledad*,[95] leading Cerdeira da Silva to comment in the following terms: 'The text draws the reader's attention to one fact: the people are not eternal, but what is eternal is what they represent;

they are therefore identical as representatives of a phenomenon which transcends them, and which speaks for them.'[96]

This apparent unchangingness in the Alentejo is given greatest prominence in the opening chapter of the novel, which nonetheless closes with a sting in its tail: on the one hand, it is narrated predominantly in the historic present tense and it focuses on the background panorama of the landscape, but even within this broad sweep there is a hint of the contrasting emphasis of the following chapters, where it is humans and animals who become the main focus of attention:

> O que mais há na terra, é paisagem. Por muito que do resto lhe falte, a paisagem sempre sobrou, abundância que só por milagre infatigável se explica, porquanto a paisagem é sem dúvida anterior ao homem, e apesar disso, de tanto existir, não se acabou ainda. (p. 11)

> [What one can see more than anything else in this land is the landscape itself. Whatever else may be missing, there was always plenty of land to look at, a wealth which can only be explained as an ever-renewing miracle, since the land was doubtless there before man, and, in spite of having been around for so long, it still has not reached the end of its days.]

In spite of the apparent unimpeachability of this striking opening statement (comparable in visual terms to the wide panoramic sweep of the camera at the beginning of a film), the emphasis on the permanence of the land conceals an ideological subcurrent which is in the interests of the landowners: for the insistence on the ephemeral nature of human settlement fits all too easily into the other-worldly rhetoric of Father Agamedes, encouraging submissiveness to authorities who act as if they owe their position to divine favour, rather than to the ugly reality of a grant of land given to an immigrant nobleman by a long-dead king in return for services rendered to the crown (p. 24).[97] In addition, however, there is a further assumption implicit in this passage, also convenient to capitalist interests, in the suggestion that the people who populate this land do so for the sake of the land, and not vice versa: from the very opening words of the novel, therefore, we are confronted with the idea that it is property which has primacy over people. This assumption then allows Lamberto Horques

Alemão, the founder of the *-berto* dynasty, to adapt biblical language and claim that 'minha é a terra e quanto nela há' (p. 26) ('mine is the land and all that it contains').[98]

The dominant social order was created against this backdrop of apparent permanence, and if this has involved human suffering, then a superficial reading of this chapter would suggest that it is simply a sad truth which cannot be changed: 'Levou séculos para chegar a isto, quem duvidará de que assim vai ficar até à consumação dos séculos?' (p. 14) ('It has taken us centuries to get this far, who can doubt that it will remain so until the end of time?'). Indeed, only in the closing sentence of the chapter is the reader invited to revalue the ideological assumptions concealed within the carefully constructed (and in many ways seductively beautiful) composition of this opening section of the text: 'Mas tudo isto pode ser contado doutra maneira' (p. 14) ('But all of this could be told in a different way').[99] The rest of the novel then sets out to demonstrate that the repetition of a natural cycle does not inevitably require the circle to come back to exactly the same point where it started,[100] and that those who wish to introduce change may be more in keeping with the inner workings of nature than those who wish to preserve and effectively fossilize society.[101]

The estates are famously described as a 'mar interior' ('internal sea') in this novel (with some variants on the precise phrasing of this image: see pp. 219, 319–20, 337, 358 and 363). Its significance is twofold: firstly, unlike the apparently unchanging landscape depicted in the first chapter of the novel, the sea is in permanent flux. Secondly, however, the importance of the sea in Portuguese history lies in the opportunity which it presented to Portugal to transform itself briefly into a world power. These two ideas become interrelated in this striking image of the land transformed into an inland sea: the Portuguese, once innovative in their explorations of unknown territories, can now move into metaphorically uncharted waters by creating a juster and more fulfilling society for themselves, as is suggested by Cerdeira da Silva:

> 'Changing times, changing wills.' ['Mudam-se os tempos, mudam-se as vontades.'] The project set to man has also changed. 'The sea has been fulfilled', now the land awaits fulfilment. ['Cumpriu-se o mar', falta cumprir-se a terra.] The sailors gave Portugal a glorious past which for centuries disguised the decay of

> the present in its nostalgia and messianism, living off the illusion of past glories and the utopia of future miracles. The whole plot of this book revolves around the discovery that the here-and-now was simply being taken away by these two false and deceptive shadows.[102]

The echoes of Camões and Pessoa here ('"Mudam-se os tempos, mudam-se as vontades"', and '"Cumpriu-se o mar", falta cumprir-se a terra') are no accident: if Camões glorified the nation's achievements in the sixteenth century, Pessoa's *Mensagem* could be said to bewail the obstacle which the awareness of those achievements had become to the healthy development of the nation in the twentieth.[103] The implicit allusion made by the critic to the last sentence of *Ano* ('falta cumprir-se a terra') is equally appropriate:[104] for it is precisely the type of 'jam tomorrow' statements repeatedly made to the nation by successive rulers (in all of their guises) that lead to the depiction of a circular conception of time obscuring the people's need for meaningful progress instead.

So, when Faustina goes to Lisbon to try to visit João in prison, she is surprised by her first view of the sea. Clearly, in spite of all the official rhetoric presenting ordinary citizens as children of the motherland when this suited the government's purpose, Faustina has never come to know one of the most important elements in the formation of the identity of this nation. Even more striking, however, is the sense of excited mystery sensed in the sea by her guide in Lisbon, who sees the water every day:

> . . . é a segunda vez que Faustina Mau-Tempo vê o mar, este ribeiro de descomunal tamanho, e a seguir outra vez de comboio até Caxias, o mar é subitamente muito maior, Ai, comadre, isto é que é o mar, e a companheira que ao Terreiro do Paço a foi esperar e vive na cidade sorri de compreensão e benevolência diante deste pouco saber e diz que sim, que aquilo é o mar, mas cala a sua própria ignorância do que o mar verdadeiramente seja, não este parco abrir de braços entre duas torres, mas uma ânsia líquida e infinita, um remexer continuado de massas de vidro e espuma, uma dureza mineral que amolece e enregela, o lugar dos grandes peixes e dos lutuosos naufrágios, poesias. (pp. 256–7)

> [. . . this is the second time that Faustina Mau-Tempo has seen the sea, this unusually long shore, and then again on the train out to Caxias, suddenly the sea is so much bigger. Ah, my companion, so this is the sea, and her friend who went to the Terreiro do Paço to

> wait for her and who lives in the city smiles with benevolent understanding of her lack of awareness and says, yes, that is the sea, but she keeps quiet about her own ignorance of what the sea really is, not just this narrow embrace between two towers, but an infinite, fluid longing, a continual flux of transparency and foam, a hard wealth of minerals which softens and freezes, the home of great fish and tragic shipwrecks, the site of poetry.]

It is evident in this passage that the concept evoked of the sea slowly moves from being one of a simple part of the city landscape to become a place of life and adventure, where both risk and beauty dwell in a way which recalls the famous verses of Fernando Pessoa:

> Deus ao mar o perigo e o abismo deu
> Mas nele é que espelhou o céu.[105]
>
> [God placed danger and the abyss in the sea,
> But he also made it heaven's mirror.]

This association links ordinary Portuguese citizens to the notion of heroism and exploration of the unknown, a motif which is a constant in the author's work.[106] The world which is there to be explored by Faustina and people like her is not a glamorous and exotic one of the type discovered by great figures of the past such as Vasco da Gama: it is the possibility of a better life and taking charge of their own destinies, an adventure enough in itself.[107] One also notes here that the recurrence of the imagery of opening one's arms (developed later in the novel, in connection with João's encounter with Ricardo Reis and Ermelinda, p. 264) is used here in relation to the sea, which may thus still prove to be the ally, rather than the perdition, of the Portuguese people. This notion is made more explicit later in the text with an episode which echoes the closing pages of *Ano*, when a group of political prisoners escape on a ship which shares the name of one of Columbus's fleet in 1492:

> Uma desgraça nunca vem só, ainda ontem fugiram aqueles presos de Peniche, os medonhos comunistas, os comedores de crianças, ai vizinha viu por aí os meus filhos, ainda ontem se agitaram as almas e os oceanos com aquela nova história de corsários, quem os fuzilasse a todos, um tão bonito barco, todo de branco vestido, Santa Maria caminhando sobre as águas como o seu divino filho. (pp. 322–3)

> [Misfortunes always come together, just yesterday those prisoners escaped from Peniche, the dreadful communists who eat babies, oh dear neighbour have you seen my children, and then yesterday as well people's souls and the seas were all shaken up by this modern-day story of pirates, I wish someone would shoot the lot of them, such a fine boat, all in white, Santa Maria sailing over the waters just like her divine son.][108]

These words (spoken from the perspective of one of the landowners, but increasingly opening themselves up to alternative interpretations, particularly once it becomes unclear whether the words 'Santa Maria' are intended to refer to the hijacked ship or to the Virgin Mary in her incarnation as an ideological support to the regime) echo the hysterical tones of official discourse which Lídia feels obliged to question when she hears her lover speaking with the words of the newspapers about communists in a later novel (see *Ano*, p. 388). Yet through them one can detect the sense of adventure which triggers the revolution at the end of *Levantado*, a revolution which might be capable of being sustained beyond April 1974 if the people of Portugal would only realize that salvation may actually lie in the very set of beliefs which is virulently rejected here.

The alternative path offered by the establishment, that of messianic faith in their order, is no real solution. The same type of religious panacea offered to the workers at Mafra after the death of Francisco Marques in *Memorial* also features here: Father Agamedes openly encourages his parishioners to welcome suffering in this world so that they may look forward to their deaths and the rewards which they will receive in heaven (*Levantado*, pp. 107–8), and the priest's attempts to use the pulpit in the 1930s to warn his flock away from the dangers of communism make implicit use of the message of Fátima in the prayers offered for the conversion of Russia (p. 120), while Salazar is said to be a living symbol of Christian morality (p. 94). At a figurative level, the threshing machine which Manuel Espada and his comrades refuse to operate is seen to disturb the air all around it, obscuring the visibility of its operators: 'Há uns vultos no meio desta névoa' ('There are some figures visible in the middle of this haze', p. 100). Not only does this represent in visual terms the same type of obscuring of human realities practised in purely linguistic terms by the description of the landscape in the opening chapter of the novel, but, in a Portuguese context, the Sebastianic echoes of the mist which envelops the workers suggest that industrialization of labour will prove to be as chimeric a benefit to the people as the type of fossilization of the ignorant rural worker in a timeless agricultural idyll envisaged by Salazar. What this industrialization really means for the workers instead is a 'violentação' ('rape', p. 100).[109]

More strikingly however, earlier in the novel, as prices rise and wages fail to go up accordingly, families are increasingly unable to feed themselves, and a worker whose family is starving appeals to Father Agamedes for advice, without receiving any reply (p. 83). This leads into reminiscences about a popular wish-fulfilling story about a treasure trove hidden under a tree; sadly, however, when the family goes to dig up the treasure they find that someone else has taken it first (p. 83). This is a negative variant on the familiar popular tale of the family who are told of buried treasure and whose diligence in digging up the soil in search of it leads them to realize that hard work will bring its own rewards;[110] what this story seems to be saying instead is that if the workers do not look out for their own interests first, then the inevitable result will be that their 'treasure' (in this case, the fruits of their labour) will have been appropriated by someone else who does not possess legitimate title to it. This chapter of the novel then closes with a clear call to the workers to seize the day:

> Caso mais claro é aquele das duas arcas de pedra enterradas pelos mouros, uma cheia de ouro, outra cheia de peste. Diz-se que, com medo de abrir por engano a arca da peste, ninguém teve ânimo para as procurar. Não tivesse sido aberta, não estava o mundo como está, tão de peste cheio. (p. 85)
>
> [A clearer story is that of the two stone chests buried by the Moors, one of them full of gold, the other one full of pestilence. It is said that out of fear of opening up the chest of pestilence by mistake nobody had the courage to seek them out. If they hadn't been opened up, the world would not be so ridden with pestilence as it actually is.]

The apparent contradiction between the final two sentences of this excerpt is, in fact, transformed into a meaningful one once this story is conflated with the preceding one: the people have been too fearful of the risks involved in seeking change to notice that the negative chest has been open all along while the positive one has been raided by those who control the means of production. Instead the workers need to realize their own potential, suggested through an oblique reference to Zeca Afonso's song which triggered the 1974 Revolution, 'Grândola, Vila Morena': 'Quem mais ordena não é quem mais pode, quem mais pode não é quem mais parece' ('It is not the person of greatest potential who is in charge, the one with the greatest potential is not the one that it seems to be', p. 119). This statement may be taken to signify that the group most given to issuing orders (the landowners) is not the group which has the greatest potential (the people) and that, as a result, the group with greatest power (the people) is not the one currently in charge. All of that will change, however, when: 'O povo é quem mais ordena/ Dentro de ti, ó cidade' ('The people are the ones who give the orders,/ Inside your walls, o city').[111]

The path to 1974 has been a long and difficult one, with many obstacles on the way. Yet the very institutions created by the establishment partly bring about its own downfall. This paradox becomes particularly evident through the figure of António Mau-Tempo, who, in common with Baltasar and Blimunda, never has a child (as is foretold to him by a soothsayer, p. 200) but who instead leaves something equally valuable to the world: an example of fruitful resistance, as he leads a protest in the army and learns of new possibilities while enduring the hard life of the emigrant worker in France, a fate which became the lot of huge numbers of young Portuguese men during the 1950s and 1960s.

António's success in this derives from his application to a different context of the very military virtues which are inculcated in young men by the army, for, in his account of the hunger strike which he led, he stresses both the disciplined solidarity of the protesters (p. 226) and their courage in facing down the guns of the enemy, in this case challenging the other soldiers to shoot them for their display of defiance (p. 227). This same fortitude and courage also leads him to challenge Father Agamedes' inappropriate speech at his sister's wedding (p. 223),[112] and, when he travels to France, he comes to realize how much he has in common with his Spanish colleague Miguel Hernández. In spite of the traditional enmity of their two countries, the two of them share similar life experiences and can learn profitably from one another's experiences (p. 289). As Saramago himself has acknowledged in another context, such cross-border solidarity cannot help but challenge the mental foundations on which both Iberian states depend for their existence in the minds of their citizens:

'Como cualquier otro portugués antiguo y moderno, fui instruido en la firme convicción de que mi enemigo natural es, y siempre habría de serlo, España' (Like any other Portuguese person, past or present, I was brought up with the clear understanding that my natural enemy was Spain and always would be Spain').[113]

In *Memorial* too, the border between the two Iberian states becomes something capable of uniting rather than dividing the ordinary people of the peninsula. Baltasar, of course, loses his hand on the border between the two countries (*Memorial*, p. 36). This location is made more meaningful when placed in the context of the recurrence of martial imagery throughout the novel, indicating that while he has fought for his king, the ruling classes have been engaged in continuous warfare against their own people: not only are the workers brought to Mafra like prisoners of war, they are maltreated and disciplined like enemies once they are there (p. 218). When the court travels to the border for the royal wedding, the description given of the celebrations could just as easily apply to an outbreak of war between the two nations:

> Salvou a artilharia, e tão combinadas estas coisas pareciam, que do outro lado da fronteira retumbaram igualmente uns tiros, era a entrada dos reis de Espanha em Badajoz, quem aqui tivesse vindo desprevenido julgaria que estaria para travar-se uma grande batalha. (p. 315)

> [The artillery gave a salvo, and things appeared to have been so well timed that a gun salute came resounding back from the other side of the frontier as the Kings of Spain made their entry into Badajoz, anyone arriving here unexpectedly would have thought that a great battle was about to take place.] (p. 302)

The real division is not between two nationalities, then, but between the ruling classes and the oppressed in each country,[114] and if the masses of workers, described in metaphorical terms as an army (p. 250), were to go into battle against their real enemies, the complacent and privileged, then the transformation of society imagined at the end of *Levantado* would be a real possibility.[115] What is required is heightened awareness, coming about slowly but surely from the very circumstances which contribute to repression itself. Thus, the incident in *Levantado* where a worker is forced by the police to fight his own father (*Levantado*, pp. 334–5) is a disturbing one, but it still teaches this worker a valuable lesson and leads him to a Proudhonian reflection on the best use of property: 'se eu sou ladrão por ir roubar bolota, ladrão é também o dono dela, que nem fabricou a terra nem plantou a árvore e a podou e limpou' ('if I am a thief for going and stealing acorns, then the owner of the tree is also a thief, for he did not build the land, nor did he plant the tree, or prune it and keep it clean', p. 334). This spirit subsequently creates the Revolution and will allow the people to succeed in the domestic wars existing in parallel with the wars mentioned by official history (in the following passage the specific reference is to the First World War):

> Correram vozes em Monte Lavre de que havia uma guerra na Europa, sítio de que pouca gente no lugar tinha notícias e luzes. Guerras também as havia ali, e não pequenas, todo o dia a trabalhar, se trabalho havia, todo o dia a ganir de fome, houvesse ou não houvesse. Só as mortes não eram tantas, e no geral os corpos iam para a cova inteiros. (p. 47)
>
> [Stories went around Monte Lavre that there was a war in Europe, a place about which hardly anyone in the village knew anything or could shed any kind of enlightenment. There were wars there too, and no mean ones, working all day if there was work to be had, yelping with hunger all day, whether there was food or not. There just weren't as many deaths, and in general the bodies were buried in one piece.]

Eventually, however, the adventures of António Mau-Tempo will lead him to France, a country central to the eighteenth-century European Enlightenment (implicitly alluded to here by the metaphorical use of the word 'luzes'), and the experiences gained there will help to bring down the dictatorship at home, just as in *Memorial* Bartolomeu has to go to freethinking Holland in order to perfect his plans for the *Passarola*.[116]

These two novels, then, offer a statement of faith in the potential of the Portuguese people: as long as ordinary people like Baltasar, Blimunda, and the various generations of the Mau-Tempo family continue searching for a better life, then the possibility remains for them to claim their birthright, as eventually happens through the youthful figure of Maria Adelaide, whose association with the April Revolution embodies hope for a better future. On that 'dia levantado e principal' ('day of rising and hope', alluded to on the final page of *Levantado*, p. 366), like the heroine of Cervantes's *La gitanilla*, the apparently lower-class girl recovers her birthright[117] and, just as the large estates collapse in part through the internal contradictions of their own power structure, so the girl who went to the spring only to be brutally raped there is succeeded by a descendant of both violator and violated, who returns to the scene of the crime, now bedecked in the flowers of springtime (p. 356), having achieved a more meaningful form of elevation than that of Cervantes' little gypsy girl, because it is done through her own efforts and those of her ancestors, male and female.[118]

The end of the novel sees a time of celebration, then. But the symbolic resurrection of the generations of dead workers as they join in the festivities in the final chapter imposes an obligation as well as providing a cause for rejoicing. For the reason why the dead must participate in this moment is that it was they who trod the long, hard road leading to the victory of 1974. Maria Adelaide's inheritance of the blue eyes of the Mau-Tempos therefore reminds the reader of all the suffering that preceded her, and that the Revolution, if it is to be meaningful, must be continually renewed under trying circumstances:

> Se estas bocas tanto amargam, foi por terem falado e esperado falar ainda melhor, se viesse a liberdade, e afinal a liberdade não veio, alguém viu a liberdade, tanto dela se disse, mas a liberdade não é mulher que ande pelos caminhos, não se senta numa pedra à espera de que a convidem para jantar ou para dormir na nossa cama o resto da vida. (p. 308)

> [If these mouths are so dry, it is because they spoke out and hoped to speak more clearly if freedom ever came, and freedom never came, has anyone ever seen liberty, so much has been said about her, but liberty is not a woman walking along the road, she does not sit down on a stone waiting to be invited to dinner or to sleep in our beds for the rest of our lives.]

This implicit rejection of images such as Delacroix's famous painting of *Liberty Guiding the People*, which presents the people as following a superhuman, messianic figure, is repeated more explicitly fifteen years later in *Cegueira*, where it is the doctor's wife, with her clothes reduced to bare rags, who presents a truly heroic image of liberty precisely through her lack of glamour and simple dedication to the good of others (see *Cegueira*, p. 225).[119]

Just as the people should not be deceived by the over-optimistic language of the landowners and their various allies regarding the desirability of Portugal before the revolution, then, it is also important to continue making the Revolution a reality beyond 1974. As also happens in so many other novels by the author (including *Cegueira*), the 'dia levantado e principal' when the text of *Levantado* comes to a close (*Levantado*, p. 366) is a beginning as well as an ending, and the narration leaves us with the people of Monte Lavre in a position to decide how that story should continue, as Ceccucci declares:

> The movements backwards and forwards, in terms of journeys and lessons learned, of generations of peasants towards the gaining of consciousness and final redemption is merely the classical 'mise-en-scène' [*sic*] for the utopian journey of humanity towards a 'just and fraternal society'; it is the development of the history of the people; it is the fulfilment of the whole project of human history.[120]

It is then left up to the protagonists of later novels and, by extension, to their readers to continue the struggle which the peasants of Monte Lavre fought so hard over several generations; it is therefore incumbent upon the people of Portugal to ensure that these sacrifices were not made in vain. The very manner of writing of *Levantado*, with its experiments in narrative technique and its multiple, shifting narrative voices, is itself part of the continuing revolution which the text itself proposes; as Sabine remarks, 'the artifice of the text represents [. . .] a belief that the literary text can serve only as a "provisional account" on which readers may draw in the dialectical construction of that Marxist vision'.[121]

NOTES

1 See Sabine, p. 92.

2 Grossegesse stresses that the earlier novels invite the reader to collaborate with the author in a creative rewriting of past history, while he suggests that the importance of a work such as *Ano* lies more in stressing the importance of understanding processes at work around us in our own lifetime; see his *Saramago Lesen*, pp. 26–7. Thus, just as Saramago recognizes that 'glib post-modernist pronouncements of "the death of history" and "the death of ideology" have not discouraged the manipulation of historical narrative for ideological ends' (Sabine, p. 96), so Saramago's continued use of the past for his own narratives must also be viewed in an ideological light; the

difference in Saramago's practice lies in the fact that the explicit textual allusions to the process of recuperation of history in his work alert the reader to the subjective elements within that process. In this sense, Ricardo Reis' lack of awareness of the currents shaping the readings of history around him in the 1930s may be read as a disturbing parable of our own blindness to developments within society in our own times; see in this connection the comments made regarding the dangers of whitewashing the past reproduced in the Introduction.

3 Oliveira Filho, p. 54. The terms are derived from a passage on p. 27 of the novel (p. 19 in English).

4 See Birmingham, p. 74.

5 Note here the self-referentiality of the text at this point, as it implicitly makes a comparison between the real-life author writing the text of *Memorial* and manual labourers such as Baltasar working on the building site of the Convent at Mafra: this functions both as a refutation of contemporary theories of the 'death of the author' (a view rejected by Saramago in other contexts; see, for example, his thoughts expressed on the relation between literary narrator and real-life author in his *Cadernos – IV*, pp. 191–2, entry for 9 August 1996), and also as a means of dignifying the seemingly humdrum labour of the unnamed workers who contributed to the construction of the convent by comparing their efforts to those of a respected contemporary author.

6 This incident has some factual credibility: Maia asserts that, on encountering some incredulity from the foreign supplier of the royal matrimonial bed as to the extravagance of the order placed, the historical D. João V simply doubled the price being offered for it; see Maia, p. 53, and p. 53, n. 1.

7 See Arnaut, '*Memorial do Convento*', pp. 39–40.

8 'Crowning/decrowning is a dualistic ambivalent ritual, expressing the inevitability and at the same time the creative power of the shift-and-renewal, the *joyful relativity* of all structure and order, or all authority and all (hierarchical) position'; see Bakhtin, p. 124; the emphases are Bakhtin's.

9 'Although Dom João V [. . .] was nicknamed "The Generous One" and had had bestowed upon him the title of "Most Faithful Ruler" by Pope Benedict XIV, rational historians consider him wasteful, hypocritical and vain' (Linhares Filho, p. 184).

10 The reference to Camões is to *Os Lusíadas*, Canto IV, Stanza 95: '"Ó glória de mandar, ó vã cobiça/ Desta vaidade a quem chamamos Fama!"' ('"O pride of power! O futile lust/ For that vanity known as fame!"'; see Camões, *Os Lusíadas*, p. 186, and *The Lusiads*, p. 96). Cerdeira da Silva identifies further verbal echoes of Camões in the same passage; see her 'Do Labirinto Textual', pp. 254–5. The same critic also points out Saramago's imitation of the epic tradition in invoking the protection for Baltasar, Bartolomeu and Blimunda of a guardian angel before the maiden flight of the *Passarola*; see *Memorial*, p. 194, and Cerdeira da Silva, 'Do Labirinto Textual', p. 253.

11 Birmingham, pp. 69–71.

12 Compare with the opening of Pessoa's poem 'O Infante D. Henrique' in his *Mensagem*:

> Em seu trono entre o brilho das esferas,
> Com seu manto de noite e solidão,
> Tem aos seus pés o mar novo e as mortas eras –
> O único imperador que tem, deveras,
> O globo mundo em sua mão.

('On his throne amidst the shining spheres/ With his blanket of night and solitude/ And at his feet the newly-discovered ocean and the epochs now past:/ The only emperor who truly has/ The globe of the world in his hand'; the translation here is mine.) Berrini speculates that Saramago's change of the 'esferas' of the first line of this poem to 'estrelas' is intended to highlight D. João V's self-imposed solitude by way of contrast with D. Henrique's reliance on science; see Berrini, p. 75. The effect in this passage of the typical Saramaguian device of hastily retracting an impression already given is to draw attention to the strong note of irony in the subsequent statement which introduces D. João V ('faz o infante D. Henrique fraca figura comparado com este D. João', p. 227) ('then Dom Henrique is a feeble monarch when compared with Dom João', p. 212), thus alerting the reader to the current king's superior material circumstances merely by way of insinuating his total lack of all the personal attributes which made Henry the Navigator one of the outstanding European figures of his time. The text of the Pessoa poem is taken from Pessoa, *Mensagem*, p. 49.

13 Lopes, '*Memorial do Convento*', p. 201.

14 Sabine sees the Church-State alliance in *Memorial* as being marked by a tension caused by the king's ambitions to extend his economic and military power through the very type of innovations (such as those proposed here by Padre Bartolomeu) which the Church, as an essentially conservative force, cannot contemplate or permit. As the novel progresses, however, it becomes apparent that the problem with the development of the *Passarola* as an assertion of liberation is that it comes far too soon; see also Sabine, pp. 151–5 and p. 133, no. 48. Saramago's vision of the possibility of the Revolution within his fiction lies far into the future, in 1974 in historical terms (as portrayed in *Levantado*), but in terms of the realization of the society which the author would really wish to see created, this prospect is seen to remain a tantalizing one and perhaps one which is unachievable in practice. This matter is discussed further in Chapter Two.

15 António Apolinário Lourenço reminds us that there is a similar fabrication of a miracle later in the text, when official discourse explains away the appearance of the *Passarola* over the convent at Mafra as a sighting of the Holy Spirit giving its blessing to the project of the convent (p. 210), although there is a counterbalancing positive sign of healthy scepticism when Álvaro Diogo, asked to confirm that he also saw the same sight, replies simply that something had

passed over the site (p. 210). See António Apolinário Lourenço, 'História, Ficção e Ideologia', p. 77.

16 The emphases here are mine.

17 Linhares Filho (p. 186) raises a minor historical problem in connection with this incident, namely that as the historical Frei António de S. José was a lay monk, he could not have heard the queen's confession; the critic bases his assertion on Serrão's *História de Portugal*, p. 272. However this is not what the text actually declares; rather that he merely communicated to the king the promise that his wife would bear him a child if he undertook to build the convent. Grossegesse makes a more telling point regarding this character: that in Portuguese popular tradition St Anthony is often the figure who supplies a miraculous outcome to a difficult situation; the choice of this particular monk to be the bearer of good news to the king therefore takes on an extra ironic twist here. See Grossegesse, 'José Saramago, *Memorial do Convento*', pp. 139–40, and p. 139 note 11. Sabine, focusing on the textual reference to the queen's 'imobilidade total' ('total immobility') and 'falta de estímulo e tempo, e cristianíssima retenção moral' (pp. 11–12) ('lack of incentive and time, and . . . her deep moral scruples', p. 3) during sexual relations with her husband, suggests that her failure to conceive a child by him may well be attributable quite simply to his failure to arouse her adequately (see Sabine, p. 111). Sabine also makes the very pertinent point in relation to the bargain apparently made between the king and God over the queen's pregnancy that the promise vouchsafed to the monarch in return for the construction of the convent in no way differs from the type of supernatural intervention which the Church persecutes in the person of Blimunda's mother Sebastiana de Jesús earlier in the text; see Sabine, pp. 124–5.

18 This etymology is pointed out by both Cerdeira da Silva (*José Saramago*, p. 262, n. 8) and Fernandes (p. 40). Gomes, Schor and Cerdeira da Silva all note that the name Maria Adelaide, that of the young woman who embodies the spirit of the 1974 Revolution at the end of the text, has Germanic origins, related to the modern German word *adel*, for 'noble', thus symbolically representing her recovery of what was her due and that of all of the people: the control of the land which had been taken away from them by generations of *-bertos*. See Gomes, p. 26; Schor, p. 46 note 7; and Cerdeira da Silva, 'Do Labirinto Textual', p. 252; Schor is, however, incorrect in saying that Maria Adelaide is the first of the common people in the novel to bear a Germanic name: Sigismundo, for example, appears before her. In addition, however, one might add that the combination of this name with the more popular Portuguese form 'Maria' suggests a successful sublimation of the native inheritance with her own Germanic genes, while the root of Faustina's first name also clearly echoes a German hero who dared to challenge seemingly impregnable authority.

19 This reference to the Hanseatic League not only strengthens Lamberto's links with northern Europe and hence his alien presence in

the region but, when borne in mind in the context of *Jangada*, it surely also contains an insinuated criticism of modern market-oriented trading groupings such as the European Union.

20 Serrão mentions D. Isabel's well-known charity and piety, but regarding legends about her he limits himself to declaring that 'the people created an aura of sanctity around her, attributing various miracles to her'; see his *Dicionário*, p. 343 (it might, of course, be thought that these legends themselves are an exercise in transhistorical propaganda, designed to elicit a favourable press for the monarchy over successive generations of exploitation of the kingdom). Regarding D. Clemência, Cerdeira da Silva discusses this passage of the novel at greater length and makes more explicit reference to the spatial distance between rich and poor, while also reminding us that the rich benefactor remains in a heated space throughout, by contrast with the children on the frozen ground below, although she does concede that D. Clemência should perhaps be given some indulgence on an individual level, as she is not hypocritical, but merely deceived by the ideological mantra of charity developed by her own social class for its own ends over many generations. See Cerdeira da Silva, *José Saramago*, pp. 205–7.

21 The emphasis here is mine.

22 One might also see in the choice of this word an evocation of the powerful socially-engaged song 'Cálice' by the Brazilian singer and poet Chico Buarque de Holanda, where the repeated interruption of the noun 'cálice' (representing the sufferings of Christ) sounds identical to the verbal imperative 'cale-se' ('shut up'). The biblical reference here is to Christ's prayer to God before his crucifixion, in Matthew 26:39 ('O my Father, if it be possible, let this cup pass from me'). All quotations and references to the Bible are based on the Authorized (King James) translation.

23 Cerdeira da Silva (*José Saramago*, p. 227) makes brief reference to the major issues in the 1958 election. See also Birmingham, pp. 173–4, and Raby, pp. 177–90. For specific discussion of the manipulation of the election results, including the reproduction of a leaked document outlining the lengths to which the government went to ensure a favourable outcome, see Raby, p. 189.

24 Grossegesse adds an interesting twist to the motif of the inherited blue eyes which run in the Mau-Tempo family, as he writes: 'One fact largely forgotten today is that the existence of eyes of this colour in Portugal was interpreted by the anthropologists of the New State as evidence of a valuable Germanic substratum'; this theory was apparently influenced by Nazi-era experiments in eugenics in Germany. See Grossegesse, 'Messianismo Telúrico', p. 208, and p. 213 note 6.

25 The competing claims of biological family versus community are a repeated motif in Saramago's novels; see Jesus' rejection of and by his mother and siblings in *Evangelho* (see *Evangelho*, pp. 254 and 328), Joana Carda's effective rebellion against the patriarchal demands of her family in *Jangada* (as well as her claim that the feminine ending of her surname derives from a female ancestor's refusal to conform

to the subordinate role expected of her; see *Jangada*, p. 159) and, in a more positive sense, the constitution of new families of association, such as that of the five travellers in the same novel, or the group led by the doctor's wife in *Cegueira*. Both that novel and *Jangada* use language relating to families to refer to groups of disparate individuals thrown together by chance but held together by goodwill (see *Cegueira*, p. 218, and *Jangada*, pp. 209, 285, 312 and 314).

26 Cerdeira da Silva, *José Saramago*, p. 235.

27 See Deut. 34: 4–5.

28 Luke 2:19.

29 This loss of an audience for a Church insensitive to the needs of its flock is a theme taken up again by Lídia in *Ano*, when she admonishes Ricardo Reis (and, by implication, the conservative forces with which he instinctively sides): 'se a igreja estivesse do lado dos pobres, para os ajudar na terra, os mesmos pobres seriam capazes de dar a vida por ela, para que ela não caísse no inferno, onde está' (*Ano*, p. 388) ('if the church were on the side of the poor and helped them on this earth, then the poor would be the first to give their lives for the church', *Year*, p. 336).

30 These comparisons to the early Christian Church are surely intended to represent the innocence of a spontaneous faith unbound by centuries of turgid dogma and increasing collaboration with established power structures.

31 Sabine fixes the events described at this point in the narrative as taking place in 1962. The references to the month of April, however, are clearly intended to point forward towards the 1974 Revolution at the climax of the novel. He also points out that it is at this moment that the novel's narrator begins to make increasing allowance for direct narration and interpretation of events by the voices of those very workers who have traditionally been cast as voiceless, even by the Neo-Realist movement; see Sabine, p. 54.

32 Cerdeira da Silva, *José Saramago*, p. 96. The wider positive implications for development of a revolutionary consensus which can be drawn from this negative are examined in Chapter Two.

33 See Sabine, pp. 143–50 and 155–6.

34 The origins of the term 'fascist' lie in the corresponding contrary truism, namely that a bunch of twigs bound together (Latin *fasces*) is harder to break than a succession of individual twigs, an etymology explicitly recalled in a later novel (see *Ano*, p. 397). It is logical, therefore, that fascism should seek to have all of its followers responding with total loyalty to the will of the leader ('Nós não somos nada', or 'We are nobody', to use the mantra repeated in the same novel; see *Ano*, particularly p. 374), while wishing to prevent such solidarity amongst its opponents. The type of democratic socialism envisaged by Saramago in the current novel relies on a unity resulting from members of the movement growing in solidarity together through debate.

35 This toponym could be interpreted both in terms of its suggestion of height, which is directly associated with the exercise of power in this

novel, and also as 'Mon-temor', that is 'the mountain of fear'. For discussion of the equation of height with power, see Frier, 'Ascent and Consent', pp. 126–9. Sabine (pp. 152–4) makes some justifiable refinements to the ideas proposed in that article.

36 See Sabine, p. 67.

37 'In certain social conditions, Marx argues, human powers, products and processes escape from the control of human subjects and come to assume an apparently autonomous existence [. . .], so that men and women submit to what are in fact products of their own activity as though they are an alien force' (Eagleton, p. 70).

38 One might see an implicit contrast in the reference to these prostitutes with Camões's idealistic account of the 'Doze de Inglaterra' in *Os Lusíadas* (Canto VI, stanzas 42–70; see *Os Lusíadas*, pp. 227–34); this possibility is supported by the fact that by the time Baltasar reaches Lisbon the group has been reduced to a dozen (p. 43).

39 This experience is shared by Saramago's depiction of Camões on his return to Lisbon in *Livro*.

40 The same point is reinforced by a suggestion made two pages previously that Lisbon 'é terra de muito crime, morre-se mais que na guerra' (p. 45) ('more people are murdered in the city than are killed in war'; p. 36).

41 See Lisboa, pp. 350–2.

42 Of course this transition to a new stage of his life is also a positive one: shortly after his arrival in Lisbon Baltasar first meets the love of his life, Blimunda. Blimunda makes a corresponding negative transition to a new stage of her life when she comes into Lisbon, also after crossing the Tagus (p. 356), and then enters widowhood as she observes Baltasar's execution at the end of the novel.

43 Cerdeira da Silva, *José Saramago*, p. 56. This idea is further developed by Sabine in terms of Marcusian conceptions of the ideal society, where labour, willing cooperation, leisure and free sexual expression coexist; see Sabine, pp. 143–50.

44 See Saramago's interview with Molina, pp. 258–9.

45 Lima rightly points out that Francisco Marques is not only killed by the stone but also symbolically castrated by it, for when his body is removed from under the cart, his penis is said to have been crushed to the point of becoming invisible (p. 259). See Vieira Lima, p. 44.

46 This minor incident might be seen as an echo of the negative trajectory followed by the Spanish picaresque hero Lazarillo de Tormes in the first three 'Tratados' of the anonymous sixteenth-century narrative bearing his name: Lazarillo moves from material dependence on a blind beggar early in the narrative through to being required to subsidize his noble (but penniless and unemployed) master in Tratado Three, before beginning an ascent in material fortunes in the latter part of the text. Indeed, the basic conception of *Memorial* bears many resemblances to picaresque novels such as *Lazarillo de Tormes*, a point made at length by Oliveira Filho, who discovers a convincing and extended frame of reference within the contemporary novel to the *Obras do Diabinho da Mão*

Furada by the eighteenth-century playwright António José da Silva. Oliveira Filho suggests that *Memorial* may be seen as the work which da Silva might have written outside the restrictive intellectual environment of eighteenth-century Portugal: for, instead of leading to a denunciation of the social ills of its time, the critic claims that the depiction of the miseries of everyday reality in his work leads merely to a disappointingly conventional work of orthodox piety, with the protagonist recognizing the truths of Christianity and renouncing all worldly pleasures (see Oliveira Filho, pp. 32–5 and 38–40). It is presumably both intentional on Saramago's part and deeply ironic, therefore, that the final scene of his novel depicts da Silva (popularly known as 'O Judeu', or 'The Jew') being burned at the stake by the Inquisition, alongside the 'sinful' Baltasar: the dramatist's attempts to conform to the orthodox morality of his time were therefore of no benefit to him in the longer term.

47 João's enforced labour with pick and shovel here forms a contrast with the voluntary (and therefore, in Marxist terms, non-alienated) search for the same implements undertaken by the doctor's wife and her comrades towards the end of *Cegueira*, where these tools are to be used for the restoration of human dignity through the burial of the old woman whose body they find in the street (see *Cegueira*, p. 286).

48 As Fernandes points out, this vision from above is contrasted within the text with João Elvas's contemplation of the other side of the royal procession to the Spanish border with its 'pedintes e outros vadiantes' ('a horde of beggars and tramps', p. 287) (see Fernandes, p. 32; the phrase quoted from the novel is at p. 301).

49 Rouanet introduces an enlightening contrast between Scarlatti's music, described as 'articulando em discurso novo o que parecera antes fragmentário e contraditório' (in a passage on p. 177 of the text) ('as if giving new expression to what had previously seemed fragmentary and dissonant', p. 165), while the king's attempts to build his miniature version of St Peter's Basilica in Rome simply put everything back into a preordained position (p. 12), leading to unchanging and predictable results (p. 277); see Rouanet, p. 61. Sabine (pp. 117–20) makes a comparison of Scarlatti's development of the sonata form to Hegelian conceptions of dialogism, before concluding that the most telling conclusion to be drawn from this parallel is that the historical novel can never fully and objectively recover the past which it seeks to represent, with any attempts to impose the neat patterns of interpretation (akin to those of the sonata) being merely window-dressing over the essentially formless and limitless array of data potentially open to our understanding. Perhaps the key point in attempting to reconcile these two apparently incompatible arguments lies in regarding Rouanet as stressing the potential existing within accounts of the past for creating new patterns of interpretation, while Sabine is correct in asserting that any such new account must be seen merely as a provisional and tentative one, a point reinforced by the emphasis on trial and error in the epigraph to the later *História*: 'Enquanto não alcançares a

verdade, não poderás corrigi-la. Porém, se a não corrigires, não a alcançarás. Entretanto, não te resignes' (*História*, dust jacket) ('Until you attain the truth, you will not be able to amend it. But if you do not amend it, you will not attain it. Meanwhile, do not resign yourself', *History*, flyleaf).

50 For further discussion of this point, see Frier, 'Ascent and Consent', pp. 126–9.

51 See Sabine, p. 60; see the same critic also, at p. 60, n. 40, for an enumeration of the specific events in Portuguese and world history alluded to in this manner.

52 Cerdeira da Silva (*José Saramago*, pp. 248–9) comments on the importance of this episode in raising the awareness of the people of their own power, making a comparison in this respect with Eisenstein's film *The Battleship Potemkin*, based on a real-life incident in 1905, when Russian soldiers rebelled against the diseased food which they were required to eat by their superior officers. Sabine (p. 88 and pp. 88–9, n. 92) views the same passage of the text in relation to the notion of sacrifice for the conquest of the sea in Pessoa's famous poem 'Mar Português'; in fact, an equally apposite point of comparison might be another Pessoa poem, 'O menino de sua mãe' which is alluded to in *Ano*, as the poet contemplates the possibility of his son by Lídia dying on some corner of a foreign field that will be forever, but futilely, Portuguese (see *Ano*, p. 390); the text of that poem itself may be found in Galhoz (ed.), pp. 83–4.

53 Cerdeira da Silva suggests that José Gato is seen within the text to be essentially a maverick rebelling against the system without shaking its foundations in any significant sense (see Cerdeira da Silva, *José Saramago*, p. 241). This would certainly fit with the unconfirmed story of his eventual co-option by the system when he takes up a position with the colonial police in Africa (p. 133).

54 The phrasing here once again recalls the fascist slogan 'Nós não somos nada' ('We are nobody'), repeated like a mantra in *Ano* (see *Ano*, particularly p. 374).

55 'Wherever you will go I will go, and where you stay I will stay' (Ruth 1:16).

56 This formulation recalls the imagery used in relation to the ants at the end of the discussion of the death in captivity of Germano Vidigal, as discussed above.

57 Dogs become a recurring motif in the author's work, appearing not only in this novel, but also in *Jangada*, *História*, *Cegueira* and *Caverna*. In those works they generally embody the qualities of loyalty and consolation. For further discussion of the use of animal imagery in this novel, see Schor, pp. 51–3, and Berrini, pp. 36–8. Berrini (pp. 36–7) sees the use of animal motifs as being partly an attempt to place the narrative in the context of rural oral tradition, which frequently makes use of anthropomorphized animals. I have excluded from my discussion of animal imagery in this novel the fanciful stories told by António Mau-Tempo (and others) inserted into various moments of the narrative; this issue is discussed by

Sabine (p. 51 and p. 51, n. 26). The same critic recalls the repeated use of ant imagery in Carlos de Oliveira's Neo-Realist *Uma Abelha na Chuva* in this connection (p. 66, n. 50).

58 See *Memorial*, pp. 118, 211, 218, 230 and 253.

59 See the comments attributed to Salazar by Avelãs Nunes (Avelãs Nunes, pp. 60 and 61, n. 15).

60 See 'Cadeira', in *Objecto*, pp. 15–34.

61 Saramago very pointedly here makes use of the Camonian phrase 'bicho da terra' ('such insects on so small a stage'; see *Os Lusíadas*, Canto I, stanza 106, at Camões, *Os Lusíadas*, p. 95 and *The Lusiads*, p. 24), but with a significant revision to the original context, in keeping with the perspective of the landowners: a phrase originally used to express the appropriate sense of humility of the human race in the face of more powerful forces has instead become a means for the powerful to dismiss the workers as being essentially of a different species: humility has therefore been transformed into humiliation in a manner which also exposes the perversion which the Portuguese establishment made of the Portuguese national epic over many generations.

62 Cerdeira da Silva uses the variation on Camões here to make a point related to Gramscian notions of cultural hegemony: 'It is like the ordinary Portuguese man taking on the poet who, for centuries, had been the great and legendary point of reference in his national culture, in order to reshape it on a new basis' (Cerdeira da Silva, *José Saramago*, p. 205).

63 See *Jangada*, p. 9 and *Lucidez*, p. 329.

64 This comparison could be related to the one used to describe the withered arm of the passive Marcenda in *Ano* as being 'como uma ave doente, asa quebrada, chumbo cravado no peito' ('an injured bird, its wing broken, a lead pellet embedded in its breast'; see *Ano*, p. 127 and *Year*, p. 104).

65 An exception to this general tendency is the description of Germano's torturer Escarrilho as a wild dog being turned upon his victim to bite and castrate him (pp. 171–2).

66 Schor interprets this repeated motif in the following terms: 'Amongst these insects some are particularly noticeable, as they hold their heads up like dogs. This positioning of the head indicates heightened awareness and greater self-awareness, so that these ants are no longer the animals which crawl around on the ground; instead their raised heads allow them to look around and thus better recognize what is going on around them' (see Schor, p. 53).

67 For details of the uprising at Beja under the leadership of General Varela Gomes, see Raby, pp. 211–3.

68 Grossegesse, *Saramago Lesen*, p. 39.

69 Schor links this dynamic perception of society to the new narrative technique adopted by the novel: 'It is no longer what is fixed that will be in the foreground, but what moves, what is dynamic. The discourse which is loyal to traditional aesthetics is abandoned in favour of an unconventional, narrative one' (Schor, p. 42). One also notes

once again the recurrence of the motif of the person who is blind because they refuse to see.

70 See Arnaut, '*Memorial do Convento*', pp. 52–7. Arnaut argues that the two versions of the names of these characters within the text permit them effectively to be different people for Baltasar and Blimunda from what they are in court circles. This may well be the case with Bartolomeu, for Arnaut correctly observes that at court his name includes the second surname 'de Gusmão', which causes some surprise to his lowly friends when they first hear it (p. 144). In the case of Scarlatti, however, the adoption of the alternative name 'Escarlate' (or 'Scarlet', as opposed to the omission of a separate element of his name) is surely simply a reflection of greater ease of pronunciation for a couple unused to dealing with foreign names, as is stated by Venâncio, who rejects Pedro Alvim's ideological reading of the revised version of the name as an allusion to Marxism on the grounds that 'this distortion in the popular version of the name would be both easy and predictable' (Venâncio, p. 113; the reference to Alvim is to a review of the novel under the title '*Memorial do Convento*: uma personagem chamada língua portuguesa', which was published in the *Diário de Lisboa* of 17 December 1982). Contrary to the statement made by Carlos Reis on the matter, the historical Bartolomeu Lourenço de Gusmão was, in fact, known by both of the names used here, as the 'de Gusmão' element (which Reis sees as having been part of his official name) did not derive from his parents, who were known as Francisco Lourenço and Dona Maria Álvares respectively (for Reis' comments, see his article '*Memorial do Convento*', p. 99, n. 6). The most probable explanation for this variation is that at some point between 1712 and 1718 he adopted the extra surname in order to honour Padre Alexandre de Gusmão, who protected the interests of the Rodrigues Álvares family in Bahia; this Alexandre de Gusmão is not to be confused with Bartolomeu's brother of the same name; see Serrão, *Dicionário*, at the entry for 'Bartolomeu Lourenço de Gusmão', III, 184–5 (p. 184). My estimated dating of the change in Bartolomeu's name is based on the title page of the preacher's 'Sermão da Virgem Maria Nossa Senhora' (dated 1712), which refers to the author simply as 'Bartolomeu Lourenço', while that of the sermon dedicated to 'Nossa Senhora do Desterro' in 1718 contains both surnames; these title pages are reproduced in Moraes, pp. 183 and 185 respectively. I gratefully acknowledge the assistance of Professor Enrique Martínez-López of the University of California at Santa Barbara for his assistance with these genealogical matters.

71 MacNab suggests that the ambivalence and social mobility of these characters functions in order to permit the reader's attention to be diverted away from the traditional focus of history at court and towards the real actors in this novel, Baltasar and Blimunda (see MacNab, p. 138).

72 Cerdeira da Silva, *José Saramago*, p. 209.

73 For further discussion of these dreams, see Cerdeira da Silva, 'O *Memorial do Convento* e a Repressão da Utopia', p. 122.

74 Cerdeira da Silva, *José Saramago,* p. 81.

75 See Berrini, p. 55, and Júlio, p. 90.

76 See Real, pp. 75–6.

77 The relevant passages are as follows, firstly from Canto III, Stanza 120 of *Os Lusíadas*: 'Naquele engano da alma, ledo e cego/ Que a Fortuna não deixa durar muito' ('In that soft deception of the soul/ That fortune never indulges long'; Camões, *Os Lusíadas,* p. 157, and *The Lusiads,* p. 72), and 'Grande desventura foi a que me fez ser triste, ou que pela ventura me fez ser leda' ('It took great misfortune to make me sad, and great happiness to bring me joy'; Ribeiro, p. 7). Garrett reproduces the lines quoted from Camões in Act I Scene I and from *Menina e Moça* in Act II Scene I of his drama respectively; see Garrett, pp. 11 and 55 respectively.

78 Ecclesiastes 1:2. In fact, D. João V himself, in a moment of weakness, implicitly reinforces this assocation through his words earlier in the text: 'Vaidade das vaidades, disse Salomão, e D. João V repete, Tudo é vaidade, vaidade é desejar, ter é vaidade' (p. 289) ('Vanity of vanities, Solomon once declared, and Dom João V repeats these words, All is vanity, to desire is vanity, to possess is vanity', p. 274). Linhares Filho compares this excerpt from the text to a reference by Oliveira Martins to the king as 'the bloated Solomon of Mafra' (from Oliveira Martins, *História de Portugal,* Lisbon: Guimarães Editores, 1972, p. 454, quoted in Linhares Filho, pp. 177–8).

79 For the definition of this distinction, see Forster, pp. 46–54.

80 Pereira points out one redeeming feature in the figure of the king, whom he sees as a 'complex and contradictory character', whose megalomaniac tendencies are counterbalanced by a wish to see Portugal catch up with the more 'advanced' countries in Europe. Against this one could also argue that as long as this attempted 'progress' is to be achieved only in terms of elite cultural figures such as Scarlatti, this will be meaningless to the ordinary man and woman. See Pereira, p. 122.

81 This ambivalence becomes more explicit in a passage relating to the king's lovers at the Convent of Odivelas, which deliberately plays on the two senses of the word 'Senhor' (see p. 156). Linhares Filho provides historical evidence for the possible factual basis for this passage (see Linhares Filho, p. 185).

82 For further discussion of this point, see Cerdeira da Silva, *José Saramago,* pp. 232–3, and Letizia, p. 159. Letizia goes on to point out Sara's extreme patience and submission (pp. 160–1) but slightly overstates the situation in stating that this figure never displays any 'sign of rebellion' (p. 160); put more accurately, dominant social structures require her to make her protests in an indirect way, for example through the assistance of Picanço (*Levantado,* pp. 48–9). Sabine (pp. 76–85) discusses the relationship between Sara and Domingos in some depth.

83 See Sabine, p. 81; the same critic also suggests that there is an

implicit parallel here to the opening of Fernando Namora's *O Trigo e o Joio* (see Sabine, p. 49). Fernandes sees a parallel between Sara and Domingos and the Sarah and Abraham of the Old Testament; this seems more tenuous than the clear allusions to Christ's nativity, both here and in relation to the birth of Domingos' own son João later in the text, not least since this Sara conceives a child on purpose, while her alleged biblical forebear initially finds the idea of her own fertility ridiculous at the age of ninety; it does appear, however, that the main purpose of Fernandes's comparison lies in the foundation of a dynasty. See Fernandes, p. 28; Genesis 17, 18 and 21:1–2; and *Levantado*, p. 24.

84 Despite this ironic treatment of the parallel with scripture here, Berrini is probably correct to see a more straightforward and serious intent in the majority of the allusions to the Bible in this novel, contributing to the heroic stature of the ordinary people of the Alentejo; see Berrini, pp. 38–49. While Sabine is correct in saying that the text draws attention to the limited nature of the applicability of the parallel made here, this parallel is nonetheless made and still has its effect upon the reader's perception of the narrative.

85 Sabine (p. 87) discusses the narrative's adoption of folk tales of werepigs and werechickens as devices to discuss instances of domestic violence. By way of contrast with the relative frankness of present-day society surrounding such issues, a conservative and patriarchal society such as that of the early twentieth-century Alentejo could only have discussed socially controversial issues like this through a refracting lens of a type which would not openly acknowledge their existence.

86 I believe that Saramago's use of the word 'risco' (which can mean either 'line' or 'risk' in Portuguese) rather than the everyday word 'linha', is deliberate in both contexts discussed here; see also Frier, 'Agouros e Oportunidades', p. 717.

87 Similarly, Letizia points out that João's sister Maria succeeds in obtaining a limited degree of personal and financial freedom in moving to Lisbon to work as a maid for a wealthy family (see Letizia, p. 166). This is very much a limited freedom, however, leaving her totally dependent on her employers for her welfare, as is demonstrated when João, newly released from prison late at night, has to rule out the possibility of seeking assistance from his sister because his bad reputation in respectable society would place her in an awkward position with her employers (Letizia, p. 262). Sánchez contrasts her immobility in staying in the same job throughout her working career with Maria Adelaide's mobility later in the novel (see Kathryn M. Sánchez, review of *Levantado*, in Tesser (ed.), pp. 15–16, p. 15). Nonetheless, it is clear that João and Faustina do what they can to coexist and raise their children in a more positive environment than that which they experienced, leading Sabine (p. 87) to refer to them as an 'idealised family observing socialist principles, countering the *Estado Novo* paradigm of a tightly disciplined patriarchal family'.

88 A further indication of the preservation of patriarchal attitudes is that, even as the revolution finally blows away political repression, young women like Maria Adelaide are still regarded with suspicion if they attempt to relate to men on their own terms rather than according to traditional codes: 'se esta Maria ou aquela Aurora não nasceram bichos de mato e com os rapazes conversam naturalmente, rindo quando é de rir, aqui d'el rei que são uma levianas e cabeças levantadas' ('if Maria over here or Aurora over there were not born in a field and chat to boys naturally, laughing when there is something to laugh at, then call out the cops, for they are loose and headstrong', p. 349). The use of the archaisms 'aqui d'el rei' (particularly with its monarchist echoes) and 'levianas' in this context clearly indicates an authorial view of such conservative sexual mores as being outdated, an impression confirmed by the reference immediately afterwards to 'cabeças levantadas', placing such behaviour firmly in the context of the same attitude of liberation as has occurred politically at this time (the phrase recalls that used in connection with the ants imagined as having the capacity earlier in the novel to disclose the uncomfortable truth about the killing of Germano Vidigal; see p. 176).

89 Cerdeira da Silva, *José Saramago*, pp. 252–3. By a process of calculating backwards from João's death, this incident can be estimated as taking place around 1950: João dies at the age of sixty-seven (p. 347) when Maria Adelaide is seventeen (p. 346), that is probably in 1972, since she is said to be nineteen at the time of the 1974 Revolution (p. 350). This would place his birth in 1905 (1904 at the very earliest), so that his release from custody in Lisbon must take place between 1948 and 1950 at the very latest, as he is said to be forty-four years old (p. 241) when he is arrested. This date would therefore allow this Ricardo Reis to have lived on for at least twelve years after the year of the death of Ricardo Reis described in the later novel. On this occasion, of course, Reis's woman is his wife Ermelinda (p. 264), not Lídia, the poet's unmarried lover, while the character himself bears little resemblance to the solitary scholar of *Ano*. Nonetheless, the choice of this name cannot be an accident: Saramago has repeatedly declared his fascination for the poetry of Reis and, in particular, his lengthy struggle with accepting the implications of the famous verse 'Sábio é o que se contenta com o espectáculo do mundo' ('Wise is he who contents himself with the spectacle of the world'); on this point see, for example, the comments made in his interview with Molina (in Molina, pp. 260–1). In the course of the same interview the novelist himself, without any prompting, brings up the character in *Levantado* when asked about the protagonist of *Ano* (see Molina, p. 261). Regardless of whether or not Ermelinda is intended to be another version of Lídia, or she is simply intended to be seen as a subsequent relationship, both she and her husband demonstrate the same spontanous and generous warmth as the hotel-maid does in the later novel, something inconceivable from Saramago's more familiar version of Ricardo Reis.

90 The same notion recurs implicitly when João, who has agreed reluctantly to attend an anti-communist rally in Évora, thinks of going to relieve himself just as one of the speakers invokes the nation in glorious terms, exploiting to the full an implicit association with divine favour: 'Onde é que eu posso mijar, ó Requinta, isto são brincadeiras, não há aqui ninguém que ouse dizer tal coisa em tão grave momento, quando a pátria, ela que não mija nunca, está a ser assim invocada por aquele bem posto senhor no palanque, que abre os braços como se nos quisesse abraçar a todos'. (p. 95) ('Where can I go for a piss, Requinta, this is just a joke, nobody here would dare say anything like that at such a serious moment, when the Fatherland, which never ever pisses, is being invoked by that elegant gentleman up on the platform who is opening up his arms as if he wanted to embrace us all'.) The speaker's body movements here echo Ermelinda's actions in welcoming João into her home (p. 264); the similarities are presumably meant to stop there, since this speaker's actions express a false affection designed for effect, as opposed to Ermelinda's simple and honest generosity of spirit. Specifically regarding the motif of urination, this Rabelaisian incident also relates to the excremental imagery used in Baltasar's imaginary letter to the king in *Memorial* (p. 287), and this relationship thus reinforces the subversive potential of that letter.

91 Cerdeira da Silva, *José Saramago*, p. 204.

92 Avelãs Nunes (pp. 60 and 61, n. 15) derives the quotation by Salazar from Fernando Rosas, 'Salazar. Os anos de chumbo', in *Fim de Semana/ O Diário* ('Suplemento'), no. 4408 (27 May 1989), pp. 1–23 (pp. 7–8).

93 Cerdeira da Silva, *José Saramago*, p. 208. The critic derives this association from the text of the novel itself: 'whether or not the shepherd may be thinking more about the stomachs of the sheep than about the interests of his master Berto, that is, the hidden one' (*Levantado*, p. 275; see Cerdeira da Silva, *José Saramago*, p. 262, n. 12).

94 See Luke 3:23–38.

95 As the Colombian novel was first published in 1967, it would be possible to posit some influence from it over Saramago's practice in the naming of his characters. An equally likely source of influence, however, is Alves Redol's *Barranco de Cegos* of 1961, which features a character named Chico Bem-Fadado (corresponding here to the Mau-Tempos). As regards the humorous names given to the policemen, Vítor Viçoso suggests that they may have been influenced by Raul Brandão's *Húmus*, a work which includes names such as D. Ninharia, D. Insolência and D. Teles das Teles e Reles (see Viçoso, p. 247). Sabine makes a brief examination of the deeper thematic links existing between *Levantado* and *Cien años de soledad* (see Sabine, p. 89).

96 Cerdeira da Silva, *José Saramago*, p. 209. The same critic returns to this point later in her study: 'The means of depersonalizing these agents of power is to strip them of their individual attributes and reduce them to mere representatives for a force which they endorse and

whose will they carry out. Thus they lose their own names which are reduced to formal repetitions of their character [. . .] In this way, their personal names, deprived of their referential function, that of identifying and individualizing the characters, take on instead a semantic content which destroys their inherent arbitrariness.' (p. 222)

97 The issue of the control of Portuguese soil being granted to foreign opportunists resurfaces briefly in *Jangada*, where the poor of the Algarve occupy holiday homes abandoned by the tourist industry (*Jangada*, pp. 98–105), and, more prominently still, in *História*, where Raimundo Silva's account of the final days of the siege has the ordinary Portuguese soldiers demanding parity with the few foreign crusaders who remain with Afonso Henriques and who stand to make substantial gains from the sacking of the city; see *História*, pp. 342–3.

98 Saramago appears to allude here to either of two biblical passages: 'Behold, the heaven and the heaven of heavens is the LORD'S thy God, the earth also, with all that therein is' (Deut. 10:14) and 'The earth is the LORD'S, and the fulness thereof; the world, and they that dwell therein' (Psalms 24:1). The exploitation of such rhetoric, however, simply begs the question of the justification for the specific and exclusive claims laid to the land by the *-bertos*.

99 Sabine (p. 50) provides a detailed and convincing argument for viewing the transformation in narrative stance in the novel as a gradual process, but this does not invalidate the supposition that the first chapter deliberately sets out to contrast a 'traditional' narrative perspective with the increasingly pluridiscursive chapters which follow it. The subtler transitions which Sabine outlines may still be possible within the later chapters of the novel after a sharp break with its opening section.

100 Cerdeira da Silva makes essentially the same point about this novel when she writes of it as 'a return, not a circular one, but a spiral' (see Cerdeira da Silva, 'Saramago e Redol', p. 38). Sabine reinforces the novel's suggestion of progression within the apparently eternal recurrence of the seasons through a discussion of the comparison made by the text of the earth to a watch; in later novels, such as *Memorial*, however, he sees progression posited primarily on a hypothetical or utopian plane (see Sabine, pp. 71, 92 and 105 respectively), although he also acknowledges textual anachronisms hinting at positive developments to emerge in the twentieth century (see Sabine, p. 116).

101 Fernandes sees a contrast between the agitation of the 'mar interior' developed over the course of the novel as a whole and the essentially bucolic and stable nature of the Portuguese countryside depicted by Cesário Verde. While this contrast has some validity, Verde's idyllic imagery was intended to function as social criticism in itself, by setting up a (perhaps over-utopian) positive counterpoint to his vision of the ills of the nineteenth-century city; as Fernandes points out, Verde's peasant (unlike Saramago's) 'does not speak, the poet

speaks for him' (Fernandes, p. 71). For her discussion of Verde in general in relation to *Levantado*, see Fernandes, pp. 69–71.

102 Cerdeira da Silva, *José Saramago*, p. 194. The same critic also makes further discussion of imagery relating to the sea in her article 'Saramago e Redol' (pp. 45–7), while similar points are also made by MacNab (p. 139) and Sánchez (in her review of *Levantado* in Tesser (ed.), 16–18, p. 17).

103 The allusions here are respectively to Camões' sonnet 'Mudam-se os tempos, mudam-se as vontades' (in Camões, *Versos e Alguma Prosa*, p. 45) and to the final two lines of 'O Infante' in Pessoa's *Mensagem*: 'Cumpriu-se o Mar, e o Império se desfez./ Senhor, falta cumprir-se Portugal!' ('The Sea was won, the Empire undone./ Lord, we must still win Portugal!) (in *Mensagem*, p. 57; the English translation is from Zenith, p. 273).

104 'Aqui, onde o mar se acabou e a terra espera' ('Here where the sea ends and the earth awaits', *Ano*, p. 415, and *Year*, p. 358).

105 Pessoa, 'Mar Português', in *Mensagem*, p. 70; the English translation is from Zenith, p. 278.

106 See *Conto*, especially pp. 31–9.

107 Cerdeira da Silva explicitly relates even the title of the novel to a theme derived from Camões's commemoration of the journey of Vasco da Gama, expressed in Canto I, Stanza 3 of *Os Lusíadas*:

> Que eu canto o peito ilustre Lusitano,
> A quem Neptuno e Marte obedeceram.
> Cesse tudo o que a Musa antiga canta,
> Que outro valor mais alto se alevanta.

('I sing of the famous Portuguese/ To whom both Mars and Neptune bowed./ Abandon all the ancient Muse revered,/ A loftier code of honour has appeared'; Camões, *Os Lusíadas*, p. 69, and *The Lusiads*, p. 3). See Cerdeira da Silva, 'No Paraíso da Memória', p. 263.

108 Saramago appears to be conflating two separate incidents here. The hijacking of the cruise liner *Santa Maria* was carried out by exiled Portuguese dissidents in Venezuela on 22 January 1961, bringing discontent with Salazar's regime to the world's attention (see Raby, pp. 208–9.) The reference to the escape of communists from imprisonment at Peniche presumably refers to the jailbreak carried out by Álvaro Cunhal and nine other Party members on 3 January 1960 (see Raby, pp. 130–1).

109 The use of the image of rape in terms of labour relations effectively intertwines issues of sexual politics with the brutality of the dominant economic system: the rape of the peasant girl at the spring effectively founds the *-berto* dynasty and creates the oppression of both men and women. This abuse is eventually redeemed by the symbolic triumph of Maria Adelaide over the forces of privilege at the same spring centuries later, in the final chapter of the novel.

110 This story is given the catalogue number H588.7 by Stith Thompson, III, p. 431.

111 Lyrics taken from the web pages of the Universidade do Minho,

http://natura.di.uminho.pt/~jj/musica/html/zecafonso-grandola.html (web page consulted on 2 November 2005).

112 This incident is a key one in the development of the popular voice in the novel. In spite of his alliance with the landowners, on this occasion Agamedes is rebuked by Norberto for his strategic error in raising the subject of the recent strike at an occasion such as a popular wedding, whose social function from the perspective of the landowners is to be the entertainment which pacifies the populace after a period of difficult relations: 'Não foi nada boa ideia, senhor padre Agamedes, disse mais tarde Norberto, que lembrança a sua, ir recordar essas coisas, é o mesmo que falar de corda em casa de enforcado' ('That was a lousy idea, Father Agamedes, Norberto said later, whatever gave you that idea, bringing up those issues, that's really sticking your foot in it'; p. 223). Norberto's choice of imagery in adapting the popular saying 'não se fala de corda em casa de enforcado' (literally, 'don't mention rope in the house of the man who has been hung') might be seen as another strategic error, in that it creates an association with brutality to the official response to this strike, although this is clearly a choice on the part of the author in order to give Norberto in his turn enough rope to hang himself in the reader's eyes.

113 Saramago, 'Mi iberismo', p. 5.

114 This false mock-up of warfare might also be compared to the fake bombing-raid carried out over Lisbon in *Ano* (*Ano*, pp. 336–9), which, of course, merely prefigured another (very real) bombing raid often regarded by historians as a trial run: the bombing of the Basque town of Guernica by the Luftwaffe during the Spanish Civil War, generally viewed as having been a useful experiment for the Nazis in preparing for saturation bombing of other civilian targets during World War II. The major difference between the incident in Lisbon and the bombing of Guernica is that there were mass fatalities in the latter case; the link between the false raid over Lisbon and real raids to come in the future is stressed by the fact that at the end of the 'attack' the planes wheel away in the direction of Badajoz (p. 339), the scene of another real massacre mentioned later in the text (pp. 390–1). The point implicitly made, then, is that simulated warfare cannot be described as harmless if it actually enables real warfare to be carried out more effectively.

115 Cavaliere, in fact, points out a further similar instance of imagery suggesting that ordinary people have unwittingly been caught up in warfare in peacetime: during the transportation of the giant stone from Pêro Pinheiro to Mafra, the workers are said to be returning from a 'guerra perdida, sujos, esfarrapados, sem riquezas' ('some disastrous battle, dirty, ragged, and bereft of spoils', *Memorial*, p. 264; *Baltasar*, p. 249); see Cavaliere, p. 201.

116 Sabine also notes the significance of the use of the word 'luzes' here, but places the emphasis more on the backwardness of Portuguese

society than on the opportunities for enlightenment available outside the constrictive world of twentieth-century Portugal (see Sabine, p. 60).

117 This type of plot structure adopted by Cervantes is reflected on in more explicit terms earlier in the novel in connection with Maria Adelaide's mother Gracinda, with the twist that on this occasion royalty are seen to want to take possession of the child: 'Fiquemos por aqui, debaixo da azinheira, abanando o rostinho da criança que quer dormir, com este galho, porque as moscas já tornam e também para evitar um desgosto aos pais, não vá passar por aqui cortejo de reis e cavaleiros, ver a aia da rainha estéril este anjinho deitado e levar a Gracinda para o palácio' ('Let's stay here, beneath the oak tree, fanning the face of the child who wants to sleep with this branch, because the flies are coming back, and also to avoid any upset to the parents, we wouldn't want the party of kings and knights to go past, letting the queen's barren chambermaid see this angel lying here and then take Gracinda away to the palace', p. 185). Nonetheless, since the child's inherent beauty is visualized as leading the royal party to wish to abduct her, this story (which casts a more democratic light on the type of pattern used in stories such as *La gitanilla*, where the gypsy girl's adoptive parents sacrifice their own emotions and give ready assent to her removal to a higher social class) symbolically prefigures Maria Adelaide's claim to have access to property, privilege and control of her own life.

118 Letizia cites the presence of orange branches in this scene and develops a comparison of the figure of Maria Adelaide to a bride on her wedding day, with the groom being the new Portugal in which she and other women can now play a fuller part (see Letizia, p. 175). The young woman's symbolic victory in this incident also reawakens cultural memories of another famous Alentejan woman who was sexually used and abandoned by her foreign lover: Mariana Alcoforado, whose *Lettres Portugaises* were a 'succès de scandale' in seventeenth-century Europe. As *Levantado* was written when memories of the controversy surrounding the Three Marias' *Novas Cartas Portuguesas* (a revindication of the abandoned nun from Beja) were still fresh in the mind, it seems inconceivable that Saramago would not have been well aware of such an implicit link in this incident. Sabine (p. 85) comments on the use of the marigold as an image of liberation in relation both to Maria Adelaide as a woman in the passage alluded to here and to the spread of workers' occupations of estates across the Alentejo at the time a few pages later (*Levantado*, p. 361); in doing so, he suggests that Maria Adelaide's garland 'crowns the sequence of intimations [. . .] of progress towards female emancipation as one facet of the fulfilment of the telos of a free and harmonious society' (see Sabine, p. 85).

119 Sabine also comments on Saramago's use of Delacroix's image of Liberty in *Levantado*, but he does so specifically in the context of rejecting excessive romanticization or idealization of women; see Sabine, p. 61, n. 41.

[120] Ceccucci, 'L'utopia saramaghiana', p. 214.
[121] Sabine, p. 40.

Chapter Two

'Além da conversa das mulheres, são os sonhos que seguram o mundo na sua órbita': Centripetal and Centrifugal Forces

1. Introduction

The quotation reproduced in the title of this chapter occurs approximately one third of the way through *Memorial* (p. 115).[1] Its enigmatic assertion is more significant than it may seem: the importance of the conversation of women will become clear in the final section of the present chapter, dealing with the relevance of Gramscian socialism to Saramago's conception of the Revolution, but this conversation (and therefore also that Revolution) would not even be possible without the human capacity for independent thought and imagination.

The notion expressed of keeping the world up in its orbit is, of course, especially relevant to *Memorial* and in particular to the chapter which is opened by this statement, where Bartolomeu returns to Portugal after three years in the Netherlands (p. 115), revealing to Baltasar and Blimunda the astonishing secret of the fuel which will power his flying machine: the wills of ordinary people (pp. 123–4). The *Passarola*, the outstanding symbol in all of the novelist's creation for the concept of liberation, is important because it will allow ordinary people to escape the 'Terra solta, pedrisco, calhau que a pólvora ou o alvião arrancaram ao pedernal profundo' (p. 239) ('Loose soil, gravel, and pebbles that the gunpowder or the pick had prised from the stony ground', p. 224), which are their everyday lot otherwise in a kingdom said to be badly governed (p. 189).

The struggle for the ordinary people in this work, therefore, is between staying rooted to the earth (in which, in a later novel, the old woman who attempts in vain to eke out an independent existence amidst an epidemic of blindness has to be buried; *Cegueira*, p. 285) and escaping the humdrum in order to achieve something greater, for themselves and for the rest of humanity. This is why the attack by the 'authorities' of the New State on the *Afonso de Albuquerque* at the end of *Ano* becomes significant: for Daniel and his comrades aboard this ship are attempting to escape the land (also expressed as 'terra' in Portuguese) in order to help bring liberation to Spain, no longer seen as the traditional enemy of the Portuguese people, but instead as brothers in a transnational struggle against dictatorship and the repression of the human spirit.[2]

This spirit of rebellion should not, however, be seen in a purely ideological context, although clearly the novelist's own political views give these conflicts a particular slant, certainly in the case of *Ano*. Nonetheless, throughout Saramago's work, the notion of an escape from the dead weight of authority, of paternalistic control, and indeed the search for an independent and authentic existence become ever more urgent and pressing considerations. These ideas have been examined in recent years (in terms of the increasing exploitation of the individual as consumer within a market-oriented society) in *Caverna*, and (in terms of ideological conditioning and the restrictions on the freedom of thought of the individual, even within modern pluralistic societies) in his controversial *Lucidez*, which expresses in practice some of the author's misgivings about Western concepts of democracy.[3]

This chapter, therefore, will explore the contrast between conformity and independence, principally as they find expression in three novels: *História*, *Evangelho*, and *Jangada*. The sections on these texts will then lead into a concluding section outlining the positive path identified in a number of works to lead towards the writer's ideal of personal and political emancipation. These ideas will be expanded in the Conclusion into a vision of a struggle between the impulse towards life in its fullest sense and the death of mere existence.

2. 'No' News is Good News: *História do Cerco de Lisboa* and *O Evangelho Segundo Jesus Cristo*

This association between the refusal to cooperate with an overwhelming presence of apparently irresistible domination and the need to maintain one's own existential validity is not a new one in Saramago's writing: as was noted in the previous chapter, the title of his first genuinely successful novel, *Levantado do Chão* (*Risen from the Soil*) implicitly stresses the notion of organic growth, with the political emancipation of the workers of the Alentejo forming a parallel to the inevitable ripening of the crops which they harvest.

Other works since *Levantado* also bear witness to this message of defiance and, indeed, hints of it may be found even in works written before 1980: this section of this chapter will, therefore, include also brief reflections on the author's collection of short stories *Objecto Quase* of 1977. Of all the author's works of the 1980s and 1990s, however, it is in *História* and *Evangelho* that the issue of resistance to a stultifying self-proclaimed 'authority' becomes most prominent. These works form an interesting contrast to one another, in the sense that whereas Raimundo Silva, the protagonist of *História*, eventually succeeds in reinventing himself in a way which looks forward to the unexpected voyage of discovery and liberation later undertaken by the anonymous couple in *Conto*, Saramago's Jesus, in a radical rewriting of the traditional gospel story, becomes the sacrificial victim more of his own lack of self-belief and ambition than of the sins of humanity. Both works raise questions about authority: *História* more in the realm of knowledge, *Evangelho* in the sense of authority as a mask for the exercise of power to intimidate others into submission and to thwart their inner growth. However, even if the ending of *Evangelho* is a negative one in terms of plot resolution, this work still highlights the need for its readers to face up to their own challenges in a more positive manner than that adopted by this version of Jesus.

História opens with a disorienting dialogue between an anonymous historian and an unnamed proofreader of his work;[4] the latter figure is presumably intended to be identified with the apparently innocuous Raimundo, who realizes the inadequacies of a work of conventional history and distorts it by the gratuitous insertion of the word 'não' ('not') into a key sentence of the book, then proceeding to rewrite the history of the twelfth-century siege of Lisbon from that counterfactual premise and being rewarded for his efforts in the end by the love of his supervisor, Maria Sara, the very figure whose professional responsibility it would normally be to prevent any such acts of rebellion against established order. In this way he succeeds in breaking the circular pattern (represented to him by the 'delete' symbol used in the course of his work, compared by the text to an upper-case Q, the initial letter of most interrogatives in Portuguese; see p. 11) which Schor identifies with the serpent eating its own tail, an implicit allusion to Nietzschean notions of the eternal repetition of human history.[5]

In Saramago's subsequent novel, *Evangelho*, the author once again challenges established hierarchies, not only in his negative presentation of the Christian God, but perhaps more radically in the fact that he centres Jesus' earthly life around the figure of the prostitute Mary Magdalene, thus placing the human Jesus above the divine one that he could choose to be if he simply resigned himself to the fulfilment of his Father's will, as the biblical Jesus does. Thus, Jesus' experiences of a loving and sexual relationship with Mary Magdalene give him his greatest sense of personal fulfilment, and under her guidance, for example, he realizes the futility of bringing Lazarus back from the dead only for him to have to face the same fate for a second time (*Evangelho*, p. 428); in this way Jesus defies what the modern reader knows has become the accepted biblical version of this episode, and Saramago effectively leads the reader to question the 'truth' of the whole orthodox understanding of the Christian story.

The potentially positive factor lying at the heart of both of these novels is that of the fulfilment of the human capacity for individual growth and for love for another. The negative counterpoint to this, however, is the peril of the erasure of the self: in *História* this danger is evident in the early Raimundo's personal vanity which leads him to dye his hair in a bid to hide his true self (*História*, p. 56); towards the end of *Evangelho*, however, this process becomes an openly menacing one in one of the author's most memorable passages, where, in a reversal of orthodox belief, it is humanity (in the form of Jesus) who calls God to account for His actions, requiring Him to account for all the martyrdoms, wars and cruelty which will be perpetrated in the name of the Church to be founded in Jesus' name after his own death (*Evangelho*, pp. 380–5). This passage is, in fact, more than just an exercise in the author demonstrating the fruits of his research into the subject (impressive though these are): in the context of a story which we know will end (so to speak) in a crucifiction, it amounts to a reminder of the stunting of human potential at the heart of the voluntary subjection of the self to the will of any abstract go(o)d. For this Jesus has discovered human love, has struggled with his conscience over a decision made in his name (Joseph's failure to warn other parents when he took his own wife and child away from the imminent slaughter of the innocents in Bethlehem), and has witnessed at first hand in his conversations with the rabbis in the Temple the logical contradictions into which human reasoning is led when it attempts to describe and define the ineffable in terms of simplistic human attributes which are given the false status of unchanging values (*Evangelho*, pp. 207–13).

The fact that Jesus is still young when he confounds the so-called experts is more than a reflection of the biblical source of this incident;[6] it is a reminder that authority derives from wisdom and not vice versa. In these novels, then, we find an assertion of the primacy of individual growth over loyalty to pre-existing hierarchies, whether these are located in the 'truths' of religious doctrine, in the biblical commandment to honour one's father and mother (which Saramago's Jesus most emphatically fails to keep, as his relations with his mother deteriorate throughout the text); in patriotic sentiment (called into question in *História*, as Raimundo debates whether the site of his present-day home would have lain within Muslim Lisbon or in the encampment of the Christian besiegers of the city in 1147; *História*, pp. 75 and 267); or even in commitment to mere factual accuracy as a marker of truth, as Raimundo's 'não' becomes not an erasure of the past, but a door into the future, enabling him to pass from the status of mere keeper or guardian of other people's truths into being the author of his own (p. 300). This is a development which, of course, places him in a similar light to the humble archivist Sr José in the later *Todos*, whose personal growth transforms the Kafkaesque/Orwellian structure of the Registry from a depersonalized mausoleum into a place where the past continues to be adaptable for the benefit of the living.

Despite these apparent similarities between the conception of *História* and *Evangelho*, however, their outcomes are in stark contrast to one another: whereas Raimundo is last seen in the contentment of creative and amorous fulfilment with Maria Sara, the subsequent novel is in many respects Saramago's darkest, for, even if *Cegueira* plumbs the depths of man's inhumanity to man, the uplift at the end of that work contrasts with Jesus' realization that he has been the victim of a divine confidence trick, with God's will being imposed on him at the end of the novel (*Evangelho*, p. 444), in spite of his earlier efforts to prevent the fulfilment of the prophecies made to him on the Sea of Galilee.

The reasons for this pessimistic ending are twofold: firstly, before we even begin the novel, we know that Jesus will die on the cross, so that (short of creating a Resurrection story, which would go against the author's well-publicized atheistic scepticism) Saramago is simply not in a position to create a positive finale in terms of the storyline. At a more fundamental level, however, Saramago's Jesus fails to address the real problem which he faces, which is not that the God whom he rejects with distaste is insuperable but that he treats this God as being insuperable. More simply, Raimundo has the courage to reject accepted assumptions and reform his own life by rewriting history already past, but Jesus (who has the opportunity to affect the future) fails because he cannot or will not see a real alternative to the script which has been prepared for him by others.

These positive and negative examples are marked by brief evocations of the work of the poet most closely associated with Lisbon, Fernando Pessoa, as well as by brief allusions to the Brazilian poet Drummond de Andrade and the epic tradition of Camões. Early in *História* and immediately before he hands over his altered proofs to the publishers, Raimundo looks out at a mist-free Lisbon, 'pessoanamente' ('in the manner of Fernando Pessoa'), thinking, by way of contrast with this landscape, how everything else is 'vago e vário' ('vague and uncertain'; *História*, p. 52, and *History*, pp. 42–3). The poem alluded to here may be 'Tenho em mim como uma bruma', written under Pessoa's own name in 1934,[7] but the Lisbon setting, the sense of aimlessness in Raimundo's life and the image of the cigarette burning away as his own life threatens to drift into nothingness, all evoke the figure of Pessoa's most ambitious, yet also his most enigmatic and frustrated heteronym, Álvaro de Campos. At this point, all is vague and uncertain for Raimundo, as he still has time to correct his illicit alteration to the manuscript and he has therefore (like Pessoa) still to give himself real form, he still has to decide which of Pessoa's heteronyms he will seek to emulate: the self-effacing and meticulous Reis (who in another of Saramago's novels is appalled by the idea that anyone might want to tamper with the truth; see *Ano*, p. 388), or the unambitious Caeiro; or will he, in common with Campos, choose to become more than he has been up till now?

Paradoxically, however, after Maria Sara has issued her challenge to him to rewrite Portuguese history, he settles down to write his new version of events in a Caeiran manner, by natural daylight 'o mistério da escrita está em não haver nela mistério nenhum, verificação que, ao ser aceite, nos conduziria à conclusão de que se não há mistério na escrita, tão-pouco o haverá no escritor' ('the mystery of writing lies in the absence of any mystery whatsoever, which if accepted, might lead us to the conclusion that if there is no mystery about writing, neither can there be any mystery about the writer'; *História*, p. 181, and *History*, p. 160).[8] Raimundo here has become an amalgam of the best of both Campos and Caeiro: the resignation of Caeiro is lost, along with the agonizing self-doubt of Hamlet de Campos,[9] and in its place one finds the desire of Campos (represented not least in Raimundo's growing longing for Maria Sara), alongside Caeiro's determination to follow through to the end of the road (an image used more than once by Caeiro himself in his portrayal of the life lived according to nature[10]) his decision to rewrite the history of his country by working out according to simple logic how it would have developed without the historical burden of a unitary, imposed 'truth' as its sole foundational principle.

The treatment of the imagery relating to Raimundo's view out of the windows of his flat bears some examination, and, in general, the lights from the other side of the Tagus burn brightly when either Raimundo the author is working on his alternative version of national history or Raimundo the lover is developing his relationship with Maria Sara:[11] for if, at times, the view is obscured by mist or cloud, in these moments he is either still preoccupied with mere factual accuracy of a nit-picking nature (see, for example, *História*, p. 36, where he is determined to establish the etymological link between the word *balear*, meaning 'an archer', and the Balearic Islands) or overwhelmed by despair at the enormity of the task facing him to rewrite Portuguese history (p. 117). By contrast, however, most of the scenes where we see Raimundo looking out of his window present a view that is clear, if sometimes cold: twice early in the text (pp. 58 and 67), this view offers him encouragement as he reflects on his recent 'crime' of inserting the word 'não' into the text, and, in the latter of these two contexts, the effect of that insertion comes to be a comforting one, as his action appears to have been the catalyst for the disappearance of the mist outside and, indeed, of any more significant threat to his happiness:

> [. . .] apesar da grande distância, percebe-se a serenidade que há nele, adivinha-se mesmo o voo pulsante das gaivotas sobre o rebrilhante caminhar das águas. Se fosse verdade estarem cinco barcos de cruzados além, certamente que já teriam começado a bombardear a cidade inerme, mas tal não poderá acontecer, que nós bem sabemos que desse lado não virá perigo aos mouros. (p. 67)

> [[. . .] despite the great distance, you can sense the serenity out there and imagine the throbbing flight of seagulls over the gleaming highway of the waters. If it were true that there are five ships carrying crusaders out there, they would almost certainly have started to bombard the defenceless city, but no such thing will happen, because we know very well that from this side no harm will come to the Moors.] (p. 57)

Raimundo implicitly sides with the Moors here rather than with the Christians, in an indication of his nascent spirit of unorthodoxy. More subversive than this, however, is that the allusion to the possibility of there being hostile boats in Lisbon harbour is surely intended to remind us of the rebel sailors at the end of *Ano*, but with a twist: for, in spite of the dominant rhetoric of the Salazar era, the threat posed by the *Afonso de Albuquerque* in that context is not to the city of Lisbon, but to a self-appointed, all-powerful clique of vested interests, comparable to the early Afonso Henriques in this novel, before Raimundo's rewritten version of history forces the King into making egalitarian concessions to the ordinary people which would have been unthinkable in the twelfth century (and which, of course, Salazar's regime would never have agreed to in 1936), but which were certainly conceivable at the time of writing of this novel. At any rate, any prospect of a threat from across the water is now seen to have been removed by Raimundo's actions (since the event denied by his version of history is the assistance offered to Afonso Henriques by the foreign Crusaders from the sea), and so Raimundo can gaze out to sea, secure in the knowledge that his altered version of the nation's past is now keeping him safe in his own time.

Raimundo's defenceless state does, of course, mean that he is now open to invasion of a less hostile form, so that the mention of the flight of the seagulls in this passage might also be seen to be an allusion to the famous poem 'Gaivota' by Alexandre O'Neill, with its evocation of a love longed for at a distance, which is the best that Raimundo can hope for in his personal life at this point in the novel.[12] The clarity of the view available to him does, however, indicate that we should hold out better prospects for him in the longer term, and the reader surely senses that the traditional frustrated Portuguese seaside longing of the medieval *Cantigas de Amigo* may be supplanted by a successful love (the usual conclusion to Saramago's novels), through a force as yet unknown to Raimundo but which will eventually overpower him with her healing love, Maria Sara (Saramago makes play here on the association of her name with the Portuguese verb *sarar*, meaning 'to cure'), as is indicated when he returns home after his first meeting with her and opens his windows to allow some fresh air into his home and his life:

> A casa tornou-se subitamente pequena, até a própria janela aberta para as três vastidões, a da cidade, a do rio, a do céu, lhe pareceu como um postigo cego, e é verdade que não havia nevoeiro, e mesmo a frialdade da noite era retemperadora frescura. Não foi neste momento, mas antes, que Raimundo Silva pensou, Como se chamará ela. (p. 96)
>
> [The apartment suddenly became small, even the window open to those three vast entities, the city, the river, and the sky, now looked like a blind peep-hole, and it is true that there was no mist and the night chill brought a revigorating freshness. It was not at that moment, but before then, that Raimundo Silva thought to himself, I wonder what she's called.] (p. 84)

There is surely a further poetic allusion here, this time to Drummond de Andrade's famous 'Poema de sete faces' of 1928, where he expresses a similar sense of awe in the face of the seemingly inexhaustible reality around him:

> Mundo mundo vasto mundo
> se eu me chamasse Raimundo
> seria uma rima, não seria uma solução.
> Mundo mundo vasto mundo,
> mais vasto é meu coração.[13]
>
> [World world enormous world,/ if I were called Raimundo/ that would just be a rhyme and not a solution./ World world enormous world,/ My heart is even bigger.]

Unlike Drummond's poetic persona, who ends up looking out at the moon and admitting defeat by this greater world as he drowns his sorrows in brandy, Saramago's protagonist (who is, in fact, called Raimundo and who discovers a real identity within himself rather than accepting that his name functions merely as a label) eventually finds the solution for his heart in the world beyond the self, in the company of Maria Sara. It is appropriate, therefore, that the same type of clear, chill air experienced by Raimundo at this moment should be said to return both when she offers him a ride home in her car[14] and, implicitly also, on future occasions when they remember the growth of their feelings for one another (p. 173). This type of air is also noted when the couple cautiously edge towards one another as they look out over the old city of Lisbon from Raimundo's window ledge (p. 265) in an incident which forms a vivid contrast with the awkward and fleeting moment of apparent communion between Ricardo Reis and Lídia, observable only from the outside and not in the real experiences of the characters themselves, in *Ano* (*Ano*, pp. 58–9), when hotel guest and chambermaid look out of the window together at the flooding in the street below.

In common with the presence of Pessoa's Campos and of Drummond's famous 'gauche' within the text, as discussed above, the allusion to Camões is also an implicit rather than an explicit one, based on a pseudo-epic phrasing which lends a heroic atmosphere to Raimundo's undertaking:

> Apesar de adiantada, a primavera ainda não se resolvera a abrir as portas ao calor, ao Austro morno que leva a desafogar os colos e subir as mangas [. . .] este abril húmido, gris, [. . .] felizmente a casa vira as costas ao Bóreas, que é quem neste momento está soprando. (*História*, p. 242)

> [Although advanced, spring had not yet decided to open its doors to the heat, to the warm southern wind, that encourages us to unfasten our collars and roll up our sleeves [. . .] this damp, grey April, [. . .] fortunately his apartment was protected from the north wind blowing at this moment.] (*History*, p. 215)

One notes here not only the use of classical names for the north and south winds, but also their epic anthropomorphization (and that of the spring); in a specifically Portuguese context, the setting of this incident on a dull April day also reminds the reader of the 1974 Revolution (presumably, given the dull weather and the late date in the month of the fall of the dictatorship, this moment is visualized as being before the twenty-fifth of the month) and thus serves to lend a heroic overtone to the subversive project on which the character is engaged, while the reference to loosening shirt-collars and rolling up sleeves places his heroic endeavours in a clearly modern context, with a slight hint of the iconography of the socialist propaganda artwork which was so common in the streets of Lisbon in the 1970s and 1980s.

As the novel progresses (with a possible echo of the poem 'Caminos' by another poet much admired by Saramago, the Spaniard Antonio Machado[15]), Raimundo proceeds to explore the city, within and without the Moorish walls; he takes on the inner citadel of the publishers (personified in Maria Sara, whom he extracts from her position as his professional superior to become his equal partner, thus overcoming the challenge to the queen and the hermit to relate to one another in a purely natural way which remains unresolved in Manuel Milho's story in *Memorial*). He also grows in confidence to the point where he would be in a position to challenge a supposedly expert historian in debate along the lines developed in the opening chapter of the novel (thus also prefiguring Jesus' debate with the rabbis in *Evangelho*). In this way, it may be observed, he might perhaps be able to perform a miracle beyond Machado's powers and beyond the will of Saramago's Jesus, that of creating life where previously death appeared to reign supreme: for the novelist's Jesus seems only too content to join Machado's Leonor (mourned in the final line of 'Caminos') in the grave,[16] while Raimundo instead exposes himself to the healing powers of love through a Maria Sara, linked by her name to the novelist's Mary Magdalene, one of whose first actions in *Evangelho* is to heal the cuts on Jesus' feet (*Evangelho*, p. 278).[17]

The declaration near the end of the novel that 'Lisboa estava ganha, perdera-se Lisboa' (*História*, p. 347) ('Lisbon had been conquered, Lisbon had been lost'; *History*, p. 312) thus refers to the Christians' seizure of the city from Moorish hands in the twelfth century, but also to Raimundo's new life with Maria Sara and his accomplishment in effectively banishing any sense of a naturally subordinate role from his behaviour and attitudes in general, as well as in accepting love with her in a genuinely equal partnership. Certainly the last few lines of the novel appear to support this interpretation, as the final scene sees Raimundo and Maria Sara snuggling together happily, having apparently found the contentment sought by Cipriano, his companions and his faithful dog, as they flee the Centre at the end of *Caverna*:

> Na minha ideia, Ourouna vai voltar para a Galiza, e Mogueime irá com ela, e antes de partirem acharão em Lisboa um cão escondido, que os acompanhará na viagem, Por que pensas que eles se devem ir embora, Não sei, pela lógica deveriam ficar, Deixa lá, ficamos nós. A cabeça de Maria Sara descansa no ombro de Raimundo, com a mão esquerda ela acaricia-lhe o cabelo e a face. Não adormeceram logo. Sob o alpendre da varanda respirava uma sombra. (p. 348)
>
> [As I see it, Ouroana will return to Galicia, and Mogueime will go with her, and before they leave they will find in Lisbon a dog that has survived in hiding and will accompany them on their journey. What makes you think that they should go away. Difficult to say, the logical thing would be for them to stay, Forget it, we're staying, Maria Sara's head is resting on Raimundo's shoulder, with his left hand he strokes her hair and cheek. They did not fall asleep at once. Beneath the verandah roof a shadow sighed.] (p. 312)

This ending resembles those of the later *Caverna*, and also that of the author's own previous novel, *Jangada*: is it, then, as Sabine suggests, a deliberate parody of that work, where the mysterious dog encountered in the forest clearing at Ereira leads the human protagonists to Galicia and Joaquim to his new love with Maria Guavaira?[18] On the one hand, Raimundo seems to recognize that there is no apparent logic in Mogueime and Ouroana leaving the newly founded kingdom of Portugal just after the king has reluctantly given in to the demands made of him by his local soldiers; on the other hand, Saramago does later return to exactly this type of plot resolution in *Caverna*, where there is no particular hint of satirical intent in the repetition of this denouement (and where, in fact, the topos of the casually encountered dog is pointedly recalled in the name 'Achado', or 'Found', given to Cipriano's pet). It may well be, therefore, that the recognition reached by the protagonists here is that, for the moment, in the historical circumstances prevailing in 1989 (the year of the fall of Communism all over Europe), more wide-ranging change to the dominant political order will not be possible, but a solution for issues of personal worth and sense of well-being in the world may be found. As in other works, however, the ending to *História* is not as definitive as it may seem, for a mysterious shadow is still present below the window of Raimundo's flat: the outside world has not gone away, and it will be addressed again in more idealistic terms in later novels, including *Caverna*.

Shortly after deciding to take up Maria Sara's challenge, Raimundo pays a visit to the Castelo de S. Jorge on a cold, blustery, and uninviting day to contemplate the city whose past he is trying to comprehend. From this high vantage point the castle no longer seems the intimidating structure which it must have appeared to the Christian besiegers in the twelfth century: 'Entrou no castelo, de cada vez surpreende-o que seja tão pequeno, uma coisa que parece de brincar, um outro legos ou meccano' (*História*, p. 134) ('He entered the castle, he never ceases to be surprised that it should be so small, almost like a toy castle, another Lego or Meccano set'; *History*, p. 118). Not only does this imagery suggest in advance that Raimundo will eventually triumph over the obstacles in his path (thus indicating also that the citadel of the accepted version of Portugal's history is not as impregnable as might have been thought): it also reminds the attentive reader of the mastery held by D. João V over his kingdom in *Memorial*, where he plays with models of massive churches inside the royal bedchamber just as he plays with his kingdom outside it (*Memorial*, pp. 12–13). One should remember, however, that in that earlier novel, Baltasar recalls his vision of the real convent from above as seeming far less intimidating than it did at first (p. 212), while similar observations could also be made about the Centre in *Caverna* (see *Caverna*, pp. 100–1) and the Temple in *Evangelho*:

> Aí está o Templo. Visto assim de perto, do plano inferior em que estamos, é uma construção que dá vertigens, uma montanha de pedras sobre pedras, algumas que nenhum poder do mundo pareceria ser capaz de aparelhar, levantar, assentar e ajustar, e contudo estão ali, unidas pelo próprio peso, sem argamassa, tão simplesmente como se o mundo fosse todo ele uma construção de armar, até às altíssimas cimalhas que, olhadas de baixo, parecem roçar o céu, como outra e diferente torre de Babel que a protecção de Deus, contudo, não logrará salvar, pois um igual destino a espera, ruína, confusão, sangue derramado, vozes que mil vezes perguntarão, Porquê, imaginando que há uma resposta, e que mais cedo ou mais tarde acabam por calar-se, porque só o silêncio é certo. (*Evangelho*, p. 97)
>
> [There is the Temple. Viewed at close quarters, from down below where we are standing, the building gives one vertigo, a mountain of stones upon stones which no earthly power would seem capable of dressing, lifting, laying and fitting, yet there they are, joined together by their own weight, without any mortar, as if the entire world were simply a set of building blocks, and the uppermost cornices when seen from below appear to be grazing the sky, like another and quite different Tower of Babel which even God will be unable to save because it was doomed to the same destruction, confusion and bloodshed. Voices will ask, Why, a thousand times, believing there must be an answer, but they will eventually die away for it is better to remain silent.] (*Gospel*, pp. 65–6)

As Saramago writes elsewhere, however, 'tudo isto pode ser contado doutra maneira' ('all of this could be told in a different way'; *Levantado*, p. 14): for it must be borne in mind that this description of the Temple is given from a relative position ('Visto assim de perto, do plano inferior em que estamos [. . .]'), seen through the eyes of Joseph, a character who repeatedly adopts an attitude of deferentiality before hierarchies, political, theological, or social. And there are gaps in the account of the Temple here, just as there are in its walls, which have not been solidified with cement: seen as a unit, it is intimidating, yet it is made up only of a multitude of the same stones which Jesus sees all around him in his time in the desert, and, ultimately, it is nothing more than a huge 'construção de armar', that very same term used in *Memorial* of the king's model of St Peter's Basilica in Rome (*Memorial*, p. 13). In spite of outward appearances, this 'outra e diferente torre de Babel' will not survive the ravages of time and the conflicts of history, while the huge stones ('algumas que nenhum poder do mundo pareceria ser capaz de aparelhar, levantar, assentar e ajustar') inevitably remind the reader of the 'mãe da pedra' ('the mother of all stones'; *Baltasar*, p. 230) transported from Pêro Pinheiro to Mafra in *Memorial*, under regal command but by the powers of men, who could perhaps choose to unite in defiance of the king rather than in obedience to him (p. 245). A close analysis of this description of the Temple, then, reveals it to be no more unshakeable than the walls of Lisbon were to Afonso Henriques, or, indeed, than the 'truths' of Portuguese history prove to be to Raimundo, who refuses to accept his role merely as a proofreader and recognizes that the twelfth-century Christian besiegers of Lisbon would not have used the emblem of nationhood represented on the modern Portuguese flag, just as the Moors would not have used the symbol of the crescent, which derived from the later Ottoman Empire (*História*, pp. 41–2). Equally, after he sees clear evidence that Afonso Henriques' address to his troops before battle has been subject to rhetorical revision and embellishment, probably by a Christian cleric (pp. 43–6), he and Maria Sara agree by the last page of the novel that his own, rewritten, version of Portuguese history is more satisfactory for the purposes of his life than the so-called expert one which he was first asked to check (p. 348).

What can we conclude from all of this regarding Jesus' ultimate conflict with God? In one of his conversations with Pastor (a thinly-disguised version of the Devil) in the desert, he is forced to face up to his own sexuality and the inadequacies and inconsistencies of the attempts by orthodox Jewish morality to account for it and to control it (*Evangelho*, pp. 236–8). As Pastor mocks Jesus for his conventionality and refusal to contemplate his own potential for growth, a wind blows up amongst the stones (p. 238), precisely the kind of force which could rip apart the seemingly impregnable walls of the Temple, and at the end of this scene Jesus (in spite of his earlier reluctance) follows this force of rebellion, telling Pastor as he approaches him 'Aqui estou' (p. 238) ('I'm here'; *Gospel*, p. 178). These are words which ironically mirror Caeiro's account of how God would appear to man if He chose to reveal Himself to us.[19] Yet, by the end of the novel, when God delivers to Jesus His prophecy of the future of Christianity, all motion has been banished from the scene, and He does so on the very centre of a becalmed lake (p. 364). The fact that Jesus' opening words to God in this scene are effectively the same as those which he earlier addressed to Pastor is significant: 'Cá estou' (p. 364) ('I'm here'; p. 278), for even if the less reverential tone of these words indicates some resentment of God's domination, their basic sense prefigures Jesus' eventual resubmission of himself to the divine will: 'Faça-se então em mim segundo a tua vontade' (p. 377) ('Then do with me as You will'; p. 288), words which (through their repetition not of Christ's own well-known words of resignation in the Garden of Gethsemane, but rather those of Mary's acceptance of her use by God to bear His son in the Annunciation[20]) implicitly align him by the end of the novel with his passive and submissive mother rather than with the rebellious and liberating non-conformist Mary Magdalene, who teaches him to become his own man through their love for one another. The potential for *dynamis* in Jesus and in Raimundo has, therefore, been fulfilled by the latter in his questioning of authority, but Jesus, instead, chooses to return to stasis, thus permitting control to be exercised over his life and that of countless millions of others by the unaccountable figure of God (who, in fact, represents all forms of artificial mental constructions over our lives rather than a purely theological or moral one).

In spite of his horror at the death and destruction which he is told will be meted out in his name, then, Jesus effectively submits himself to God's will: his first words of real substance to his apostles when he returns to the shore are 'o que importa não é vencer César pelas armas, mas fazer triunfar Deus pela palavra' (p. 395) ('what matters is not to conquer Caesar with arms, but to make God triumph with words'; p. 302). Yet he has been given a clear indication on the lake that the 'truth' possessed by the Christian God is no more absolute than any other when the issue is raised of Christian conflict with Islam:

> Mas então, perguntou Pastor, quem vai criar o Deus inimigo. Jesus não sabia responder, Deus, se calado estava, calado ficou, porém do nevoeiro desceu uma voz que disse, Talvez este Deus e o que há-de vir não sejam mais do que heterónimos, De quem, de quê, perguntou outra voz, De Pessoa, foi o que se percebeu, mas também podia ter sido, Da Pessoa. Jesus, Deus e o Diabo começaram por fazer de conta que não tinham ouvido. (pp. 389–90)

> [Then who will create this hostile God, asked Pastor. Jesus was at a loss for an answer and God, who had been silent, remained silent, but a voice came down from the mist and said, Perhaps this God and the one yet to come are one and the same God, Jesus, God and the Devil pretended not to hear.] (p. 297)[21]

And, after a brief moment's disquiet, none of the three pursues this question any further. In spite of the specifically Portuguese literary joke in the allusion to Pessoa, there is a serious point in this passage: that the notion of God is one which changes through the centuries, and, just as the claims to absolute veracity of Christian and Muslim theology are mutually exclusive, so the human notion of the Christian God cannot be the same in the twenty-first century as it was in the days of the Roman Empire. To that extent, God is a creation of humans and their many masks (the original meaning of the word *persona*, from which the Portuguese *Pessoa* is derived). In the end Jesus' failure to take note of the philosophical implications of this fact (namely that the God whom he will proclaim is merely a provisional truth) will lead to generations of slaughter of the innocents to be added to the initial one from which his earthly father's intervention saved him. His acts of rebellion do not go far enough: when he overturns the tables of the merchants at the Temple in the final chapters of the novel (pp. 425–6), he restricts himself to this largely symbolic act and retreats when faced by the High Priest (p. 426), an act which is in direct contrast, for example, to the challenge posed to ecclesiastical authorities by Jorge de Sena's *O Físico Prodigioso*.[22] The Temple itself, the 'centro do mundo, o umbigo dos umbigos, o santo dos santos' (p. 98) ('the centre of their world, the navel of navels, the Holy of Holies'; p. 66), remains unscathed, and the prime mover of the universe remains masked behind the heteronym of the Christian God. Presumably unaware of Platonic imagery (his undoubtedly sharp brain is, understandably, not depicted as being complemented by a classical education), the Jesus who returns to Bethlehem to visit the cave where Saramago places his birth (pp. 219–20) never comes to the realization achieved by Cipriano in *Caverna*, that he needs to flee the self-proclaimed Centre in order to achieve a fulfilling existence and to discover his own truths.

There is also a Platonic echo in *História*, as Raimundo and Maria Sara discuss their respective conceptions of truth:

> Orientamo-nos por normas geradas segundo consensos e domínios, mete-se pelos olhos dentro que variando o domínio varia o consenso, Não deixas saída, Porque não há saída, vivemos num quarto fechado e pintamos o mundo e o universo nas paredes dele, Lembra-te de que já foram homens à lua, O seu quartinho fechado foi com eles, És pessimista, Não chego a tanto, limito-me a ser céptica da espécie radical, Um céptico não ama, Pelo contrário, o amor é provavelmente a última coisa em que o céptico pode acreditar, Pode, Digamos antes que precisa. (*História*, pp. 299–300)

> [We are guided by norms based on consensus and authority obvious as it is that any variation in the authority varies the consensus, You give no leeway, Because there can be no leeway, we live cooped up in a room and paint the world and the universe on its walls, Don't forget that men have already gone to the moon, Your claustrophobic little room went with them, You're a pessimist, Not quite, I'm simply a sceptic of the radical kind, A sceptic is incapable of love, On the contrary, love is probably the last thing in the world in which the sceptic can still believe, He can, Rather let us say he has to.] (*History*, pp. 267–8)[23]

Raimundo does not appear, at least at this point, to be aware of the significance of what he is doing with his rewriting of Portuguese history, for, when Maria Sara demonstrates not only her need to love but also her willingness to do so, by refusing to let the traditional provider (the man) pay the bill, he rejects the notion that he is involved in some kind of class warfare: 'Eu não sou mais do que revisor, estou fora dessa guerra' (p. 300) ('As a simple proofreader, I'm not involved in this conflict'; p. 268). Not only does Raimundo go on during the rest of the novel to prove that he is a lot more than a mere proofreader, though: the discussion reproduced above implicitly raises Gramscian issues of cultural hegemony, as well as the fraught issues of combining the Revolution with the specific emancipation of women. It is notable in this context that Raimundo's final resolution of his version of the siege of Lisbon posits a quasi-socialist scheme for the distribution of wealth (pp. 340–2) which was not a real possibility in Portugal until the period between 25 April 1974 and 25 November 1975, and here he himself is implicitly obliged to recognize that the notion of truth as an unquestionable category may only be an intellectual tool whose limitations can never be escaped in practice. In this latter sense, then, Sabine is correct to assert that this is the only one of Saramago's novels of the 1980s which does not deal with issues of mass movements and ensuring solidarity within them; however, the achievement of at least some provisional certainty as to what the goals of any such movement should be in practice is a necessary prerequisite for the initiation of revolutionary activity.[24] This novel might be viewed to some extent, then, as the way in which two very unlikely candidates for revolutionary activity may find that their personal and intellectual development leads them towards a greater sympathy for such action than they might ever have envisaged. As Sabine also stresses, the provisional ending which Raimundo proposes for his story within a story (that of the historical lovers Mogueime and Ouroana within his version of the siege of Lisbon) sounds a little too much like an 'And they all lived happily ever-after' solution modelled on the climax to *Jangada*, without the self-avowedly open ending given to that work by its final sentence ('A vara de negrilho está verde, talvez floresça no ano que vem'; *Jangada*, p. 330) ('The elm branch is green. Perhaps it will flower again next year'; *Raft*, p. 263).[25] Raimundo and Maria Sara, in common with the lovers within their fiction, have a lot of work to do before their own island of love can become a utopian reality, for them and even more so for the society within which they live, but, in view of the resolution given to Raimundo's authored story of the siege of Lisbon, it does seem difficult to maintain that *História* 'makes *no* consideration of the revolutionary potential of mass organisations'.[26] The point, more assuredly, is (as Sabine himself implicitly acknowledges elsewhere[27]) that the successful Revolution has to be one based on the life experience and fulfilment of its own agents.

Raimundo has, then, moved a long way from his ambition (stated early in the novel) to be attached by a metaphorical umbilical cord to a simple, centralized database at his disposal which would provide him with all the answers he requires (*História*, p. 26). As with so many other male protagonists in Saramago, he does so with another symbolic string: the metaphorical Ariadne's thread offered by his female companion, whose confidence in where she is going and how she can help him is indicated by the terms of her offer to Raimundo of a ride home early in their relationship. This provides a constructive contrast with the short story 'Embargo' in *Objecto*, whose protagonist finds himself the prisoner of the will of his own car:[28] 'Deixe-me na Baixa, por favor, tomo aí um eléctrico, Ora essa, levo-o a casa, não me custa nada, Mas sai do seu caminho, Eu, não, o automóvel' (p. 173) ('Drop me off in the Baixa, please, I'll catch a tram from there, Whatever next, I'm taking you home, it isn't any trouble, But you're going out of your way, The car is, not me'; p. 153).

Maria Sara's insistence that the inconvenience involved is to her car and not to her is a reminder that she is in control of her life, and that she intends her own path through life to include Raimundo. At the same time as this is an act of simple generosity, then, this gesture is effectively the same challenge as Joana Carda issues to José to join her in *Jangada* (*Jangada*, pp. 150–1), and Raimundo must take personal responsibility for this challenge: the climax to this novel, then, is the successful conclusion of this modern-day task of Hercules.

Saramago's Jesus never learns this lesson and ultimately rejects even the love offered to him by Mary Magdalene (who struggles in vain to protect her island of love with him). In doing so, he becomes (alongside Ricardo Reis) one of only two major characters in Saramago's fiction to be overcome in the end by negativity. To Saramago, destinations are always more important than points of departure: *Janguda* plays with the reader's fear of imminent catastrophe only to hold out hope in the end for a better future, even in an Iberia of no fixed abode; *Conto* and *Caverna* both extend the possibility of fulfilment lying in a personal dynamic abstracted from the realities of contemporary society and its institutions; and, in spite of Baltasar's ultimate failure in *Memorial,* he and Blimunda (and not the king) are seen to possess the spirit which once led Portugal to undertake great voyages of discovery. Such voyages of exploration (conducted in that spirit of love which Maria Sara sees as the only alternative to total pessimism) will allow humans genuinely and productively to revise their 'truths' and cast off the blindness which later affects an entire city in *Cegueira.* Raimundo's persistence (represented in his own story by the eventual fall of Lisbon to the Portuguese invaders) in effect makes the subsequent (to Afonso Henriques) and historical (to Raimundo) Portuguese explorations of the globe possible, for, as Schor points out, the historical work which Raimundo initially sets out to proofread gives an impression of dependence on supposedly superior northern European technology and ingenuity, so that it would be hard from that account to believe what we all know to be true, that it was the Portuguese and not the Germans,

French or English who first systematically explored the non-European space.[29]

The link of this historical motif to more personal concerns is represented by the use in the text of the popular Portuguese proverb 'tantas vezes o cântaro vai à fonte que por fim lá deixa a asa' (p. 316) ('when the pitcher goes too often to the well it is broken at last'; p. 283) at the very moment when the walls of Lisbon are finally scaled: the obvious romantic and sexual overtones of the fundamental motif of conquest used in the title of the novel are thus accentuated by the sexual overtones associated with this proverb, recalling medieval love-lyrics comparing the act of going to collect water from the spring with sexual intercourse.[30] The use of this proverb here therefore provides a more positive counterpoint to the generally negative connotation of the spring in *Levantado* as the site for the forcible subjection of a local girl to the will of a German overlord, and it is thus recuperated in *História* to indicate that, just as a better social order may be postulated for the past than the one which is generally held to have existed, so, too, a tradition of a more equitable relationship between the sexes may be found useful for the establishment of harmony in the future.[31]

This link between love and establishing an appropriate social order is further reinforced by the quotation from Marx and Engels reproduced at the beginning of *Objecto*: 'Se o homem é formado pelas circunstâncias, é necessário formar as circunstâncias humanamente' ('If man is formed by his circumstances, it is necessary to form those circumstances in a human manner'; *Objecto*, p. 11).

In fact, three of the stories in that collection also appear to support the line of analysis developed here. The science fiction story entitled 'Coisas' depicts an anonymous, functional society where people and objects are referred to by acronyms rather than names; inexplicably, an apocalyptic tale develops of mysteriously disappearing objects and disintegrating buildings, climaxing in the destruction of all the buildings of the city. At this point the story's protagonist (who has fled from the city centre to its periphery in the countryside, as if in imitation of the storytellers in Boccaccio's Florence) finally realizes what has really been happening when he hears a brief dialogue between two of the 'terrorists' responsible for these strange events:

– Agora é preciso reconstruir tudo.

E uma mulher disse:

– Não tínhamos outro remédio, quando as coisas éramos nós. Não voltarão os homens a ser postos no lugar das coisas. (*Objecto*, p. 109)

[– Now we must rebuild everything.

And a woman replied:

– There was no other remedy since we were those things. Never again will men be treated as things.] ('Things', p. 243)

The moral of the story, therefore, is that people should be placed at the heart of all social planning and not the interests of the state or those of capital. In a similar fashion, the king in 'Refluxo' who attempts to enforce centralized burial of all of his country's dead in one location in the exact centre of the country is eventually obliged to accept the failure of his plan, when life obstinately emerges from the space which he has decreed as being that of death, as all sorts of facilities for the living spring up around the quarter of the dead. In the end, when his own hour of death arrives, he gives orders that he should be buried in a forest, where life will grow naturally out of his own remains (*Objecto*, p. 68).

Raimundo succeeds in rebuilding his city (and, indeed, his country) from scratch, learning that mere historical accuracy for its own sake (that is, treating our origins in the departed past with the type of reverence offered to them by Saramago's version of Ricardo Reis) is less important than building a better future which views people as an end in themselves. In this sense, whatever the historical accuracy of his own account of the siege of Lisbon (or, indeed, that which he proofreads in the earlier part of the text, since both treat of a period which is all but irrecuperably lost in a past, surviving only in archaeological remains and written sources of debatable authority), such accuracy can only be provisional, for, as Sabine points out, Raimundo becomes increasingly aware of the very partial nature of the knowledge which can ever be gathered, even about his own immediate surroundings.[32]

In the final story of *Objecto*, 'Desforra', a boy witnesses the castration of a pig and learns the need for his own fulfilment, as he is impelled to lose his own virginity in response to this negative spectacle (p. 138). This is a rather more drastic and traumatic experience (not least for the pig) than that which leads Raimundo to achieve his fulfilment in *História,* but it does form a valid parallel to it. Sadly Saramago's Jesus will have a long way to go before he will be able to construct a genuine City of God: effectively he allows himself to be neutered by the overwhelming presence of his heavenly Father, who will not permit him to escape the centre of the stagnant Sea of Galilee (*Evangelho,* p. 364) and join in the spirit of the adventurers of the Iberian Peninsula on their Atlantic exploration in *Jangada.* The evidence offered by the stories of *Objecto* and by the examples of Raimundo in *História,* Cipriano in *Caverna* and Tertuliano Máximo Afonso in *Homem* would seem to suggest, however, that the author maintains faith in the capacity of ordinary people to renew the world around them through spontaneous growth and their ability to grow away from their circumstances (as represented in the case of *Homem* by the eventual failure of Tertuliano's apparent *Doppelgänger* to turn their apparent physical identity into a merging of personal identities). This faith should not be taken, however, to signify a lack of threat to the growth of the individual in modern society, a need which preoccupies Saramago greatly in works such as *Evangelho, Caverna* and *Ano.*

3. From the Plough Buried in the Sand to the Hidden Flying Machine: Opportunities for Escape

In the preface to his collection of short stories of 1963 *Jogos de Azar,* José Cardoso Pires exploits the sight of a rotting plough, abandoned on a beach in the Algarve, to give expression to what he saw as the incongruity of widespread hunger and exclusion in the modern era, when such problems were clear in their nature and capable of resolution through the scientific, economic and technical resources available to humanity.[33] The solution which he saw to this (one which could be expressed only cautiously under the prevailing censorship of the New State) was therefore one of political will and ideology, shaped by the need for a recognition of the inherent worth of the individual human being, and this line of thought is clearly evident throughout the stories which followed this piece.

Four decades have passed from that date, and similar problems continue to exist in a world of even greater technological sophistication than that which Cardoso Pires wrote about, yet Saramago echoes the same comments made by him in an interview with the Spanish magazine *Cambio 16* in 2000:

> All the serious problems of hunger, poverty, and lack of dignity in which millions of people live could be resolved. It is also very clear that wealth is in fewer and fewer hands while poverty is taking hold of an increasing number of people.[34]

As a first step to address these issues, Saramago has repeatedly asserted that it is not only the right, but the duty, of each and every citizen of our modern democracies to be vigilant over the preservation of the rights which we do possess in a world where unaccountable, transnational organizations frequently wield power over the democratically-elected national governments which we would like to think enable us to exert some control over our own lives. This was, for example, the central theme of presentations which he gave to audiences in London in July 1999 and in Murcia, in Spain, in February 2000, and it is also given expression in an interview with his fellow-novelist Baptista Bastos, published in 1996, already quoted in the Introduction.[35]

Just because Marxism is no longer in favour, therefore, Saramago does not believe that it has lost its relevance any more than Christians would forsake their faith because we live in what is now predominantly a secular society:

> In fact, we live in a period of economic liberalism and consumerism and a loss of ethical values, so that Marxism appears to have no relevance and no place within that. But if we think in historical terms and if we realize that nothing in human thoughts and actions has died out, it is hard to see why Marxism should be an exception, and become completely extinct. And since there was someone who came back from the dead on the third day, it may well be that my form of Marxism comes back three centuries from now.[36]

In terms of reflecting what Saramago would view as the naivety of the oft-quoted assumption that free markets and democracy go hand in hand, it is worth noting that in his *Caverna*, for example, the all-consuming Centre appears to exist as the sole power in existence within the society described: its security guards are in effect the police, and no higher power is visible which could call the Centre into line if required. There is, therefore, no state authority in *Caverna,* nobody to whom citizens may turn in protest against its actions; this is merely a fictionalization of an opinion expressed to a Brazilian magazine in November 2005 that even President Bush is governed by capitalism.[37] It is considerations such as these which lead Saramago to declare that 'the only organized power is economic and financial power, which doesn't give a damn about anything: religion, ideologies, culture, languages, anything'.[38] Once viewed in contexts such as this, Saramago's apparently obdurate refusal to accept what many of those brought up during the Cold War would regard as the inherent superiority of so-called democratic capitalism over communism perhaps seems less eccentric than it might do at first.[39]

In attempting to understand such thinking it is important to realize first of all the impossibility of simply dividing twentieth-century Portuguese cultural history into clear and distinctive categories corresponding to 'before' and 'after' the 1974 Revolution. This was, in fact, a revolution which was widely anticipated in Portugal, and certainly in some respects the climate which the country experienced from the (literal) fall of Salazar in 1968 to the advent of democracy in the spring of 1974 was already a more liberated one than that which had existed under the country's long-term dictator; equally, however, the fact that this was a peaceful revolution perhaps meant that many of the changes which the country experienced were perhaps superficial rather than far-reaching, with many officials continuing in the same positions as before the transition and with no clearly visible change in prevailing attitudes and mentalities.[40] This is certainly a fear given expression in literary form by writers such as the Three Marias in their *Novas Cartas Portuguesas* of 1973,[41] and by Lídia Jorge in a work such as *O Dia dos Prodígios,* published in 1980.[42]

More fundamental than this, however, remains Saramago's passionate conviction that there are certain practices which are fundamentally right and certain others which remain unjustifiable, regardless of the circumstances in which they occur: it is perhaps no surprise to find him denouncing the Clinton–Blair–Schröder type project of the so-called 'Third Way' as lacking in intellectual coherence and basic honesty to the public in terms of its underpinning assumptions and objectives, even if it is questionable whether or not he actually ever envisages the creation of a Marxist society in fact.[43] But this does not abolish the relevance of a Marxist consciousness, whose role is to question the underlying assumptions of a world order that naively proclaims the end of history and is then caught off guard by events such as those of 11 September 2001. Saramago's ideological coherence therefore lies precisely and paradoxically in the non-dogmatic nature of his Marxism: it is a form of Marxism which exists for him as a means and not as an end and which he believes enables him to make sense of a world where human needs are too often sacrificed on the altar of other principles, as he states in an interview with Reis:

> As far as I am concerned, my way of understanding society and the world is linked to Marxist concepts and analysis. [. . .] Marxism is useful to me as a means of understanding the world in a way which makes total sense. What I mean by that is that Marxism, at least for me, is not dead and continues to be useful: I live in it, and I cannot even imagine any other way of trying to understand the functioning of human societies.[44]

The usefulness which the writer detects in Marxism is not, therefore, a programmatic one: it exists rather as a means of identifying what is wrong with the society in which we live, and thus in enabling the ordinary citizen to call to account those who attempt to exercise power over him or her, be they political leaders such as Tony Blair, or powerful businessmen such as Bill Gates.

Saramago's sense of disillusionment at the apparent loss of the gains which the April Revolution promised for a period of some eighteen months does not, therefore, imply defeat: just as springtime comes round once a year, so the successors of Maria Adelaide may also experience the same fresh arrival of new life and new hope in the future; and if the ending of *Levantado* does not offer guarantees of the success of the Revolution, then equally the tentative recovery of eyesight towards the end of *Cegueira* reminds us that hope remains as long as there are humans prepared to struggle for a better future. Works such as *Cegueira* and *Caverna* should, therefore, be viewed as worst-case scenarios designed to warn his readers of danger rather than suggestions that the world has lapsed into absolute catastrophe (in spite of the pessimistic views which the author has occasionally declared[45]).

The outstanding representation of hope in the author's novels remains the flying machine which Baltasar and Blimunda help to build and power under Bartolomeu's supervision in *Memorial*.

The fact that the *Passarola* flies only twice during the novel (and, indeed, on the second occasion by accident, as Baltasar unwittingly releases it from its moorings) is not important; indeed, its own inventor's difficulty in controlling it on its maiden flight is actually significant, as an indication that the time for this type of freedom has not yet come: many more generations of Portuguese people will have to suffer tyranny and oppression before their descendants achieve fulfilment.[46]

Instead Saramago turns this tale of thwarted ambition into one of postponed endeavour, by making the flying machine a parallel for the genuine people's revolution which was promised by the April Revolution but which remained undelivered by successive governments, for the *Passarola* (whose proposed method of propulsion as a historical phenomenon remains vague from the descriptions left to us by the real-life Gusmão[47]) is powered in the novel by the wills of ordinary people, as collected by the mysterious Blimunda, and, even when the ship is abandoned by its designer, it is lovingly tended for future use by Baltasar and Blimunda. When it is accidentally flown again by Baltasar, all we know is that he is captured and executed by the Inquisition: the ship itself with its subversive intent, defying and outstripping the heights reached even by the gigantic project at Mafra, may perhaps lie buried somewhere in the soil of Portugal across which Blimunda wanders in search of her lost husband in the final chapter of the novel, all the while preaching a new gospel of nonconformity to any who will listen.

It is then worth considering that this lost will to fly may be what leads the Iberian peninsula astray in another of the author's most famous works, *Jangada.* This possibility seems particularly inviting, not only because the author himself declared (in an interview published to coincide with the publication of this novel) that 'My books are linked to one another by situations which are either repeated or which are inserted into the contexts of other ones. That spirit of continuity means that the end of one book forms a link to the beginning of the next one',[48] but also in that this novel posits a utopian reversal of roles in comparison to *Memorial*: the victim crushed by a stone in the earlier novel (Francisco Marques) is succeeded here by ordinary Iberians, who instead choose to ride on top of the stone raft which their land has become.[49]

Here Spain and Portugal, just at the moment which many political leaders described as the fulfilment of their national destinies in joining the European Union, are instead led away from this trading block based on the hierarchies of economic power and into a more profound meditation on what it means to be Spanish or Portuguese, to be a man entering into a fruitful relationship with a woman or a woman entering into a childbearing relationship with a man, all on terms of apparent equality. All the time, as external political and financial leaders, from the White House to international financial authorities, seek to return the two Iberian nations to some form of stability (in other words, control), these two rebellious children of Europe look inwards to seek their own autochthonous solutions. Is this merely an idealistic pipe dream? Perhaps so, but *Jangada* may be seen as the furthest point to which Saramago's exploration of national history may take him: indeed, the only subsequent novel which he has written on explicitly Portuguese subject matter (*História*), even as it charts a course into the future for Raimundo, has to delve into the nation's past in order to do so. *Jangada* is in many respects what might happen if Gusmão's flying machine could have been brought back to life in the more liberated (but still far from perfect) 1980s, as the various characters discover what unites them all as human beings from their different parts of the Iberian Peninsula, as well as what differentiates them and what allows them to live together in acknowledgement of these differences.

The most significant aspect of *Jangada* is not, in fact, the one which makes the greatest initial impact (the separation and unpredictable meanderings of the Iberian Peninsula across the Atlantic), but the way in which the novel is slowly taken over by the personal relationships among the five principal characters, just as, in *Memorial*, the king's project at Mafra ultimately recedes from view while the love of Baltasar and Blimunda (and their cooperation on Bartolomeu's flying machine) take centre stage. In fact, what becomes evident as the novel progresses is that the extent to which the two Iberian nations are dependent on their own governments or foreign intervention to determine their fate decreases as the ordinary Iberians take increasing control of their own personal destinies. This is, in fact, implicit in the statement (or is it really a question?) almost at the end of the novel which deliberately plays on both the spatial and the fatalistic senses of the Portuguese word 'destino': 'Os homens e as mulheres, estes, seguirão o seu caminho, que futuro, que tempo, que destino' (*Jangada*, p. 330) ('As for the other men and women, they will travel on their way, who knows what future awaits them, how much time, what destiny'; *Raft*, p. 263).

This speculative sentence not only leaves the ending of the story open, it also prompts questions such as: are our futures set out for us, or do we create them ourselves, just as the movements of the Iberian Peninsula within the fiction belie our usual assumption that we inhabit a fixed environment? Do we have a path, or do we create it and it becomes fixed only after we have marked it, as Joana Carda does with her elm-wand, which after that initial event never performs any further useful purpose, other perhaps than giving her confidence in making a new life for herself? The teleological readings of history implied in the simple use of phrases such as 'o seu caminho' are thus questioned, and this question mark applies as much to visions of history which view the Revolution as inevitable as to those believing that the fall of the Berlin Wall meant the definitive triumph of Western capitalism.

It is important to bear in mind the essentially utopian nature of this novel, which, while it depicts growing understanding among its principal protagonists, does not really address head-on the often troubled relationship between Portugal and Spain (for individuals can interact in a different way face to face from their responses to other groups *en masse*), nor, as Sabine points out, does the novel really address a multitude of other contentious issues which may rear their heads again after the immediate crisis recounted in the novel has passed; this critic is therefore correct to state that the novel leaves the peninsula 'at a crossroads between consolidation and fragmentation'.[50] And Saramago is well aware that, in spite of the increasing cross-border traffic within Europe in recent years, the categories of the nation-state and inherited conceptions of national identity (Anderson's 'imagined communities') remain as much a part of our capacity for making mental maps of the world as they ever did.[51]

Nonetheless, the weakening of the fixed nature of these categories can begin only in the discovery of the non-alien within what is apparently alien, and the life-experience gained by the Andalusian Pedro Orce certainly enables him to 'reconhecer na melancolia aparente da cidade [Lisbon] a imagem fiel da sua própria tristeza íntima' (p. 109) ('Pedro Orce could now recognize in the apparent melancholy of the city the faithful image of his own intimate sadness'; p. 83). It is therefore also worth remembering that the journey which the travellers take around the peninsula is precisely that, a journey *around* the peninsula: they avoid the traditional seat of power and influence (Castile) and explore instead the periphery, by travelling through Portugal, Galicia, Andalusia and the Pyrenees. Presumably, the reader is intended to understand that, just as the novel jokingly foresees the possibility of Europe fragmenting to the extent that all of it that is left is Switzerland (p. 162), then eventually the traditionally centralist tendencies of Castile (alluded to on p. 298 of the novel) may recede to the extent that this traditionally dominant power will accept its role as merely one among a multitude of Iberian identities. It is probably fair to say, however, that this novel, while making a bold assertion of the right of Iberians (and, by implication, others) to be themselves instead of conforming to a 'European' identity which conceals as much as it asserts, effectively succeeds only in positing a similar uniformity within the peninsula to that which it seeks to refute within Europe. This does not invalidate the essential point made by the novel, that identities, alliances and fixed beliefs about the organization of human society are, in fact, in flux as much as our turbulent earth, which masks geological instability with an apparently fixed map, disturbed only by occasional eruptions such as that which brought the Icelandic island of Surtsey into existence in the 1960s, or by the major redrawing of political lines which took place in Europe from 1990 onwards: but it does open the door to the possible challenge of an endless process of fragmentation which would render problematic the very universalities which the author seeks to identify in some of his later works.

There is some value, then, in the focus on the peripheral regions of Portugal and Spain as a reminder that established orders do not possess any sacred quality, and, similarly, once again the traditionally weaker sex call the men to order, rather than vice versa: Joana by challenging José Anaiço to step over the line which keeps them as separate individuals rather than becoming a couple (pp. 150–1), and Maria Guavaira more visually, by effectively hauling Joaquim Sassa in towards her with her endless ball of twine (p. 185), an action which leads the narrator to effectively compare her to the classical Ariadne even as he denies any such parallel: 'Maria Guavaira não se chama Ariadne, com este fio não sairemos do laberinto, acaso com ele conseguiremos enfim perder-nos. A ponta, onde está' (p. 18) ('Maria Guavaira is not called Ariadne, with this thread we shall not emerge from the labyrinth, perhaps it will help us to succeed at last in losing ourselves. Where is the end of this thread'; p. 9).

This type of playing with the expectations of the reader is evident at length within this novel. For not only do the worst projections about the fate of the Iberian Peninsula not come to pass (the collapse of the economy, the collision with the Azores, the breakdown of discipline and social order), but, in fact, gradually the prospect of a new order arises from the initial vision of chaos, and the only genuinely disturbing incident is the brutal execution by the military of the solitary sailor who accidentally penetrates a deserted Lisbon during the state of emergency decreed as the peninsula approaches the Azores (p. 234), in an action which prefigures the paranoid killing of the car thief in *Cegueira* and the cold-blooded elimination of the doctor's wife in *Lucidez*. Disaster, then, is in the eye of the beholder, for, of the dire forecasts made, only the potential collision with the Azores would be unequivocally negative in its outcome: other negative judgements made are given from points of view which could hardly be described as disinterested (the proprietorial outrage at the occupation of holiday hotels in the Algarve by the homeless, or the almost literal flight of capital implicit in the rush by the rich to book up every airline seat available out of the peninsula once the definitive nature of the separation becomes apparent; pp. 105–6) and, as Sabine points out, even the possible collision with the Azores harks back to American attempts to thwart the ideals of the 25 April Revolution shortly after it occurred through pressure exerted in relation to the US air force base on the islands.[52] In this sense, then, the shock of the possible collision with the islands should perhaps be viewed metaphorically as a warning of the constant threat of disruption to Utopia rather than as the mass humanitarian crisis which it appears to be in a literal reading of the text.[53]

Instead, the focus of the novel moves increasingly onto the principal characters and the ways in which they seek to create meaning out of apparent formlessness: even as the clock is wound back and the characters resort to small-scale bartering and trading to make a living (a development which forms a clear contrast with the centrally-controlled, large-scale trading favoured by the European Union[54]), and even as they resort to a horse and cart to replace Joaquim's Citroën Deux Chevaux (a car manufactured in the heart of the European Union), the clock has not been reversed permanently. The first priority for these people is to come to satisfactory relationships with one another (a challenge which they face up to with some success, most notably in the crisis provoked by Maria and Joana's decision to make love to Pedro; pp. 290–3[55]), and then all of the old conveniences of modern life can be restored with the new terms of engagement established both internally, within this community, and externally, with the wider world. This redefinition of the terms of engagement between men and women thus parallels that between the peninsula and the wider world: implicitly, therefore, it is the rest of the world which will have to become accustomed to dealing with an itinerant Iberia and not vice versa (which, indeed, would be merely the logical corollary to the rhetoric so commonly espoused by the major players on the world stage regarding the need to spread democracy across the globe).

In fact, many of the apparent problems in the earlier part of the novel, once examined closely, contain a hint also of their own positive potential. Thus, while much of the earlier part of the novel is taken up by discussion of French, Spanish and international reactions to the breach which has appeared in the Pyrenees, a closer examination of these reactions demonstrates them to be, generally speaking, a mixture of panic, short-term planning, and token gestures in the face of a superhuman force. Thus, when cement is poured into the gap at the border at Collado de Pertuis, the Portuguese contribution to this effort at crisis management is dismissed in a rather patronizing tone:

> . . . até de Portugal, esse pequeno país, saiu um comboio de dez betoneiras, estrada fora, têm à sua frente uma longa viagem, mais de mil e quinhentos quilómetros, esforço extraordinário, não vai ser preciso o betão que trazem, mas a história registrará o simbólico gesto. (p. 29)

> [. . . even from Portugal, that tiny country, a convoy of ten concrete mixers set out, there is a long journey ahead, more than one thousand five hundred kilometres, an extraordinary achievement, the cement they are carrying won't be necessary, but history will remember their symbolic gesture.] (p. 18)

One notes here not only the simulated patronizing narrative voice which is so ignorant of Portuguese history that it regards a journey of 1,500 kilometres as requiring extraordinary effort on the part of this small nation (and, one is tempted to ask, just how much shorter a journey of 1,500 kilometres would be for a train departing from Paris or Berlin?), but also that the cement turns out to be useless in a sense other than the immediately apparent one: it is useless, not because the gap has already been filled in by the time the cement mixers arrive, but because within minutes it becomes apparent that this gap has widened and is now incapable of being filled in at all; the reflection is not really, therefore, on the puniness of Portugal, but on the vulnerability of all of humanity to the forces of nature which control us. Similarly, the fireworks set off to celebrate the human triumph over nature in closing this breach (p. 29) are first rendered redundant by the continued separation of Iberia from the rest of Europe and then outshone by the unplanned fireworks display created by the fall of electricity cables stretched to breaking point (p. 39), with the related blackout of the whole peninsula provoking the apocalyptic but ultimately ironic narratorial comment 'não houve mais dúvidas: o fim de tudo chegara' (p. 37) ('then there was no longer any doubt, everything was coming to an end'; p. 26).

The narrator of these early sections of the text, who occasionally hints at his superior knowledge of the events still to be recounted, distances himself from the efforts made to save the land link with Europe, frequently ridiculing the human institutions attempting to deal with the situation. Indeed, this cool approach to an apparent crisis leads the narrator to describe the split as being totally natural: 'Não podia a humana força nada a favor de uma cordilheira que se abria como uma romã, sem dor aparente, e apenas, quem somos nós para o saber, porque amadurecera e chegara o seu tempo' (p. 33) ('Human strength could do nothing on behalf of a cordillera which was opening up like a pomegranate, without any apparent suffering, and simply, who are we to know, because it had matured and its time had come'; p. 22).[56] Whereas it might be found puzzling that the futile labours of the cement mixers at the border are also presented as almost a natural phenomenon ('essas interessantes máquinas que, com os seus movimentos simultáneos, fazem lembrar a terra no espaço, rotação, translação'; p. 28) ('those interesting machines, which with their simultaneous movements, remind one of earth in space, rotation, removal'; p. 18), this language looks forward to the later reference to the peninsula revolving in the sea like a child revolving in its mother's waters immediately before birth (p. 319).

The events of *Jangada* effectively become an intellectual maze, for the reader, whose apocalyptic expectations are repeatedly frustrated, and for the characters themselves, who do not know as events unfold that the peninsula will not collide with the Azores during its own attempts to escape the encounter with the symbolic Minotaur. Certainly references to labyrinths abound in the text: the streets of Seville form a 'dédalo de ruas' (p. 77) for the two Portuguese visitors who are unacquainted with its complexities ('this labyrinth of streets'; p. 58), a comparison repeated (implicitly rather than explicitly) in both the approach to Ereira (p. 144) and in Oporto (p. 177); when Pedro Orce leaves the two couples to their amorous pursuits in Maria's house, he finds himself in a 'labirinto de pedras' (p. 193) on the Galician shore ('this labyrinth of stones'; p. 150). And finally, at a deeper level, Maria and Joana are left to proclaim the mysteries of life and death over Pedro's body just as the group of travellers then has to negotiate their way around Orce, whose houses are compared to 'paredes de labirinto' (p. 328) in the darkness of the Andalusian night ('the walls of a labyrinth'; p. 261).

This exploitation of the image of the labyrinth (and the allusion to Ariadne earlier in the text) therefore provide a quasi-visual representation (albeit communicated to the reader through words) of the two models of history seen by Sabine as being placed into confrontation with one another in this text: the rectilinear one favoured by prophets of the political left as much as the right, and the cyclical one (which, implicitly, can conceive of no lasting improvement in the human lot).[57] If one path leads into a seemingly endless cycle of repetition, then the other, represented by Maria's ball of wool (admittedly once straightened out) will lead out of the maze. Sabine goes on to point out that the movement of Joaquim Sassa's stone when he sends it spinning an improbable distance into the sea at the beginning of the text combines both patterns: that of progression and that of circular movement on its own axis, just as later on the peninsula itself, having sailed out into the ocean and turned away from the Azores to avert disaster, ends up revolving within the sea.[58] It is, however, also worth noting the effect when the stone finally disappears from Joaquim's sight:

> Uma onda muito alta veio do largo, espumejando e rebentando, afinal a pedra sempre caiu ao mar, este é o efeito conhecido desde

> os rios da infância de quem na infância teve rios, a ondulação concêntrica que as pedras atiradas causam (p. 13).
>
> (A very high wave came in from the open sea, foaming and gushing, the stone finally dropped into the water, this is known from the rivers of childhood by anyone who had rivers in their childhood, the concentric undulation caused by stones thrown into the water.) (pp. 4–5)

Perhaps, then, the tentative solution to the debate between these two visions of time is that to some extent history has been cyclical (hence the association of the workers of the Alentejo with the cycles of nature in *Levantado*, for example), but that each action which we take is capable of moving the centre of the circle to a different point. Seen in this sense, the effective 'neglect' of the centre of the peninsula by this novel may be viewed instead as an expression of the responsibility of its peripheral regions to move Iberia to a new location where it may make a new start, as if in a spatial–historical representation of Hegelian dialectical formulae.

In one sense, the narrator is correct initially to reject the comparison of Maria Guavaira to Ariadne, for as the novel progresses, she develops greater similarities to another classical figure, Penelope. Just as Maria Guavaira unravels an old stocking to create the enormous ball of wool which will lead Joaquim Sassa to her, Ulysses, in Homer's *Odyssey*, is able to reclaim his place as Penelope's husband, because during all the years of his absence at the Trojan War Penelope has promised other suitors that she will accept a second husband only when she has finished her tapestry, a potentially never-ending project, as every night she undoes the work completed during the course of the day (thus creating her own cyclical pattern of history). This connection is strengthened when one considers the links in European cultural tradition between the motif of the woman weaving and her wait for the fulfilment to be brought to her by her long-lost lover.[59] One might also view Joaquim's initial act of throwing the stone as a parallel to Ulysses' claim in the *Odyssey* to be able to throw a javelin 'farther than anyone else can shoot an arrow',[60] thus prompting suggestions that, even if he is perhaps not destined to meet Maria in any deterministic sense (he makes a number of choices later in the text which, if not made, might lead him away from her rather than to her), this is his appropriate destination, and also that, through his classical forebear's legendary associations with the city of Lisbon, he may be one of the founders of a new nation.

Furthermore, in the *Odyssey* it is the hero's old dog Argos which first recognizes him on his return home, while in *Jangada* it is the mysterious dog Constante/Ardent which leads Joaquim to the woman who then becomes his lover.[61] The key point in this novel, however, is surely that accounts of history (more accurately, stories) do not have to repeat themselves and follow a pattern: history develops in accordance with what we make of it. In this sense, unsatisfactory as the lovemaking with Pedro may seem as part of a psychologically convincing depiction of a growing relationship between Maria and Joana on the one hand and their respective lovers on the other, it does at least suggest that perhaps (to adapt a familiar feminist slogan) these women (who before long will bear the next generation of Iberians) can aim to 'have it all': past and future, tradition and innovation, renewal and continuity. For Saramago's 'rewriting' of Ulysses' return to Ithaca here involves a more active role for the woman, who does not act as a spinster, waiting at home for her man to return: instead she sends out her dog to summon him. Maria Guavaira might therefore be said to be throwing her own stone (like Joaquim) and moving the cyclical story of their relationship (essentially the oldest human story in existence, that of 'boy meets girl') into a new phase, where girl arranges to meet boy. The stone, once thrown, creates a new reality, but that is a story to be completed by Maria and Joaquim themselves. Under this model 'rectilinear' does not necessarily mean 'teleological', however: this is the mistake made by Saramago's two most negative fictional protagonists, Ricardo Reis and Jesus, both of whom resign themselves (unnecessarily) to a fate that is less ineluctable than it might at first seem.

The characters' uncertainty in interpreting events is an experience which therefore decreases in importance as they come to terms with the changed circumstances of their homelands and with the accelerated process of coming to know one another under unusual circumstances. Thus, when José and Joaquim first meet Pedro, it is unclear if his old-fashioned approach to pharmacy indicates that he is merely a traditionalist or that he is engaging in some kind of alchemist's trickery (p. 82). In fact, in view of Madruga's observation that Scarlatti's touch makes the *Passarola* vibrate in *Memorial*,[62] it might be best to conclude that Pedro is merely following in the tradition of visionaries presented in the earlier text and that the vibrating ground which he feels beneath his feet is merely a sign of the flying machine taking off once more in the form of a giant stone raft, and it is noticeable that his travelling companions soon adapt with remarkable *sang-froid* both to Pedro himself and to the eccentric behaviour of their native soil.

In similar fashion, in her first encounter with José, Joana briefly considers that her stick could be used for self-defence if necessary (p. 121), while for the males it is unclear whether her 'vara de condão' (pp. 140–1) ('magic wand'; pp. 108–9) could indicate that she is a good fairy or, as the nickname of 'Dona Olhos Não Sei Bem' (p. 129) ('Little Joana Strange Eyes'; p. 100) bestowed on her might also indicate, some kind of witch, who in Pedro's eyes may be luring them into a trap (p. 140). Even if it is accepted that she is an ordinary human being, however, should she be seen as a 'menina' or a 'virago' (p. 146) ('girl' and 'harpy' respectively; p. 113), or is she just what she says she is, neither of these two extremes? Once again, Joana's story is surely in general terms a rectilinear one (in common with her stick), of the growth of the individual, but the precise nature of that line remains to be defined, and there is no evidence within the text to impose the teleological (and absurdly pessimistic) interpretation imposed on her by Joaquim and José's initial fears, which are surely based more on the prospect of moving into the unknown than on knowing anything about the mysteries which Joana (and later) Maria will hold for them.

In the context of José's early relationship with Joana, as in so many of his other texts, Saramago allows the allusions to Portugal's maritime past to mount up: clouds seen in the sky 'navegam no espaço como galeões, os homens, estes e todos os outros, olham estas coisas diversas e, como de costume, não as entendem bem' (p. 49) ('navigate through space, like galleons, the men, they as well as all others, look at these different things, and, as usual, do not really understand them'; p. 35).[63] As Pedro and the two Portuguese men set out from Venta Micena on their journey we are reminded that this area provided many of those who sailed overseas in the past (p. 85), and the possible collision of the peninsula with the Azores is seen as a looming shipwreck (p. 217). And, just as also happens in *Conto*, this idea of maritime exploration, with its inherent uncertainties and risks, is associated with the amorous 'conquest' of the other, no longer in an imperialist sense, but in the same reciprocal sense as that developed in *História*, of the discovery of a fruitful and mutually beneficial relationship. Even, then, if Pedro, the old man, who represents where Iberia has been and the unfortunate hierarchical relationships with the outside world which it has developed in the past, has failed to achieve this kind of successful union with the other in his life (as he confesses to Joaquim shortly before going to explore the beach near Maria Guavaira's house; p. 191), his time is past and his successors, Joaquim and José, may prove to be more adaptable in that sense than he has been.

History, then, is waiting to be shaped by this new generation of Iberians. The comparison of Maria Guavaira to Penelope does have its coherence in the sense that rather than having to choose between completing her tapestry and having her husband, as happens to the queen in the *Odyssey*, Maria will be free to put together her tapestry in the company of her freely-chosen husband if he has the courage to join her. Similarly, Camões' Island of Love, the reward for Vasco da Gama's bold men in Canto IX of *Os Lusíadas*, is superseded in the mass pregnancy at the end of *Jangada* by a productive and fertile '(Pen)ínsula de amor' ('[pen]insula of love'), where the love is not a reward for reaching a predestined goal, but a symbolic representation of a hermaphrodite community constantly renewing itself by inserting its penis into its own fertile 'ínsula' ('island'), in order to create a new future for the next generation.

The openness and speculative nature of the ending to this work has prompted most critics (including myself[64]) to view *Jangada* as a work marked by hope more than despair. In this sense Sabine's overall interpretation of the work may be found surprising: for he claims that 'the novel's empty and inconclusive close represents a deep scepticism regarding the human capacity to improve social organisation'.[65] A major part of this critic's more cautious view of the text is based on the conception of gender roles within it, and he is correct in asserting that the novel attempts to move on from clichés (however useful they may have been to their authors in their original contexts) such as Unamuno's one of Spain playing the male to Portugal's female.[66] In fact, as the same critic also points out,[67] national identity is perhaps capable of being reformed as much as personal identity, and in the contemporary era, with the benefits of modern developments which have helped to make women more independent than ever before of their biological specificity,[68] so the Portugal of the 1980s should not have to be held captive by what the nation may or may not have been in 1578, 1755, or any other significant date in the country's past.

Sabine goes on to argue that the mass pregnancy towards the end of the novel is not the positive development which some critics have seen it to be. I would certainly agree with him that this unexpected plot development constitutes the 'acid test of their [Maria's and Joana's] relationships with their partners',[69] a test most clearly left open by the concluding pages of the novel, which focus on the end of one cycle (Pedro's life) rather than on the opening of this spectacularly new one. In this particular sense, the novel seems to suggest neither a positive nor a negative outcome; it merely leaves the reader with the challenge itself. The main grounds which sway Sabine towards a negative reading of this bizarre parody of the miraculous divine impregnation of Mary in the Bible are what he himself confesses to be a 'literal, historicist vein' of reading which would see large-scale unplanned pregnancy as a liability in terms of women's rights and opportunities in a context such as that of 1980s Iberia.[70] However, *Jangada* is anything but a sociological account of its own times, and it would surely be more realistic to view the unhappiness brought about by Pedro's earlier love-making with both Maria and Joana as being like a symbolic expulsion from Eden,[71] so that the subsequent 'explosão genesíaca' (p. 321) ('genetic explosion'; p. 255) is a warning signal that this 'new' Iberia will now have to adapt to life on its own, without the imposition of externally-imposed solutions, whether these derive from other more powerful countries following their own agendas, from non-governmental institutions, or from belief-systems such as religion.

Indeed, in the unlikely event of every woman of childbearing age in Portugal and Spain becoming pregnant, it is conceivable that this very fact might in itself help to change the character of gender relations within the two countries. Certainly the two female protagonists of this novel are not people to be dominated easily, so that Sabine's caution about this aspect of the ending of the novel may have been given excessive importance in terms of determining the possible responses to the work as a whole. The quotation from the Cuban writer Alejo Carpentier which is used as an epigraph for this novel ('Todo futuro es fabuloso'[72]) is clearly utopian rather than pessimistic in nature, even if Sabine is correct to state that it also constitutes a reminder that that future offers no guarantees of the fulfilment of dreams.[73]

The challenge is therefore implicitly made to José, Joaquim, Joana and Maria, along with the other inhabitants of Iberia, to ensure that this new island (built on love, rather than merely having love as its reward, as Camões would have had it) is not taken over by the rulers of the modern games of international politics and economics, which seek to inhibit meaningful democracy through restrictive trading arrangements and hierarchical relationships which will control the history of nations, rather than to build upon it as a foundation for a truly human society.

As an illustration of this point, one should perhaps bear in mind the full significance of the historical anecdote which José tells Joaquim about the imaginary island given by D. João II of Portugal to a nobleman, who then became an object of popular derision by setting out to sea to find it (p. 65); quite apart from any implicit allusions here to the scepticism which surrounded Columbus' plans before he left Spain on his first voyage to America, to those who are acquainted with Cervantes' *Don Quijote*, José's question 'diga-me você se sabe doutro país onde pudesse ter acontecido uma história como esta' (p. 65) ('do you know of any other nation where such a thing could happen'; p. 48) will prompt an instant answer. In Part II, chapters 42–53 of *Don Quijote*, as part of their entertainment, the Duke and Duchess set up a false island kingdom for Sancho Panza to govern, in accordance with the promises made to him throughout the work by his master. In the end, Sancho's kingdom is brought to its knees as a result of interference from the rulers of the game and Sancho's own wish to return to his old life, rather than through any particularly poor performance by him as ruler of the island.[74] Could Sancho, could the Iberians, Saramago appears to be asking, perhaps be trusted to run things better on their own than some outsiders (and even some insiders) may believe?

There would, of course, be only one way to find out the answer to such a question: the potential benefits of the society which might arise out of the (perhaps utopian) purely human relationships postulated here lie in their spontaneity. For even if the society which emerges from the split in the Pyrenees proves to match a Marxist one in form, the key point is that it should not have been constructed with ideological considerations in mind, but as the natural expression of its people. The openness of the ending of the novel is therefore important for exactly the same reason as Bertolt Brecht chose to make his 1941 account of the ascent of Arturo Ui (a thinly disguised version of Hitler) a resistable one: namely that it is left to the reader or spectator to ensure that happy endings are created in our world, where they matter, rather than in a fictional context, where they are merely aesthetically pleasing.

A practical application of Saramago's ideas in the real world might be called into question on the grounds that, at least in the case of *Jangada*, there is no clear vision of how this ideal might actually be realized. Similarly, the final chapter of *Caverna* sees Cipriano Algor and his family flee from the Centre into the countryside, heading towards an uncertain future, thus creating an open ending to the work similar to that of *Cegueira* or *Jangada*:

> A furgoneta fez a manobra e desceu a ladeira. Chegando à Estrada virou à esquerda. Marta chorava com os olhos secos, Isaura abraçava-a, enquanto o Achado se enroscava a um canto do assento por não saber a quem acudir. Alguns quilómetros andados, Marçal disse, Escreverei aos meus pais quando pararmos para almoçar. E logo, dirigindo-se a Isaura e ao sogro, Havia um cartaz, daqueles grandes, na fachada do Centro, são capazes de adivinhar o que ele dizia, perguntou, Não temos ideia, responderam ambos, e então Marçal disse, como se recitasse, BREVEMENTE, ABERTURA AO PÚBLICO DA CAVERNA DE PLATÃO, ATRACÇÃO EXCLUSIVA, ÚNICA NO MUNDO, COMPRE JÁ A SUA ENTRADA. (*Caverna*, pp. 349–50)

> [The engine started and the van went down the hill. When they got to the road, it turned left. Marta, though dry-eyed, was sobbing. Isaura had her arms about her, while Found lay curled up in one corner of the seat, not knowing who to comfort first. After a few kilometers, Marçal said, I'll write to my parents when we stop for lunch. And then, addressing Isaura and his father-in-law, There was a poster, one of those really big ones outside the Center, can you guess what it said, he asked. We've no idea, they replied, and, as if he were reciting something, Marçal said, COMING SOON, PUBLIC OPENING OF PLATO'S CAVE, AN EXCLUSIVE ATTRACTION, UNIQUE IN THE WORLD, BUY YOUR TICKET NOW.] (*Cave*, p. 307)

In one sense this negative flight might be seen as an abdication of responsibility on Saramago's part in his failure to identify a real alternative to the tempting but ultimately hollow existence on offer within the Centre, just as the children born of the mass pregnancies in *Jangada* will take years to grow up and help shape their new countries in their own image. This, however, is to fall into a reductivist reading of this novel purely as a satire on the failings of global capitalism; for any requirement for a specific alternative environment here would posit the state-controlled economy or the ecologically conscious society (to mention only two possible alternative orders) as offering in themselves the same type of messianic solutions which have long hindered the people of Portugal. If these people are not to be merely stones (the state in which the doctor's wife finds her companions when she brings them food in *Cegueira*; see *Cegueira*, p. 227) but rather the pilots of stone rafts, then they must discover what works for themselves, be it within a Marxist order, a less ruthless capitalist order, or any other. If Cipriano's flight from the Centre is really in search of Bartolomeu's flying machine, then we must remember that its fuel is not any specific form of belief, but the wills of individuals expressed in harmony together as they progress to their own journey's goal through the uncharted course of human life in its full variety. It will take time to construct a meaningful alternative to the Centre, but the first step is surely to move away from its menacing shadow.

4. From Blimunda to the Doctor's Wife: Gramsci and the Transformation of Portugal

The final chapter of *Memorial* sees Blimunda searching the length and breadth of Portugal for any trace of her common-law husband Baltasar, who has mysteriously disappeared from her life. What is particularly interesting about this section of the novel, however, is not only the devotion of the lover who has lost her other half, but also her apparent distraction from the task at hand:

> Durante nove anos, Blimunda procurou Baltasar. Conheceu todos os caminhos de pó e da lama, a branda areia, a pedra aguda, tantas vezes a geada rangente e assassina, dois nevões de que só saiu viva porque ainda não queria morrer. [. . .] Julgavam-na doida, mas, se ela se deixava ficar por ali uns tempos, viam-na tão sensata em todas as mais palavras e acções que duvidavam da primeira suspeita de pouco siso. [. . .] Sentava-se às portas, a conversar com as

mulheres do lugar, ouvia-lhes as lamentações, os ais, menos vezes as alegrias, por serem poucas, [. . .] Por onde passava, ficava um fermento de desassossego, os homens não reconheciam as suas mulheres, que subitamente se punham a olhar para eles, com pena de que não tivessem desaparecido, para enfim poderem procurá-los. [. . .] Os padres que ouviam falar dela mandavam-lhe recados para que viesse à confissão, curiosos de saber que mistérios se ocultavam naquela romeira e peregrina, [. . .] A esses mandava dizer que fizera promessa de só se confessar quando se sentisse pecadora, não poderia encontrar resposta que mais escandalizasse, se pecadores todos nós somos, porém, não era raro que falando sobre isto com outras mulheres as deixasse pensativas, afinal, que faltas são essas nossas, as tuas, as minhas, se nós somos, mulheres, verdadeiramente, o cordeiro que tirará o pecado do mundo, no dia em que isto for compreendido vai ser preciso começar outra vez tudo. (*Memorial*, pp. 353–4)

[For nine long years, Blimunda searched for Baltasar. She came to know every road and every track from the dust and mud, the sandy soil and treacherous stones, experienced many severe frosts and two blizzards, which she survived only because she had no intention of dying just yet. [. . .] People thought that she must be mad, but if she lingered there for any time they found her so rational in everything else she said and she did that they began to doubt their initial impression that she was unsound of mind. [. . .] She would sit in doorways conversing with the women, who confided their grievances and woes, less frequently their joys, which were all too few, [. . .] Wherever she passed, there remained a ferment of disquiet, the men did not recognise their womenfolk, who suddenly began to stare at them, sorry that they, too, had not disappeared so that they, too, might go in search of them. [. . .] Priests, upon hearing speak of her, sent messages urging Blimunda to come and be confessed, anxious to probe the mysteries surrounding this wandering pilgrim. [. . .] She sent word back to the priests that she would accept their offer whenever she had some sin to confess, no reply could have provoked a greater scandal, since we are all sinners, but when she discussed this matter with other women, she often gave them food for thought, after all, what are these sins of ours, of yours, of mine, if we women are truly the lamb that will take away the sins of the world, the day when this message is understood, it will be necessary to start everything anew.] (*Baltasar*, pp. 339–40)

The intertextuality of this passage is striking: here we have a female Don Quixote, an idealist whose quest, in the end, leads her interlocutors to realize that perhaps she is not so crazy after all; here Garrett's D. João de Portugal of *Frei Luís de Sousa*, the lonely pilgrim ('romeira') seeks to return to her long-lost love; here we have a predecessor to the *Livro do Desassossego* written by Pessoa's semi-heteronym Bernardo Soares, whipping up discontent where previously nobody questioned the apparently settled ways of the world; and here, finally, and most audaciously, we have Blimunda as Christ reincarnate, as the lamb who will take away the sins of the world.

When we look more closely at these various role models, however, we find that all four of them have been transformed into women in Blimunda. While this fact has its own significance, there are however other more profound changes at work here too, for this Don Quixote does eventually, albeit briefly, find her Dulcinea, as the novel closes with her rediscovery of Baltasar during his execution by the Inquisition. This D. João de Portugal finds the will of her spouse coming readily to her (p. 357) rather than rejecting her in the manner in which Madalena rejects Garrett's pilgrim; this Soares does not withdraw from the world into an internal reality which contrasts with the surrounding bustle of the city of Lisbon, but engages actively with the world, even as she seeks the one reality (Baltasar) which means more to her personally than any other; and this lamb of God rejects not only the ministers of Christ, but also his teaching, as she declares herself effectively to be free of sin. Moreover, a closer analysis of Blimunda's refusal to pay homage to ecclesiastical authority reveals that it is due to more than just a sense of personal worth which does not need to be confirmed by a power structure which her own experiences have led her to view as corrupt: for the nature of the state of forgiveness preached by the priests, even if taken on purely doctrinal terms and thus without its devaluation by the actions of representatives of the Church within the text, implies an acceptance of stasis which would sit ill at ease with this essentially dynamic character, whose understanding of the world has moved from one of truth as wisdom revealed from on high to one based on a quasi-Hegelian dialectic: 'no dia em que isto for compreendido vai ser preciso começar outra vez tudo', a quotation recalling the words of the final paragraph of Saramago's *Viagem*, first published one year before this novel and reproduced in the Introduction.

It is a commonplace of criticism of Saramago's novels that his female characters are both more powerful and capable of greater initiative than his male ones.[75] More striking still, however, is the apparently marginal and unqualified nature of the particular women fulfilling this role in his work: Blimunda, the daughter of a woman condemned to exile in Africa for sins of witchcraft and possible crypto-Judaism, fits into the same tradition as the enigmatic Joana Carda of *Jangada*, who teaches the schoolmaster José Anaiço valuable lessons about love, commitment, and the unpredictable nature of human life; just as Mary Magdalene, the social outcast in *Evangelho*, becomes the teacher of the man generally thought of as the Son of God and leads him to discover love, self-respect and a willingness to question the accepted order; just as the doctor's wife in *Cegueira* leads her comrades to a means of overcoming their blindness when her husband is left helpless by the apparent inexplicability of the epidemic and by his own blindness; and just as the old lady whom Sr José attempts to bully into offering him the information which he requires forces him instead to face up to the truth about the nature of his own quest (*Todos*, pp. 194–5).

This recurrent pattern of the subaltern leading the supposedly superior to greater insight has much in common with the ideas of the Italian revolutionary thinker Antonio Gramsci, two of whose principal ideas were the importance of what he described as 'cultural hegemony', and the contrast between what he called 'organic' and 'traditional' intellectuals. While the concern of primary relevance in the current context is the latter question, in Gramsci's conception of the Revolution, this could not be achieved without the assertion of the cultural hegemony of the workers over the traditional ruling classes, that is, the need for establishing a cultural environment defined by informed popular consent, the dreams and the aspirations arising from the people as a whole and not being defined for them by a cultured elite. Until the working and peasant classes recognized that they too needed to participate in this process instead of succumbing to agendas set by traditional intellectuals, the latter group would simply preserve the unjust status quo (unjust because it was first formed by that group in pursuit of its own interests):

> The most typical of these categories of intellectuals is that of the ecclesiastics, who for a long time [. . .] held a monopoly of a

> number of important services: religious ideology, that is the philosophy and science of the age, together with schools, education, morality, justice, charity, good works, etc. The category of ecclesiastics can be considered the category of intellectuals organically bound to the landed aristocracy. [. . .] Since these various categories of traditional intellectuals experience through an 'esprit de corps' their uninterrupted historical continuity and their special qualification, they thus put themselves forward as autonomous and independent of the dominant social group. This self-assessment is not without consequences in the ideological and political field. [. . .] The whole of idealist philosophy can easily be connected with this position assumed by the social complex of intellectuals and can be defined as the expression of that social utopia by which the intellectuals think of themselves as 'independent', autonomous, endowed with a character of their own, etc.[76]

One notes in the above the clear centrality in terms of a Gramscian-based interpretation of Saramago's work of the categorization of figures such as the Father Agamedes of *Levantado* as 'ecclesiastics' but also, more alarmingly, even of the apparently innocuous Ricardo Reis, whose characterization indicates a man who falsely considers himself to be '"independent', autonomous, endowed with a character of [his] own', amply demonstrated by his inability even to comprehend Lídia's interpretation of events in Spain, never mind accept it (see *Ano*, p. 388). The fact that he is not technically an ecclesiastic and that he looks down his nose at Christianity almost as much as he does at his social inferiors such as Lídia does not remove from him any of the attributes which would lead Gramsci to view him as having essentially the same function as Agamedes; it merely indicates once more his own blindness to the content which lies behind form: 'Ricardo Reis não chegou a compreender as verdadeiras razões do alvoroço popular, nem isto deverá espantar-nos, a nós e a ele, que só tinha os jornais para sua informação' (*Ano*, p. 388) ('Ricardo Reis does not fully grasp the reason for the uprising, which need not surprise either us or him, because he has only the newspapers to rely on for information'; *Year*, p. 336).

In order to achieve the shift in cultural hegemony which he viewed as necessary for the achievement of a juster society, therefore, Gramsci saw it as necessary that the traditional intellectuals (such as university professors, writers, and members of the cultured elites in general) should be continually complemented or challenged by rising thinkers who did not enjoy these privileges and whose interests were therefore not vested in the preservation of the status quo: 'There is no human activity from which every form of intellectual participation can be excluded: *homo faber* cannot be separated from *homo sapiens*'.[77] Indeed, he saw it both as inevitable and vital to the ongoing health of society that its everyday practices spontaneously stimulate the rise of thinkers from among workers whose basic job description is of a more modest nature:

> The problem of creating a new stratum of intellectuals consists therefore in the critical elaboration of the intellectual activity that exists in everyone at a certain degree of development, modifying its relationship with the muscular–nervous effort towards a new equilibrium, and ensuring that the muscular–nervous effort itself, in so far as it is an element of general practical activity, which is perpetually innovating the physical and social world, becomes the foundation of a new and integral conception of the world.[78]

This is essentially the same concept as that embodied by Blimunda's desire to 'start everything anew' whenever perfection appears to have been reached; this is essentially an expression of the true nature, in terms used by Marxist intellectuals, of 'democratic centralism', as opposed to 'bureaucratic centralism' (the latter being the form of communism which, alas, dominated the Soviet bloc and consisted essentially of a secular version of Moses' tablets of stone being revealed to the people by the prophets of the party). This is a version of socialism where the ordinary person such as Blimunda can and should question, debate, and define new 'truths', which in turn become the thesis to be placed into a dialectical relationship with a new antithesis, as part of a never-ending approximation to the truth.

Perhaps it would be going too far to describe Blimunda as what Gramsci labelled the 'organic intellectual', someone who would form part of a regular process of 'insertion of elements thrown up from the depths of the rank and file into the solid framework of the leadership apparatus';[79] people like Blimunda (and later Lídia) do not belong to any formalized structure of resistance, but certainly their unwillingness to be coerced into silence by authority figures such as priests or educated poets turns them into something akin to what Gramsci envisaged; and certainly one notes in the reference to Blimunda's stimulation of a 'fermento de desassossego' at the end of *Memorial* an echo, whether deliberate or not, of Gramsci's view that 'it is essential that if it [the political and intellectual leadership of the political party] is destroyed it should leave as its heritage a ferment from which it may be recreated'.[80]

Essentially, therefore, Gramsci rejects the inevitability of that specialization within society which had been propounded by Plato (this is also why the role of the guards at the Centre in Saramago's *Caverna* is so inimical to the author, as it presupposes the very type of specialization and ranking of forms of labour which Gramscian thought abhors) only to be bemoaned by nineteenth-century German philosophers such as Schiller and Marx. Indeed, Gramsci's key contribution in this respect may be seen as his attempt to find a more thoroughgoing remedy for the Marxist concept of alienation than that which is advanced merely by having the state take over the ownership of the means of production. As Ransome writes:

> For Gramsci, in other words, the categorisation of a particular task or individual as 'intellectual' should not be based on the fact that some activities are intrinsically more cognitive than others, but rather on the *relative function* they perform within social practice. Since in every activity 'even the most degraded and mechanical, there exists a minimum of technical qualification, that is, a minimum of creative intellectual activity [. . .] all men are intellectuals, but not all men have in society the function of intellectuals'.[81]

This amounts, then, to a valorization of all forms of experience, proletarian or patrician, gained in menial labour or in serene contemplation of the world. To those familiar with Saramago's major novels, it should come as no surprise, therefore, that *Ano* offers us one of the most striking instances of a figure comparable to Gramsci's organic intellectual: that of the chambermaid Lídia, who proves in the end to be anything but the unworthy companion for the erudite Dr Reis we might have thought her to be when they first establish sexual relations in the early part of the novel. Indeed, it can be argued that Lídia has the potential to keep resistance alive to the fascist regime which her lover unwittingly serves in his naive indifference to the ever-changing world around him: he spends most of the novel living in a mental world of seemingly immutable truths, only to be woken up rather too late to the uncomfortable reality that those who do not learn to adapt to changing circumstances not only die themselves but may do incalculable damage to others. If Reis himself has to depart for the serenity of death, then in the process his silence at the developing situation around him leads to the death of Lídia's revolutionary brother Daniel, for he functions as the child sacrificed to the good of the symbolic parent which is the nation, but, once Daniel has gone, it is Lídia who, in a sense, will keep both him and the revolution alive.

It is only with the death of Daniel, however, that Reis first realizes that he is also an actor within history, and that the apparent truths of classical wisdom to which he has clung have receded so far behind the form given to them under fascism that there is no longer any content discernible in them at all. Thus, the dominant tone of large parts of his return to Lisbon is one of futility, evident in episodes such as his pseudo-pilgrimage to the shrine of Fátima, where he goes, not in search of the life-giving Maria, but in search of the moribund Marcenda, or in his attendance at a state-sponsored political rally, which ought to remind him of his own poetry in its suppression of content in favour of classical form:

> em todo o caminho não pensara no que tinha visto e ouvido, julgara que sim, que viera a pensar, mas querendo recordar agora não encontrava uma única ideia, uma reflexão, um comentário, era como se tivesse sido transportado por uma nuvem, nuvem ele próprio, apenas pairando. [. . .] A comícios não torno (*Ano*, p. 398).
>
> [he realized that during the long walk home he had not thought once about what he had seen and heard in the arena. He could not remember a single idea, reflection, comment, it was almost as if he had been carried on a cloud, or transformed into a cloud hovering in midair. [. . .] No more political rallies for me.] (*Year*, p. 344)

The reason why he does not detect any real substance in either of these events lies, one might suggest, in Gramsci's analysis of the functioning of cultural hegemony, as summed up by Ransome:

> There is therefore a *dialectal strategy* available to the dominant group in society. Either it can use direct physical force by such means as the army and the penal system to overcome its opponents, or it can gain their support as it were 'voluntarily' by

> persuading them to accept and assimilate the norms and values of its own prevailing world-view.[82]

This is where Ricardo Reis really fails his country: when faced with unpalatable truths and challenged to make choices by his two most intimate companions, Lídia, who represents life, and the already deceased Fernando Pessoa, whose only hope for further achievement in the world lies in his poetic offspring, such as Reis, all he can do is look out on the world as a spectator, as Pessoa himself tells him: 'você anda a flutuar no Atlântico, nem lá, nem cá' (p. 361) ('You are floating [. . .] in midocean, neither here nor there'; p. 312). This comment is partly an allusion to Reis' recent return to his homeland from Brazil, but Cirlot would also take this as suggesting that he is somewhere between life and death: 'The symbolic significance of the sea corresponds to that of the "Lower Ocean" – the waters in flux, the transitional and mediatory agent between the non-formal (air and gases) and the formal (earth and solids) and, by analogy, between life and death'.[83]

If Pessoa's incarnation of Reis famously wrote 'Sábio é o que se contenta com o espectáculo do mundo' ('Wise is the man who contents himself with the spectacle of the world'),[84] then Saramago's Reis does not take adequate note of the epigraph to a later novel: 'Se podes olhar, vê. Se podes ver, repara' (*Cegueira,* dust jacket) ('If you can see, look. If you can look, observe'; *Blindness,* flyleaf). What he sees (and becomes transfixed by) after one of his encounters with Pessoa are the characteristic Lisbon parallel tramlines, which recede into the distance (*Ano,* p. 83): this image (reinforced in the following chapter by a reminder that the tram which he hears may be the final one; p. 99) prefigures his ultimate choice in favour of death over life, as he voluntarily moves into infinity and merges with his creator rather than remaining on earth with Lídia, whose advances he rejects as coldly as his poetic persona on one occasion tells her to take her hand away from him.[85] In one final allusion to Camões, the figure of Adamastor on the Alto de Santa Catarina closes the novel by crying out in impotent rage (as he also does in *Os Lusíadas*[86]) at the point where the sea ends and the 'terra espera' (*Ano,* p. 415) ('the earth awaits'; *Year,* p. 358), but, once more, what Reis fails to notice in his static vision of the world is that while he himself has returned home, the rebellious spirit of Adamastor is no longer in

Africa but now in Portugal, uniting the colonized and the colonial power in a roar of frustration at the prospect of a further thirty-eight years of control by a 'New State', which, paradoxically, seeks nothing more than to perpetuate an old Portugal. In this sense one might evoke here Boaventura de Sousa Santos' analysis of Portugal as a 'semi-peripheral' nation in order to suggest that, behind the bombast of Salazarian rhetoric of Empire, Portugal needs to wake up to the reality that the former colonial power now finds itself the plaything of more powerful masters in Europe and elsewhere, just as Adamastor represents the futility of African resistance to the seemingly ineluctable will of the Portuguese explorers in *Os Lusíadas*.[87]

If Ricardo Reis fails to live up to his responsibilities, then the same cannot be said of most of Saramago's female characters, and, indeed, many of the male ones including, in *Levantado*, humble peasants such as Germano Vidigal and José Adelino dos Santos, victims of oppression to whom the novel is dedicated (*Levantado*, p. 7). What is being emphasized in this way is that power has now reached out even to those who have been traditionally under the greatest oppression: for a large part of the novel the female members of the peasant classes have been doubly disadvantaged not only by the same poverty and lack of opportunities for social and professional advancement open to those who are born into wealth, but also by a conservative mindset in terms of gender relations which has been internalized by women such as Sara da Conceição as much as it has been by Domingos Mau-Tempo, Father Agamades, or Salazar himself. In this sense, the youthful, hopeful figure of Maria Adelaide (with her associations with love and springtime) is herself a figure of revolutionary power: for the new dispensation after 25 April will grant her the same legal and political authority as men, indicating that hegemony now lies with all of the oppressed and that the various social hierarchies outlined in Chapter One have now been abolished, so that Portuguese society will not be able to go back so easily to its old, hierarchical structures and gender stereotyping.

There are others, men and women, who perform the role of leader and inspiration in Saramago's fiction: M. in *Manual*, who in spite of the relative anonymity of her name becomes the first of H.'s lovers to be treated as a full human being and who contributes to his self-realization as writer and person and to Portugal's liberation from dictatorship; Maria Sara in *História*; Maria Guavaira and Joana Carda, the two female protagonists of *Jangada* (but also, in the same novel, Pedro Orce, and perhaps even to a limited extent the simple peasant Roque Lozano); the mysterious unknown woman who, without even ever knowing of Sr José's very existence, nonetheless leads him to a more fulfilling existence and (indirectly) to the rehumanization of the sepulchral Registry in *Todos*; the mathematics teacher in *Homem*, whose encouragement leads Tertuliano Máximo Afonso into his quest to achieve unity and integrity; and, above all, the doctor's wife in *Cegueira*. Not all of these figures should be seen in political terms, but all of them serve at least as catalysts for change in helping bring the awareness of the main protagonists on to the issues which should really be concerning them. This does not, however, preclude the possibility of viewing these exemplary characters in both roles: as assistants in the tradition of the quest narrative, and, potentially at least, as political activists.

In some respects, the figure of the doctor's wife is a less clear-cut figure for a Gramscian analysis of the novels than Lídia or Blimunda: unlike either of these women, who arise from very clearly subaltern segments of society at times when modern ideals of universal literacy were not even paid lip service in Portugal, the glimpses of her normal lifestyle which we obtain indicate clearly that she is middle-class, educated and intelligent. There is no visible sign of inferior status or preparation here, save for the fact that she is married to an ophthalmologist amid a mass outbreak of blindness, in which she is the only person spared. In that sense, of relative qualifications vis-à-vis her husband, she is clearly in the inferior position, and yet she is effectively acting as the cobbler did to Apelles in commenting on his body above the ankle. Similarly, when the doctor's wife returns in a later novel (*Lucidez*), she and the other citizens of the capital city effectively identify the Emperor's new clothes in the crisis which is not only allowed to develop but actively stimulated by the paranoia and cynicism of national government: politics, one might say, is too important an activity in Saramago's view to be left to the professional politicians.

Equally, however, the interventions made by the doctor's wife in *Cegueira* are not of a nature which we could consider ideological as such, unless, that is, one interprets the idea of the Republic in its strict etymological sense of the Latin *res publica*, that is, that of all current affairs. It is precisely because she recognizes in *Cegueira* that the foundations for a healthy state lie in full respect for the individual, regardless of his or her status, that she becomes such a threat to the Establishment in *Lucidez*. Her essential intervention in *Cegueira* is humanitarian and humanistic in nature: she ensures that others have enough to eat (*Cegueira*, pp. 220–4); she encourages the blind writer in his somewhat quixotic aspiration to record on paper, even in his blindness, the experiences which he has encountered (pp. 277–9); and she offers what appears (by its prominent positioning) to be the recommended authorial interpretation of the attack of blindness on the final page of the text: 'Penso que não cegámos, penso que estamos cegos, Cegos que vêem, Cegos que, vendo, não vêem' (p. 310) ('I don't think we did go blind, I think we are blind, Blind but seeing, Blind people who can see, but do not see'; *Blindness*, p. 309).

At one level, then, the doctor's wife merely teaches her fellow humans to see again a truth which has threatened to become lost in the course of this sorry tale, the truth of universal humanity and the need to maintain respect for others, not only for their sake, but also for one's own. If engagement with the city ('polis' in Greek) is moral, then these acts become, by their very nature, political, and it is only to the shame of the government of the unnamed country in *Lucidez* that this shining example of far-sightedness is eliminated in what eventually goes back to being the country of the blind, where no awkward questions are asked of authority, as the final page of that novel sees the state-sponsored assassination of both the doctor's wife and her dog, to the satisfaction of two blind men:

> Então um cego perguntou, Ouviste alguma coisa, Três tiros, respondeu outro, Mas havia também um cão aos uivos, Já se calou, deve ter sido o terceiro tiro, Ainda bem, detesto ouvir os cães a uivar (*Lucidez*, p. 329).
>
> [And then a blind man asked, Did you hear something, Three shots, replied another blind man, But there was also a dog howling. It's shut up, that must have been the third shot, Just as well, I hate hearing dogs howling.]

The dog imagery adopted here, of course, recalls that of the ants and dogs with their heads held high in *Levantado*, while the epigraph to the novel ('Uivemos, disse o cão', or 'Let us howl, said the dog'; *Lucidez*, dust jacket) explicitly reminds the reader that we should not allow this seemingly decisive ending to be repeated in the real world.

If we return to the literary echoes of the passage cited from the final chapter of *Memorial* at the opening of this section, then Blimunda (who, in common with the doctor's wife, can see where others cannot) makes sense as a transformed, latter-day version of Don Quixote, D. João de Portugal, Bernardo Soares, and even of Christ. She differs from Don Quixote only in that her ideals would be capable of realization in a better Portugal, whereas those of the Knight of the Sad Countenance are not. In the role of D. João de Portugal, she surely eventually recognizes the futility in practical terms of seeking out Baltasar once more, and this is why she interrupts her search for him to preach a new gospel to the women whom she encounters: for she does not wish any of them to have to face in the future what she has had to face in her own life. Her final ingestion of Baltasar's will is therefore meaningful and forward-looking and not based on the empty nostalgia which marks Garrett's pilgrim and which could easily become simply a mental habit for Portugal if the nation does not seek to shake off the habits of the past by following the example of its own soil in making a clean break with the past in *Jangada*. She is a Soares whose mental torment leads not to an ever-deepening mental and emotional labyrinth, but to a renewal of the spirit which led to the flights of the *Passarola*, for her disquiet is contextualized within the Gramscian ferment which resembles the vortex from which God in Genesis launched creation: a better world is possible.

There remains, finally, the role of Blimunda (and by implication) other women as lambs who will take away the sins of the world. To assess this parallel, it is necessary to consider her implicit similarity to the Virgin Mary. It is abundantly clear from the text that Blimunda is no virgin, but noticeably in this passage she does declare herself to be without sin, and, if the Virgin bears a child without making love, then Blimunda's special nature allows her to make love repeatedly, in an age with very limited possibilities of artificial contraception compared to today, without giving birth (as one of Baltasar's family does not hesitate to remind her near the end of the novel; see *Memorial*, p. 350). This role reversal is probably no accident: for what Saramago is surely suggesting here is a revision of traditional conceptions of virtue and productive behaviour. In the case of this novel, the 'child' which Blimunda bears is the lesson which she gives in generosity, legitimate pride in her own judgement, and insight into the minds and souls of those around her, to her contemporaries and to us as readers.

If we examine Saramago's presentation of women's fertility more broadly, we will find an attitude which recognizes orthodox Catholic reverence for women's reproductive capacities while also rejecting the specifically sexual doctrines controlling them, so that his novels demonstrate repeatedly that sexual relations and, more particularly, pregnancies arising from them are amongst the most fulfilling transformations possible in human life: this pattern of fertilization is one which is repeated, for example, in *Ano*, *Jangada*, and *Caverna*, and, significantly, in all of these cases, pregnancy becomes a prominent motif. Along with their role as something resembling Gramsci's organic intellectual, then, in Saramago's fiction women perform the most organic role possible to human beings, that of bringing new life into the world, just as the biblical Mary does, but in the specific case of Blimunda this is represented in metaphorical rather than literal terms.

I would argue, therefore, that even if, at a purely literal level, Saramago's portrayal of women borders in some respects on romanticized idealization, the function which he assigns to them is an eminently practical one, that of ensuring that the revolution of which men talk in such idealistic terms becomes a reality in practice: for women, traditionally the subordinate, the outsider, have at least the advantage of being able to keep alive the alternative discourses traditionally excluded from the tables of power. In short, the everyday practical conversation of women will complement others' dreams to help keep the world in its orbit, that is, away from the entropy of being pulled in by the gravitational pull of the earth, here representing the traditional forces which have shaped the lives of men and women down through the ages. Such a task requires a Blimunda, and not someone like Saramago's version of Ricardo Reis, whose obsession with perfect form leads him to ignore the real substance of the nation, its people. Lídia and her unborn son will have to wait until 1974 for liberation, but in the meantime no amount of government repression will succeed in destroying the demand for freedom, for, as Garrett told the Conservatório Real in Lisbon in justification of his attempts to engage ordinary people as well as the elite through his *Frei Luís de Sousa* in 1843: 'é povo, quer verdade' ('this is the people, and they want the truth').[88] Garrett, of course, famously dismissed in 1830 the patronizing notion that Portugal was not yet ready for full democracy;[89] Saramago is of the same school, claiming that Garrett could have written the same words if he had still been alive in the early 1970s.[90] In the same article Saramago himself identified the need for Portuguese fiction to engage in a real dialogue with Portuguese realities in order to revitalize the novel in Portugal;[91] he has, of course, done more than his fair share in completing both of those agendas.

NOTES

1 The quotation ('Besides the conversation of women, it is dreams that keep the world in orbit'; *Baltasar*, p. 107) refers back to another passage on p. 109 of the text, which declares 'não fosse falarem as mulheres umas com as outras, já os homens teriam perdido o sentido da casa e do planeta' ('if women did not converse with one another, men would long ago have lost all sense of home and of the world at large'; p. 101).

2 This sense of the peoples of the Iberian Peninsula having more in common with one another than what differs between the two nations is given expression most prominently throughout *Jangada*; but it also recurs in implicit form in the opening passage of *Viagem*, where the anonymous traveller (clearly a version of Saramago himself) opens the narrative standing with one foot inside Spain and the other inside Portugal, reflecting on the significance of this invisible line; see *Viagem*, p. 15.

3 For a detailed discussion of my interpretation of *Caverna*, see Frier, 'Viagem Para as Ilhas do Sul'. The focus of *Lucidez* is primarily on the manipulation of public opinion within the context of a Western democracy, but the recurrence of references to the Iraq war in interviews given by the novelist at the time of the launch of this work suggests that this specific issue was heavily on his mind at the time; for Saramago's opposition to the war itself, see his 'Quieren la guerra, pero no les vamos a dejar en paz'.

4 Arnaut points out that Raimundo is not actually named within the novel until the third chapter, when he starts to rebel against the 'authority' of the text which he is proofreading. See Arnaut, 'Viagem ao Centro da Escrita', p. 332, n. 2.

5 Schor correctly points out that while the text refers to the serpent deciding not to bite its own tail, the publishers' decision to release the book which Raimundo proofreads along with an 'erratum' slip in

order to negate his insertion of the word 'não' into the text effectively ensures that the serpent of self-perpetuating historical untruth is preserved, in spite of his efforts to break this cycle. See Schor, p. 159.

6 See Luke 2:39–52. This incident does display some significant alterations from its biblical prototype: Joseph is already dead, and Jesus, therefore, while still very young, is significantly older in Saramago's account than in the biblical version (where Joseph is clearly still alive). In addition, while the biblical account speaks of the 'wisdom' which Jesus displays, it offers no suggestion of any challenge posed by Him to established beliefs, nor does it quote any precise words used by Him. The change to Jesus' age is presumably made by Saramago to give credibility to the type of awkward and searching questions posed by him.

7 Reproduced in Pessoa, *Poesias Inéditas (1930–1935)*, p. 154.

8 The allusion here may be to either of two poems in Caeiro's *O Guardador de Rebanhos*: in Poem XXXIX we find 'Porque o único sentido oculto das coisas/ É elas não terem sentido oculto nenhum' ('For the only hidden meaning of things/ Is that they have no hidden meaning at all'), while Poem V has 'O único sentido íntimo das coisas/ É elas não terem sentido íntimo nenhum' ('The only inner meaning of things/ Is that they have no inner meaning at all'). Poem XXXIX is reproduced in Pessoa, *Selected Poems*, pp. 131–2. Poem V is contained in Galhoz (ed.), p. 173 (the translation of the lines from this poem is from Zenith, p. 50).

9 There is a brief and humorous allusion to Raimundo as a latter-day Hamlet within the text on p. 72, as the protagonist walks around Lisbon letting his mind wander at the sights of the city around him and wondering if his real vocation is as a philosopher, with a brief allusion to Hamlet's contemplation of the skull of Yorick in Act V Scene I of *Hamlet*, a passage also alluded to in *Manual* (see *Manual*, p. 232). Arnaut mentions further allusions to Shakespeare's play on pp. 68 and 86 of *História*, but it is not clear what these are; see Arnaut, 'Viagem ao Centro da Escrita', p. 333, n. 7.

10 See, for example, poem XLII of *O Guardador de Rebanhos*, which is reproduced in Galhoz (ed.), p. 182.

11 Parra Bañón also comments on the importance of windows here in stressing the degree to which the individual can be affected by the outside world (see Parra Bañón, pp. 181–7). Sabine also comments on the use of windows, pointing out that Saramago uses them to reverse a common cultural stereotype 'of a hero's penetration of a woman's sanctuary or prison'; in his view, therefore, Raimundo effectively plays Juliet here to Maria Sara's Romeo (see Sabine, p. 294). Windows are also a common image used by Pessoa (particularly when writing as Campos, but also on at least one occasion as Caeiro) to convey the difficulty of bridging the distance between separate existences.

12 This poem was popularized, above all, by Amália Rodrigues' recording of it to Alain Oulman's music; the lyrics are reproduced at

http://natura.di.uminho.pt/~jj/musica/html/amalia-06.html (website consulted on 7 November 2005).

13 'Poema de sete faces' in Andrade, pp. 3–4, p. 4.

14 Sabine (p. 294) sees this episode as a parody of 1950s Hollywood seductions; once again, as in the same critic's comments on Saramago's use of the balcony, however, the respective gender roles have been reversed.

15 See 'Caminos', in Machado, pp. 107–8.

16 The undoubted presence of allusions to Machado in the novelist's work implicitly recalls the Spanish poet's sense of the need for the individual to overcome the diverse, but interrelated challenges of national renewal, achieving a sense of purpose in one's personal life, and facing up to the passage of time, an issue addressed also in *Jangada, Ano* and *Intermitências.* For a fuller discussion of echoes of Machado in Saramago, particularly in *Jangada, Manual* and *História,* see Grossegesse, 'Journey to the Iberian God'.

17 Sabine's observations on Manuel Milho's story here are also pertinent: he argues that Manuel's incomplete storyline leads to debate among those who have previously merely been receptors of stories as to likely outcomes, thus leading to comprehension and active 'reading' of events rather than mere reception of the interpretation offered by others (see Sabine, pp. 100–1). Similarly, it could be argued that one of the most important lessons learned by Raimundo in the course of the novel, and one never learned by Saramago's Jesus, is that no story is ever guaranteed to have the ending which we might expect.

18 See Sabine, p. 296.

19 The allusion to Caeiro is to Poem V of his *O Guardador de Rebanhos* (reproduced in Galhoz, pp. 173–5, p. 173):

> Não acredito em Deus porque nunca o vi.
> Se ele quisesse que eu acreditasse nele,
> Sem dúvida que viria falar comigo
> E entraria pela minha porta dentro
> Dizendo-me 'Aqui estou'.

('I don't believe in God because I've never seen him./ If he wanted me to believe in him,/ Then surely he'd come and speak with me./ He would enter by the door/ Saying "Here I am!"'; the translation is from Zenith, pp. 49–51, p. 50.)

20 Jesus' words in Gethsemane are: 'O my Father, if this cup may not pass away from me, except I drink it, thy will be done' (Matthew 26:42), while Mary's words after the Annunciation are 'Behold the handmaid of the Lord; be it unto me according to thy word' (Luke 1:38).

21 The published translation does not attempt to repeat the allusion made to Pessoa's heteronyms in this passage.

22 See Sena, p. 39.

23 At the beginning of this excerpt, I have altered the translator's 'Let's be guided' to the more literal 'We are guided'.

24 See Sabine, p. 291.

25 See Sabine, p. 282. The choice of the name Ouroana for the heroine within Raimundo's fiction may be intended to recall the powerful figure of Oriana in the medieval Iberian epic *Amadís de Gaula*, as is hinted, but not explicitly stated, by Cerdeira da Silva; see her 'Mulheres e Revolução', p. 214.

26 See Sabine, p. 291; the emphasis here is mine.

27 See Sabine, p. 262.

28 Sabine views this story (and another one in the same collection, 'Centauro') as a satire on Salazarist nostalgia for empire; see Sabine, p. 232, n. 41. Such interpretations are, however, perhaps more tenable in the case of 'Centauro' than in that of 'Embargo', which I would view as being more akin to the dystopia developed in *Cegueira*; see my article 'Righting Wrongs', p. 102. The story itself is contained in *Objecto*, pp. 35–50.

29 See Schor, pp. 158–9.

30 This popular proverb is also used in *Memorial* and *Evangelho* with a clearly sexual connotation (see *Memorial*, p. 13, and *Evangelho*, p. 131). In the case of *Memorial*, this is a prime case of what Arnaut refers to as the mixing of oral and official registers in order to satirize the validity of the declarations made by those with power (see Arnaut, '*Memorial do Convento*', pp. 37–41).

31 The parallel suggested here between the respective love affairs of Mogueime–Ouroana and Raimundo–Maria Sara give further support to Sabine's comments (in relation to *Memorial*) that the old city walls of Lisbon may be viewed as having allowed the Moorish and Christian parts of the city to penetrate one another rather than keeping them apart; see Sabine, p. 104.

32 See Sabine, p. 272.

33 Cardoso Pires, 'A Charrua Entre os Corvos', in *Jogos de Azar*, pp. 7–12; the phrase quoted is from p. 9.

34 Quoted in Cristóbal, p. 58.

35 Baptista Bastos, pp. 50–1.

36 Reis, *Diálogos com José Saramago*, p. 78.

37 'Até mesmo George W. Bush está submetido aos desígnios do Grande Capital', interview with *Época* magazine, *http://revistaepoca.globo.com/Epoca/0,6993,EPT1061569–1666–2.00html* (website consulted on 24 November 2005).

38 Quoted in Arias, p. 118.

39 Such scepticism is repeated in the novelist's interview with Arias; see Arias, pp. 112–20.

40 See Eduardo Lourenço, pp. 58–9.

41 See Owen, 'Writing the Unfinished Revolution', in *Portuguese Women's Writing*, pp. 115–22.

42 See Lígia Silva, especially pp. 23–4.

43 See Baptista Bastos, pp. 47–8.

44 Reis, *Diálogos com José Saramago*, p. 78.

45 In an interview to coincide with the publication of *Cegueira*, Saramago declared: 'We get more and more blind, because we are increasingly unwilling to see. Basically, what this book tries to say is

precisely that all of us are blind in a rational sense' (Saramago, 'O escritor vidente', p. 16). On Saramago's disillusionment with the real achievements of the April Revolution in Portugal, see, for example, his 'O terceiro governo', originally published in *Extra* on 16 February 1978 and reproduced in his *Folhas Políticas*, pp. 79–81, where he writes of a 'coup against the Constitution' (p. 79) as part of a plan to induce Portugal into playing a bit part in an idealized social-democratic Europe (p. 80).

46 Sabine reaches similar conclusions regarding the significance of the *Passarola*; see Sabine, pp. 151 ff.

47 The most famous extant document by Gusmão on the subject is his initial request to D. João V for permission to work on the project, which promises spectacular results in terms of governance of the king's extensive domains and the potential advantages to be gained over foreign rivals, but it is vague on the details of how the ship would actually work. Wilhelm claims that there is also a longer document in the possession of the University of Coimbra which goes into some detail regarding the functioning of the machine, which appears to have been based on the same hot-air principle as that used later in the eighteenth century by the Montgolfier brothers in France; see Wilhelm, pp. 123–32. It is entirely credible, of course, that particularly in the early stages of his work Gusmão and the king should have wanted to keep the most essential information about it confidential. The advantage which this gives Saramago as a creative writer is that he is thus free to have his version of the *Passarola* powered by whatever means works best for the development of his novel. For further discussion of the historical figure of Bartolomeu Lourenço de Gusmão and the way in which Saramago develops him within his fiction, see Frier, 'Padre Bartolomeu Lourenço de Gusmão', pp. 56–68.

48 Saramago, 'A Facilidade de Ser Ibérico', pp. 37–8.

49 The protagonist of the novel written between these two works (*Ano*) remains essentially indecisive, neither joining the ships which sail out to sea from Lisbon harbour at the end of the text nor being crushed by the oppressive Salazar regime, choosing instead to head into the classical underworld of his own accord; in this sense he 'fica a ver navios' (a Portuguese expression, literally meaning 'being left to watch the ships' and corresponding approximately to the English idiom of 'missing the boat').

50 See Sabine, p. 228. Sabine enumerates some of the awkward territorial questions which the novel evades at pp. 227–8 (although the text can be regarded as functioning effectively in terms of its general impact, in spite of these omissions: total comprehensiveness, while desirable in terms of political correctness, might easily prove tedious).

51 See Saramago, 'A Península Ibérica', p. 6.

52 See Sabine, p. 242.

53 See Sabine, pp. 242–3.

54 In interviews given at the time of publication of *Jangada*, Saramago

was keen to stress that his concerns were as much cultural as political or economic in nature: on the one hand, he declares that 'it has still to be demonstrated that the European Community is our salvation [. . .], even from an economic perspective' (in 'Fantástico é apenas aquilo que não se sabe'), but in his interview with Jordi Costa, he sees the cultural needs of the Iberian nations as lying in their historical links with Latin America and Africa (see 'La isla ibérica', p. 57).

55 The actual lovemaking takes place on pp. 288–9. As they go to make love with Pedro, both Maria and Joana mysteriously announce that they are going to look for aprons, a symbol of settled domesticity; could this allusion be intended to signify the women's ironic refusal to accept a role as mere domestic providers with no desires of their own? Such an interpretation would fit in with Ferreira's interpretation of Lídia in *Ano* as a figure who subverts prevailing attitudes all the more profoundly by performing many of the roles traditionally associated with the subordinate female while in other areas of her life behaving in nothing like the manner expected of the purely domestic female; see Ferreira, pp. 230–1. Schor sees the significance of the lovemaking with Pedro as lying in the cultural expectation that non-Iberians might have in this situation that the betrayed partners would resort to honour killings (in the tradition of Spanish Golden Age drama) as a response to being cuckolded; the fact that they do not do so and, in fact, that harmony is restored to the group within a few pages of this episode demonstrates a greater capacity for generosity of spirit among Iberian males than such expectations would allow for; see Schor, p. 123.

56 The reference to pomegranates here might be seen as an allusion to the classical legend of Persephone, which attempts to account for the eternal cycle of the seasons; once again, therefore, the point is made implicitly that nothing in the relationship between Iberia and the rest of Europe should be regarded as fixed and permanent: cultural, economic and political relationships should be viewed as flexible, organic, and shifting arrangements open to constant review and development in changing circumstances.

57 See Sabine, p. 246.

58 See Sabine, p. 246. Schor suggests that Joaquim's stone recalls the one which the biblical David uses to kill Goliath (1 Samuel:49–50), reminding us that Goliath was a Philistine, presumably suggesting that this stone is a blow being struck against the purely economic and political structures of Europe. See Schor, pp. 113–4.

59 This tradition is represented by apocryphal images of the Virgin Mary weaving at the Annunciation; see, for example, a thirteenth-century image depicted in one of the windows of the Cathedral at Lyon (reproduced in an illustrative handout in connection with a guest lecture by Professor Alan Deyermond, 'Weaving the text: the *chansons de toile* and some analogues', given at the University of Leeds on 1 December 2004).

60 Homer, Book VIII, p. 106.

61 The story of Ulysses' return home dominates the last twelve books of

the *Odyssey*. Penelope's secret is revealed in Book XXIV (Homer, pp. 340–1), and the recognition of the lost king by his dog Argos may be found in Book XVII (Homer, pp. 249–50).

62 See Madruga, p. 75; she refers incorrectly to this event taking place on p. 169 of the text (the correct reference is to p. 168).

63 One notes here also, in the allusion to the potential for human misunderstanding of signs, an allusion to the classical trope of the wrong readings given to the statements of the Oracle at Delphi.

64 See Frier, 'Ascent and Consent', pp. 136–7.

65 Sabine, p. 204.

66 Sabine refers here to Unamuno's identification of Portugal with the unfortunate Inês de Castro (although both he and Unamuno appear to overlook the fact that the historical Inês was executed precisely because she was *not* Portuguese); see Sabine, pp. 235–6, and Unamuno, *Por tierras de Portugal y de España*, p. 10.

67 See Sabine, p. 236.

68 Sabine argues that Blimunda's killing of the Dominican friar towards the end of *Memorial* might be viewed as an assertion of her capacity to act like a male as well as a female; see Sabine, p. 160.

69 See Sabine, p. 254.

70 See Sabine, p. 254.

71 See Schor, p. 128. Schor's suggestion is supported by Saramago's own notebook on the composition of *Jangada* (donated to the Portuguese National Library), where he writes that he conceives of his characters as being like a new version of Adam and Eve, 'os primeiros da sua espécie' ('the first of their species'). See sheet 11 of the reproduction of this notebook at the end of Seixo (ed.); there are no page numbers given to this section of the journal.

72 'Every future is fabulous'; the quotation is at *Jangada*, p. 7 and *Raft*, flyleaf. The two epigraphs on the dust jacket of the novel describe the Iberian peninsula respectively as being shaped like an oxhide (a remark attributed to the Greek scholar of the first century BC Strabo) and like a raft (attributed to an anonymous Portuguese person); the sequence of these two quotations (the latter being invented by Saramago) debunks the slightly sneering tone of the external perspective and instead favours the view expressing confidence in autochthonous ability to shape the peninsula according to the needs of its own people, just as Maria Guavaira will be free to knit new garments with the wool from her sock, which is presumably more or less totally unravelled by the end of the novel. The edition of Strabo consulted (in Spanish) uses merely the word *piel* ('skin') to describe the shape of the peninsula; Portuguese translations may specify the animal used, or it could be that Saramago added the name of the animal to give ironic reinforcement to the primitive impression made by the quotation. This explanation would certainly fit with Schor's assertion that *Jangada* is intended in part to demonstrate that 'the contribution of Spain and Portugal to cultural history consists of more than bullfighting'; see Schor, p. 137. For the quotation from Strabo, see Strabo, p. 56 (section III, 1, 3).

73 Sabine has also stated (correctly) that a sense of Utopia is not inconsistent with a pessimistic perspective regarding the possibilities of realizing that Utopia (private e-mail correspondence, 2 February 2006).

74 The fall of Sancho's island is recounted in chapter LIII of the Second Part of *Don Quijote* (see Cervantes, II, pp. 959–64). The basic storyline of D. João's unusual grant to the nobleman is echoed almost exactly in Saramago's later short story *Conto*, with the only difference being that the island eventually discovered is not a physical place, but the love between the male protagonist and the cleaning lady.

75 Losada makes brief reference to this topic, referring (in the cases of *Ano, Memorial, Cegueira, Jangada* and *História*) to Saramago's creation of 'very powerful women, with no story told and no aura of sainthood around them' (Losada, p. 37). Saramago himself describes his attitude towards women as one of respect rather than veneration, and he explicitly rejects romantic notions such as those of the 'eternal feminine'; instead he stresses his own experience of women's goodwill which he sees as coexisting with an 'instintive critical sense' towards artificially constituted authority; see his interview with Berrini (Berrini, p. 240). Cerdeira da Silva also discusses the question of women in Saramago's work in her 'Mulheres e Revolução', viewing his presentation of them as filling a gap in representation of the potential strength of the female in Portuguese literature from the Middle Ages onwards, while Letizia gives an in-depth analysis of the rise of women specifically in *Levantado.*

76 Gramsci, pp. 7–8.

77 Gramsci, p. 9.

78 Gramsci, p. 9.

79 Gramsci, pp. 188–9.

80 See Gramsci, p. 153. Sabine (p. 72) also quotes precisely the same passage, but he does so specifically in relation to *Levantado.*

81 Ransome, p. 187; the emphases are Ransome's.

82 Ransome, p. 135; the italics are his.

83 Cirlot, p. 268.

84 See Reis' poem 'Sábio é o que se contenta com o espectáculo do mundo', in Galhoz (ed.), p. 211.

85 See the poem 'Vem sentar-te comigo, Lídia, à beira do rio', in Pessoa, *Selected Poems,* p. 146.

86 See Camões, *Os Lusíadas,* Canto V, stanza 60 (p. 206).

87 See Boaventura de Sousa Santos, 'State and Society in Portugal', in Kaufman and Klobucka (eds), pp. 31–72, at p. 34. These issues are also discussed by Sabine (pp. 181–2).

88 Garrett, p. 156.

89 Saramago himself quotes Garrett to this effect in his 'Situação do Romance Português', pp. 219–20; the allusion is to Garrett's *Portugal na Balança da Europa* of 1830. In general, Saramago is a great admirer of Garrett, parodying the title of his predecessor's famous *Viagens na Minha Terra* in his own *Viagem,* while also dedicating the work as a whole to him; see *Viagem,* p. 7.

90 Saramago, 'Situação do Romance Português', pp. 222–3.
91 Saramago, 'Situação do Romance Português', pp. 225–6.

Conclusion

Death, the Ultimate Injustice; Love, the Ultimate Triumph

1. *As Intermitências da Morte*: Skeletons and Moths[1]

There is no escaping the grim reality of death in Saramago's novels: the inevitable fact of human mortality recurs as a significant feature in almost all of his novels, even if its precise role within each text is sometimes a surprising one. Thus, *Todos* closes with the unassuming mortal, Sr José, apparently having brought the mysterious (dead) woman of his quest symbolically back to life, while, by contrast, the supposedly divine Jesus not only appears to die definitively on the cross in Saramago's reincarnation of him, but he actually refuses to carry out one of the most famous miracles for which his biblical namesake was known, the resurrection of Lazarus from the dead (*Evangelho*, p. 428). In general terms, the novelist leaves Juan Arias in no doubt as to the significance of the question of human mortality to him:

> It's all about the hard fact of death, that we all have to die and how that casts a certain light, or rather darkness, on the life which each one of us has. Everything is involved there: life, love, everything is summed up in that ending, and everything you may say or have done is directed towards that conclusion.[2]

It is not surprising, then, that at the age of eighty-two, in his most recent work, *Intermitências*, the writer should deal explicitly with the question of death and implicitly with the age-old human yearning for eternal life. As so often in his earlier work, Saramago has discovered a new and original perspective on this universal of human existence: there is no going back here on his earlier rejection of religious notions of an afterlife; equally, there is no cloyingly sentimental love interest to form an aesthetically dissatisfying *deus ex machina* and disguise the naked fact of death (the love-interest which does develop here is, in fact, a much more ambiguous and potentially disturbing one); nor does the dying protagonist stage a rebellious cry of resistance on his way down into the underworld, such as that voiced by Mozart and da Ponte's version of Don Giovanni. Instead his focus lies on the phenomenon of death as a surprise, and, through resorting to an ingenious rewriting and subversion of the medieval *topos* of the Dance of Death, Saramago succeeds in provoking a perspective at once strangely comforting and yet still bleakly resigned to the eventual extinction of the self.

In common with the other novel by the author which mentions death in its title (*Ano*), the work is given a circular structure by a verbal echo of its own opening line ('No dia seguinte ninguém morreu', 'On the next day nobody died'; *Intermitências*, p. 13) in its closure, which repeats exactly the same sentence (p. 214). And thus the cycle of the novel is completed, just as the cycle of life is completed by death in accordance with the familiar funeral formula of 'ashes to ashes, dust to dust', reminding the listener that the void from which we emerge is matched by the one to which we must all eventually move on.

However, as in other cases where such circular motifs appear in Saramago's work, this circularity is apparent rather than real, for, by the end of the text, the reader has travelled the road of observing the alarming practical results of a dearth of deaths, and, while the novel can do nothing to change the realities of human mortality itself, its imaginative journey leaves the reader torn between a sense of reassurance and the familiar fear of extinction. Once more, then, Saramago's fiction depicts a cross between the circular and the rectilinear understandings of time pondered by Sabine and Daniel,[3] offering the individual an opportunity for lasting presence on this earth, while the text simultaneously recognizes the necessity and the inevitability of personal passing.

The earlier chapters depict the mysterious scenario (again, a development typical of the author's creativity, where an impossible premise is accepted as a plausible and necessary point of departure for the rest of the narrative), whereby an unnamed country enters the new year with the discovery that nobody is dying within its boundaries. Again, as with previous 'fantastic' novels (such as *Jangada* and *Cegueira*), the consequences of this new reality are developed with some logical rigour: funeral agencies become preoccupied with their loss of earnings (*Intermitências*, p. 28); the government faces crises in terms of the provision of health care and nursing homes for an increasingly aged population (pp. 30 and 32 respectively); republican movements voice their concerns as the state is faced with having to provide eternal subsidies for a royal family which will not only continue to grow but which will cease to provide any remotely useful functions for the king's descendants (p. 88); and the leading religious groups have to redefine their roles in a society where, apparently, nobody ever goes to meet their maker (pp. 37–8).

In one sense, then, the positing of a society without death might be said to be a mechanism for Saramago to demonstrate what he views as the essential irrelevance to the real interests of humanity of traditional pillars of society such as religious bodies and the monarchy. For some time the novel is dominated by these issues, as those chapters which focus on national institutions merely repeat (although in less cynical mode than in *Lucidez*) a now familiar vision of official insensitivity, incompetence and hypocrisy in the face of the unexpected. In fact, the text briefly seems to become bogged down in speculation as to the criminal activities of an organization known as the 'máphia' (the unusual spelling is adopted deliberately; see p. 54) which arranges for the bodies of ailing relatives to be illegally transported over the country's borders to other countries where death has continued as normal, thus permitting an unusual practice of euthanasia (to which the government turns a blind eye), and which later turns to running protection rackets when death is restored (pp. 125–6). While there is a certain amount of black comedy in these sections and, of course, the author is justified in pointing out how human greed will always find a way to profit from any situation, these chapters contribute little of originality to contemporary moral and social debates regarding human control of mortality and serve rather merely to highlight the undesirability (for all concerned) of eternal life, at least in any conventional earthly sense. Even if this section of the novel could be somewhat shorter, the establishment of this perspective is, however, necessary for the successful functioning of the latter stages of the novel, which becomes one of the most haunting and yet unusual of the writer's love narratives, bearing comparison with the powerful love of Blimunda for Baltasar recounted in *Memorial*, as the narrative focus shifts from the general to the particular and to the fate of one man.[4]

The turning point in the text comes when it is established that death has not, in fact, been abolished in this country, but instead that it (or, more accurately, she) has been moving to a new set of practices, whereby the end of life is announced in irrevocable fashion to her victims precisely one week in advance of the intended date of death, by means of a letter mysteriously delivered to its recipient in a lilac-coloured envelope (p. 130).[5] The intention of this change in arrangements is to allow the victims time to put their affairs in order, to bid farewell to their loved ones, and to effect any reconciliation necessary with enemies made during the course of their lives (p. 131).

This new 'personalized' system of death may have the advantage of removing the factor of the unexpected and allowing satisfactory completion of life's business, but, as one can imagine, it achieves its stated goals only imperfectly (p. 132), and it merely stimulates a factor of immediate fear where none existed before (p. 131). The new procedures are then demonstrated to be as flawed as the more familiar ones when (for reasons unexplained in a literal reading of the text) the letter intended for one particular recipient (a cellist in an orchestra) is repeatedly returned to its sender (pp. 141, 146, 149 and 170). This introduces what is probably the most original development of the plot, in that instead of the rest of the novel focusing on the mortal making his way unwittingly towards an inexorable fate, the process of seduction of the cellist is largely focused through the consciousness of his seducer, death herself.[6] In many respects, therefore, *Intermitências* becomes the mirror image of *Todos*, which centres on Sr José's quest for his (deceased) beloved: here it is not any particular dead woman who is sought out by the man, but death herself who pursues the living.

Having set out to discover this unknowingly resistant victim, it is not long before death becomes fascinated with him and is sucked into increasingly sinister and bizarre conversations with him (pp. 204–6 and 211), all the while concocting a cunning trap to ensnare him after he completes his performance at a concert, effectively by making him desire her (a feeling to which he eventually confesses when he speaks to her in the park; p. 211).

There are signs even from the beginning of the execution of her schemes, however, that she is displaying some human weakness as soon as she has taken on human form: she scolds herself for her teasing of the people she encounters (pp. 194–5); she seems taken by her own appearance as an attractive woman in her mid-thirties (p. 189); at one point she is said to no longer know who she is (p. 207); and when she attends the cellist's concert she cannot help feeling some sympathy for her future victim (p. 197). In the end, therefore, it is not a total surprise that it is the supernatural figure of death who is as much seduced as seductress, and, unlike the classical example of the supremely aloof Zeus with Leda, she eventually becomes prey to that most human of weaknesses and falls in love with the cellist, repeatedly making love to him and then falling asleep with him in his bed. At this point the novel closes, and it is for this reason that 'No dia seguinte ninguém morreu' ('On the next day nobody died'; p. 214).

This quest, therefore, has some echoes of the increasingly tense climax to *Homem*, which also effectively recalls the Borgesian motif of the detective-cum-victim in the Argentinian writer's 'La muerte y la brújula'.[7] Nonetheless, the apparently conclusive ending to this unusual love story is hardly any more reassuring than the open endings of works such as *Jangada*, *História* or *Cegueira*. For, if the negative circumstances still lingering at the end of *Cegueira* are intended, in Brechtian fashion, to stimulate the reader to prevent their recurrence in the real world, then equally we are obliged to recognize that the apparently reassuring ending given to this work does absolutely nothing to dispel the prospect of demise awaiting Saramago's real-life public. Other questions also remain unresolved by this ending: for death's final action in the novel before falling asleep alongside the cellist is to get up from the bed where he remains asleep and to burn the letter which she had intended to leave for her lover (p. 214). Does her decision mean that she is not going to kill him after all? Or simply that he is going to die without warning, as happens in real life, so that she is merely sparing his feelings? Or could he be left sleeping forever, like a male version of Sleeping Beauty, in a vegetative existence without value? And does the fact that nobody dies on the following day imply that death has retired once more? If so, is there any reason to believe that the consequences of this will be any more positive than they were previously? Or is this just a temporary reprieve while she rests from making love and recovers her composure?

Saramago himself has declared that the final sentence of the novel is intended to indicate that the country concerned then goes back to the problematic lack of death outlined in the earlier chapters.[8] To the reader, however, this explanation of events seems to be only one of a number of possible interpretations of the text, just as earlier works such as *História*, *Jangada* and *Cegueira* also leave their respective stories tantalizingly incomplete: it could be argued, for example, that the formal repetition of the opening of the work at its close disguises a change in emphasis from the final two words of the sentence 'ninguém morreu' ('nobody died') when it first appears, to the opening three words 'No dia seguinte' ('On the next day') at the end of the text, thus indicating a merely temporary reprieve rather than one for the foreseeable future; and, even if death is once again desisting more generally from her duties, the text does make a point of insisting that she is merely one representative (responsible purely for human beings and not for plants and animals, and only within the country described) of the greater phenomenon of 'Morte' (with an upper-case initial) which could easily supplant her in her functions if she does not carry them out adequately (pp. 79 and 118). In spite of the author's remarks, therefore, it seems fair to view the closure of this novel as an open one which perhaps temptingly invites but on closer analysis actually resists all unequivocal readings.

What is clear in the structuring of events within the text, however, is the granting of a conscience to death: in a sense, Jesus' grounds in *Evangelho* for refusing to resurrect Lazarus have thus been changed from 'Ninguém na vida teve tantos pecados que mereça morrer duas vezes' (*Evangelho*, p. 428) ('No one has committed so many sins in life that they deserve to die twice'; *Gospel*, p. 328) to simply 'Ninguém merece morrer' ('No one deserves to die'). And the cellist's sexual encounter with death (his first such relationship for some considerable time and quite probably his last; see *Intermitências*, p. 206) may perhaps be seen as the compensatory reward from the grim reaper for the fate which she has the power to inflict on him and on all of us: as Unamuno observed, the sexual imperative may be viewed as an act of rebellion against the awareness of our own mortality.[9] This interpretation would be reinforced by her apparent granting to the cellist of the power to play better than Rostropovitch when he gives her a private concert of a Bach cello suite (p. 213),[10] as an additional consolation to him before his death. Equally, however, this moment sees a subtle subversion of the idea of the Dance of Death, as on this occasion it is not, as in medieval tradition, the figure of death who plays music to lead humans to their doom, but the human whose almost divine playing distracts death from her duties.

Seen at a superficial level (whereby death appears to have been abolished, at least for this man), then, this is a comforting 'Happy ever after' ending which most of us would welcome as individuals, but which, if applied universally, would merely lead to chaos and misery as awful as that depicted in *Cegueira.* Earlier in the text, it is suggested (p. 181) that, rather than dressing up as a woman, death perhaps would be better represented as a particular type of moth (Latin name *acherontia atropos* or, in English, the death's head hawkmoth[11]), whose colouring and patterns feature a perfect representation of a bare human skull on the insect's head. This would be particularly appropriate since the cellist has some interest in entomology, and death observes him looking at an illustration of this particular type of moth (p. 180). Nonetheless, regardless of her physical disguise her threat remains undiminished for, even as she dons clothes and human skin for her secret mission, the text does not hesitate to remind the reader that 'não há nada no mundo mais nu que um esqueleto' ('there is nothing in the world more naked than a skeleton'; p. 152): as Baroque religious iconography reveals, all the beauty in the world cannot disguise the ultimate truth of our own extinction, and the scenes of lovemaking in the final chapter between death and the musician do nothing to dispel her grim potential. The triumph (if it is such) achieved by the cellist over death through his music here, then, amounts more to a symbolic than actual victory, as it reflects the capacity of even this humdrum and modest individual to make positive and meaningful transformations to his life through the force of love.

The association made here of eroticism with death in the form of the human skeleton is not, however, unique to this work in Saramago's oeuvre: in the scene in *Ano* where Ricardo Reis discusses with Fernando Pessoa his earlier confrontation with a figure of death during the carnival celebrations, his deceased creator tells him that, since he is already dead, he 'detesta a nudez absoluta que o esqueleto é' (*Ano*, p. 182) ('abhors the absolute nakedness of his skeletal form'; *Year*, p. 154). The physical intimacy which the cellist shares with death would then appear to be most likely merely the prelude to a death not foretold, a death of the type which occurs to almost all of us in real life, and which is perhaps the most blessed ending to our days after all. There is no specific evidence to indicate that the cellist will be spared death: instead death effectively allows a reprieve for a humble and solitary man, permitting him to live his final days on earth rather than merely to exist in them: his anguish over his attraction to her (which he himself describes as being ridiculous; *Intermitências*, p. 202) at least would allow him to declare, in common with Pessoa's Álvaro de Campos that:

> Só as criaturas que nunca escreveram
> Cartas de amor
> É que são
> Ridículas.
>
> ['Only those who've never written/ Love letters/ Are/ Ridiculous'.][12]

Even if the cellist must die, then, he has at least learned to live first, and effectively both death and we as readers have learned that the model of death which we all recognize (as something which we know will happen to us all, even if we know not when or how) is, indeed, the best one available in an imperfect world.

The use of the image of the moth as a possible representation of death is a pertinent one in the sense that moths are not only short-lived, but, as the text reminds us (see p. 78), they, in common with all non-human life, are unaware of their own mortality. One is thus reminded of the roses of Adonis, whom Pessoa's Ricardo Reis envies in a famous poem about death, as they have the benefit of never seeing the darkness (although this particular moth is said in the text only to appear at night; p. 180):[13] if, as Reis would have it, we could serenely spend our lives unaware even of the fact of our own mortality, then our lives would be much more content. Such an incarnation of death would offer considerable relief, but, once analysed more deeply, it becomes apparent that if the resolution of the plot by the total abolition of death would be unsustainable at a collective level, then at an individual level even the removal of the awareness of mortality would be of only superficial benefit: for Saramago's own vision of Ricardo Reis, with his pursuit of stress-free, moderated pleasures, is one of a life hardly worth living at all.

2. Ricardo Reis and the Stasis of True Death

The concept of death in Saramago means more than simply not being alive in a biological sense: in *Cegueira*, for example, the doctor's wife justifies her act of killing the ringleader of the hoodlums effectively holding the whole asylum to ransom on the grounds that killing is not only legitimate, but actually necessary 'Quando já está morto o que ainda é vivo' (*Cegueira*, p. 189) ('When what is still alive is already dead'; *Blindness*, p. 183), that is, when the perpetrator of evil has sunk so low as to no longer be capable of any kind of genuine human interaction with others. This man and his comrades have, after all, insisted that they will only release the food supplies which they have commandeered in return for the sexual services of the women around them. In contrast, she also recognizes the vestiges of human feeling which remain in those around her, thus, for example, 'forgiving' her husband for seeking some brief sexual fulfilment with the girl with the dark glasses in her presence, but in an environment which she recognizes as offering virtually nothing else to make life worthwhile (p. 171); her willingness to let this act of infidelity pass without further comment thus forms part of her general programme in the latter part of the novel for bringing the human out again in the lives of the rest of her immediate companions, and this generosity of spirit is eventually rewarded with the tentative prospect of the recovery of eyesight at the end of the novel, a 'reward' in which she shares, in that she is not blinded when the others recover their sight, as she has feared may happen (p. 310).

Equally, however, the concept of what constitutes life is frequently one which plays with our expectations: the uninhibited lovemaking of Baltasar and Blimunda in *Memorial* contrasts with the uninspiring and purely functional sexual rituals of a royal couple who are unable to bear a son, prompting existential fears in the powerful king (*Memorial*, p. 290); God's litany of martyred saints to Jesus on the boat in *Evangelho* (a presentation which makes no mention of their achieving the eternal life promised to them by the canonical Gospels) forms a contrast with Blimunda's sympathy for the silent saints as she presents them as being condemned to a form of sainthood which she sees as comparable only to damnation in *Memorial* (p. 330); the deferential attitude of Marçal's parents towards the Centre in *A Caverna* effectively casts them in the role of submitting to the quasi-mechanical processing of all human existence within its walls (*Caverna*, p. 117); while in the earlier chapters of *Intermitências*, those who have been spared death but who have passed the age at which they would otherwise have been expected to die effectively survive only in a vegetable-like existence of little use either to them or their loved ones (*Intermitências*, p. 30).

However, no major figure in Saramago's fiction is less alive in any meaningful sense than his version of Pessoa's Ricardo Reis: he is repeatedly given the opportunity to reject his status as heteronym and come to life as a rounded human being, but time after time he rejects this option. When the novel opens with Reis returning to his native continent and his homeland in late 1935, he finds them in a state of considerable flux and instability, with ideological differences at home reflecting the uncertainties of a burgeoning conflict in neighbouring Spain.[14] Instability and flux, of course, are qualities inimical to Pessoa's patrician heteronym Reis, whose poetry sees the poet's calling as one of giving voice to eternal truths in an environment of tranquility, regardless of whatever clamour may be intruding from outside, with the observer being a passive figure who absorbs impressions only to record them as he waits for his own death.

Since he was so fond of stability and passivity, it is no wonder, then, that Saramago's Reis is so fascinated by the statues of the capital, which, on the surface at least, embody the unchanging glory of the nation, recalling as they do the period of the Discoveries (Adamastor and Camões), prominent figures of the country's history (D. Sebastião), or previous cultural geniuses of the nation (Camões again, and Eça de Queirós). The real problem with Reis' admiration, however, is that, as Sapega suggests, statues of the great and the good (whatever their origins) tend to become simply part of the familiar landscape, so that the everyday simple glance at a statue belies the depths of the reality behind each one (just as Reis appears oblivious to the real personal qualities possessed by his lover, Lídia).[15]

Unfortunately for Reis, however, the past in *Ano* obstinately refuses to stay still, even in terms of its monumental representation. Thus, viewed with any degree of objectivity, D. Sebastião's status as a national hero is at best an ambivalent one; and, Eça de Queirós, by the nature of his ferocious critique of the nation's nineteenth-century malaise, would have to be viewed as a problematic figure in terms of representing a period of national achievement. Meanwhile Camões, as depicted elsewhere by Saramago in *Livro,* is far from the unproblematic, uncritical and quietist icon of national culture which the naive brush of Salazar's cultural policy would have had him appear. Moreover as Sabine points out, disconcertingly, to Reis' eye at least, these statues are far from static objects, as some sort of action is attributed to all of them, save ironically that of the supposedly undead king D. Sebastião.[16] Are events such as these mere hallucinations, or do they perhaps illustrate Saramago's argument in the *Cadernos* that the past is always with us?

> For me, philosophically speaking, there is no present. Only time past can be *recognized*: time, even as it *comes*, precisely because it *goes* and does not stand still, does not remain present. So, for me as a writer, my job is not about 'recovering' the past, and even less about turning it into a lesson for the present. The time we have lived appears to us built into our understanding, both complete and yet continually growing. We are the indisputable result of that time as it builds up, and not of a present which can never be identified.[17]

A major part of Reis' problem on his return to Lisbon could be said to be symptomatic of a general malaise of the early twentieth-century intellectual in the period following the First World War, a crisis felt by intellectuals in many countries, who saw the Great War as some kind of cultural watershed, after which the intellectual aristocrat could never be quite the same again: this certainly applies to varying degrees to figures such as the early Thomas Mann in Germany, or in Britain Virginia Woolf (who decried the vulgarity of James Joyce's *Ulysses*[18]). Inclusion in this company therefore makes Reis less than unique (but no less static, for all that), even if the pain which he feels in general terms here is slightly more specifically akin to that experienced by another Pessoan heteronym, Álvaro de Campos, in his 'Lisbon Revisited (1926)':

> Outra vez te revejo,
> Cidade da minha infância pavorosamente perdida . . .
> [. . .] Eu? Mas sou eu o mesmo que aqui vivi, e aqui voltei [. . .]?

> Outra vez te revejo – Lisboa e Tejo e tudo –,
> Transeunte inútil de ti e de mim,
> Estrangeiro como em toda a parte, [. . .]
>
> [I see you once more,/ City of my childhood now frighteningly lost. . . / [. . .] *I* do? But am I the same one who lived here, and came back [. . .]?/ I see you once more – Lisbon and Tagus and all –,/ A pointless passer-by to you and to me,/ As much a foreigner here as anywhere, [. . .]][19]

So, too, Reis is afflicted by doubts as to why he has chosen to return to his homeland, spending much of the earlier part of the text wandering the streets of Lisbon in a seemingly aimless fashion, as if already dead: at one point he compares his return to Lisbon to an elephant seeking its graveyard (*Ano*, p. 132), while later he is said to be merely in transit, with his life in suspension, when he arrives at his hotel (p. 22). His initial choice of hotel, whose name recalls that of the deposed royal house of Bragança, is entirely appropriate for a man of his monarchist leanings, but it is also an indication of an unwillingness to let go of the past, and this choice proves to be merely a revelation of the decline suffered by the city in his absence, for this hotel (also favoured by an earlier fictional dilettante doctor, Eça's Carlos de Maia) proves to be somewhat less elegant in its surroundings in the 1930s than it had been for his predecessor in the 1880s.[20]

And so before long he decides to move out to private accommodation, taking care to avoid the cheap new housing for the growing city throngs in peripheral areas, 'lá para a Rua dos Heróis de Quionga, à Moraes Soares' (p. 201) ('near the Rua dos Heróis de Quionga, in Moraes Soares'; p. 172). Perhaps he feels a need for a greater sense of fulfilment than he can attain in the Hotel Bragança, but his decision to move out is probably also partly motivated by fear of the discovery of his relationship with Lídia and embarrassment at being called in for questioning by the secret police. At least his sexual relationship is not an incestuous one (as Carlos de Maia is), but it should be regarded as a promiscuous one, as it does involve compromise with the burgeoning proletarian masses. In fact, the love affair of which Reis actually dreams (and which remains unfulfilled) is a symbolically incestuous one (with his social equal, the uninspiring Marcenda), but, as may also happen within a restricted gene pool, there is no sign of life emerging from this potential union, either in terms of any realization of their love (the closest they come to this is a snatched kiss, after which Marcenda appears to flee from the possibility of involvement with Reis; see p. 292) or in terms of the children which they might have: for Reis' fears of his own impotence (p. 292) are matched by her withered hand.

It is not the novel, however, which decries a new age of mindless mass culture in which the sensitive intellectual no longer finds he has a place, but merely the character. Reis is an aesthete out of place on his return to Lisbon (as is illustrated by his eventual departure from life at the end of the text) but here there is no trace of the artistic self-laceration or emotional narcissism which drove Mário de Sá-Carneiro to an early suicide. And in other novels, more perhaps than this one, Saramago does not hesitate to make use of popular culture when appropriate: *Jangada* for example, contains allusions to Hitchcock's *The Birds* (*Jangada*, p. 66) and the television series *Lassie* (p. 154),[21] while other works (such as the short story 'Cadeira' in *Objecto*) strategically mingle high culture with popular culture in order to achieve their effects, in accordance with Bakhtin's recognition of the novelistic power obtained by combining the popular 'world of the ditty' with 'the world of the Schillerean dithyramb'.[22]

Reis suffers in a number of respects in this novel: in his social humiliation, as outlined above; as he is torn between two women; as he is threatened by the mysterious figure of Death at carnival time (*Ano*, p. 164); or as he goes through the awkward embarrassment of trying not to reveal his feelings for either of the women in his life in public. And to a limited extent he is a victim, as for example when he is called to account for his behaviour and even his very presence in Lisbon by the PVDE, an event which his unsuspicious nature finds simply puzzling (pp. 171–2). But in this novel, written some fifty years after the events recounted, Saramago's prime interest does not lie in analysing the finer feelings of a sensitive poet. If Reis is a victim, then like at least some of the characters in the later *Cegueira*, he is as much prey to his own myopia as to any external conspiracy. This is not, therefore, a novel which indulges the finer feelings of the lonely aesthete: even in the case of *Manual*, which does explicitly investigate the genesis of artistic creativity, the narrator H. is eventually forced into the realization that he can neither afford nor be afforded the type of solitary creative space which he might ideally desire.

Here, therefore, we do find something of the pain of the intellectual, but this is counterbalanced by other events: even if Reis' reading of the news fails to differentiate between the significance of Bovril adverts (p. 263) on the one hand and that of political activists gearing up their visible activity on the streets of Lisbon (p. 264), then at least the reader (as so often in Saramago's fiction, with the benefit of a historical hindsight denied to the participants in history) is able to see what is really significant among the various snippets which catch the attention of this particular poet in his perusal of the Portuguese press. Thus, his preoccupation with the death of King George V of Britain sits innocently alongside a cosy acceptance of German assurances of peaceful intentions within Europe (p. 146). His implicit equation in significance of these two events is intended to communicate to the reader the importance of sorting out the wheat from the chaff in our own times: for the death of a monarch (itself perhaps a warning of the imminent demise of the monarchist, who will follow him at the end of the text) changes nothing in terms of functions performed in the world, as the text itself reminds the reader of the unchanging nature of British foreign policy in relation to Portugal on the same page, but the evident dishonesty of German declarations of best intent are quite clearly negated by their own troop movements at the time, an omen apparently dismissed by Reis (through a totally inappropriate comparison to the classical myth of Zeus appearing to Juno in the form of a cloud) with a vain (and utterly unrealistic) expression of trust in others: 'querendo Deus, tudo acabará na bela harmonia' (p. 146) ('God permitting, that all will end in perfect harmony'; p. 121).

Reis' distaste for the world is based on the assumption that it is not worthwhile trying to change the inadequate reality which he observes for a better one: he meekly surrenders to the mediocrity surrounding him and even gives in to some extent to the new rules by which the mass population of his native country now live. Only very late in the novel with the death of Daniel, however, does he appear to give up on his own presumption of being set apart from the common horde; in effect, Reis attempts to fossilize himself and others in a static, unequal, and idealized Portugal which perhaps could be said to have existed in the past of Carlos de Maia, for whom only the bourgeoisie were even visible, but which was no longer sustainable in a world where political movements of all ideological backgrounds were seeking to mobilize even the poorest sections of society in favour of their respective interests.

The logical problem with the intellectual's sense of superiority to the masses, however, as Carey points out, lies in the fact that the very concept of 'the masses' is at best a useful abstraction rather than a part of objective reality and effectively, therefore, in Bakhtinian terms, an avoidance of that productive bustle which allows for the renewing effect of carnival:

> What this intellectual effort failed to acknowledge was that the masses do not exist. The mass, that is to say, is a metaphor for the unknowable and invisible. We cannot see the mass. Crowds can be seen; but the mass is the crowd in its metaphysical aspect – the sum of all possible crowds – and that can take on conceptual form only as metaphor. The metaphor of the mass serves the purposes of individual self-assertion because it turns other people into a conglomerate. It denies them the individuality which we ascribe to ourselves and to people we know.[23]

So it is with Reis: Lídia, initially at least, is seen by him as one of the lower orders, the embodiment of a threat to his dominant position; the carnival procession (with all its Bakhtinian associations with social topsy-turviness) strikes him as a tawdry excuse for cheap alcoholic and sexual self-indulgence (pp. 159–61) and culminates, after the minor indignity of his hat being knocked off his head by revellers (p. 161), in the more sinister threat made to him by the figure of Death (p. 164); later in the novel his fellow-travellers on the train to Fátima exist in his mind primarily as an invading army preparing to occupy his carefully segregated seat in first class (pp. 306–7), and then, once arrived at the holy site, he sees only commercialism (p. 317) and superstition (pp. 318–9), and, perhaps most humiliatingly, he finds himself, like the biblical Joseph and Mary, unable to find a hotel room and forced to accept the humblest hospitality available, sleeping scruffily in a tent where others snore and have sex around him (p. 320). What we should not forget, though, is that all of these activities are signs of life which contrast with his own death-in-life.

However, Reis himself is above neither alcoholic stimulation (we read frequently of his solitary glasses of wine) nor above the sexual satisfactions provided to him by a woman who knows that he does not see her as his equal (pp. 200 and 252–3), nor indeed is his superior intellect any more immune to the enticements of advertising copywriters than his plebeian compatriots are to the religious trinkets on display at Fátima: we see him fascinated, amongst other things, by publicity for Bovril, bust enhancers (p. 242) and Freire's engravers (pp. 88–9), the latter an advertisement whose complexity is compared both to a spider's web (p. 89) and to Achilles' shield in *The Iliad* (pp. 88–9), thus permitting the narrator to remind us of the vulnerability and mortality of this great hero (p. 89) and thus also of Reis himself.[24] What is perhaps most sinister about the impact which this advertisement has on Reis, though, is once again his willingness to read names, said elsewhere to be those 'curiosas palavras [. . .] as mais vazias de todas se não lhes metermos dentro um ser humano' (*Ano*, p. 377) ('the emptiest words of all unless we put human beings inside them'; p. 325), in the light of classical paradigms rather than as mere markers of convenience and convention to identify something as complex as another human being: for he surely at some level makes a subconscious association between the woman who will be his lover (Lídia) and Ovid's Arachne (from the classical kingdom of Lydia), who was punished for her arrogance in trying to compete with the goddess Palas by being transformed into a spider.[25] If we view Marcenda as the fictional equivalent of Palas, then her tantalizing (but ultimately fruitless) role in Reis' life gives him his appropriate punishment for scorning the lover who could, in fact, offer him so much more than her: for one of the kings of Lydia was Tantalus, punished in Hell by forever seeing and hungering for the grapes which he could not reach with his hands. Reis' dream of a union with Marcenda will, then, remain forever a dream, while he will have to recognize that in the twentieth century he can no longer be the ruler of Lydia/Lídia.

Schor is therefore probably correct in evoking Freud's association of *eros* (the sexual instinct) with *thanatos* (the awareness of death) in association with Reis:[26] the very same sexual instinct which draws him towards Lídia and offers him the prospect of life is what he chooses instead to see as an indicator of his own death. There can be no doubt that Lídia poses a threat to his social class and station, but he fails to see that this is to be distinguished from a threat to him as a person. In fact, however, if he is thinking of Ovid here, then once again his reading of his very own classical models is faulty, for he fails to notice that, in her transgressive and iconoclastic act of weaving (an action which, of course, recalls the positive figure of Maria Guavaira in *Jangada*), what Arachne depicts is 'the tricking by a bull's guise of Europa'.[27] In doing so, of course, she lays bare the secret which the gods (so dear to Reis) would have concealed, and this presumption leads to her punishment, leaving the reader with the disturbing moral that the illusions fostered by the powerful are not to be questioned by mere mortals. In 1936, the bull of fascism does not deceive the classical maiden Europa but the modern continent of Europe into identifying the threat of death with its ideological rival (communism) instead of seeing it hidden inside the superficially appealing disguise cast over the bull, with the resulting slaughter of thousands which Lídia decries in the bullring in Badajoz (p. 391).[28] Her punishment is not to be transformed into a spider, but merely to have her lover abandon her and their child to an uncertain fate.

When we look at Reis in relation to others as individuals, he enters into some degree of intimacy with three other people: while in professional terms Carey's analysis would have to include Reis' deceased creator Fernando Pessoa among the ranks of 'clerks, shopgirls, hairdressers' despised by the true snob (represented to Carey in this case by Graham Greene[29]) there can be no doubt that he does qualify as Reis' intellectual equal. The two women are perhaps more significant figures, though: Marcenda, the passive upper middle-class girl from conservative Coimbra, who will do nothing to go against her father's wishes, and more importantly, Lídia, who in this novel serves to show that the masses may have represented vulgar hordes for writers such as Huxley and E. M. Forster but that she can be as much an individual as Ricardo Reis or any of her social superiors.[30] It is this individuation of the ordinary or working-class character which ultimately separates Saramago from his ultra-aesthetic predecessors. Characters such as the Sr José of *Todos* and the various protagonists of *Cegueira* belong to the era of James Kelman rather than to that of T. S. Eliot: figures such as Lídia show that they can be ordinary people and capable of an inner life just as much as any members of a cultured elite.

Indeed Lídia points a possible way out of Reis' confused state of mind, existentially as well as politically. Not only does she become a credible character: she is nobody's fool (she is well aware of her lover's preference for Marcenda; p. 304), but also, and perhaps most significantly in the current context, she is prepared by her efforts to lift his new flat out of its dark and depressing squalor and turn it into a cheerful place to live (pp. 251–4). In other words, she is prepared to give Reis something that is characteristic of him as an individual and thus 'save' him from the lower middle-class mediocrity into which he fears he will be irrevocably sunk. His symbolic failure to follow Lídia's brother out to sea at the end of the novel (towards the 'Mar Aberto', or open sea, which was the working title for *Jangada* even after the publication of *Ano*[31]) thus constitutes a rejection of the potentially fruitful mingling of social classes and creation of dialogue between them which could have spared Portugal forty more years of social confrontation and misery under the New State.

This is the example which Reis will not follow, and, unlike the protagonist of *Conto,* his faint heart is not prepared to win the fair lady. His no-risk strategy leads only to his own sense of a lack of fulfilment in life: the traditions of the past (which Reis appears to wish to venerate and embody) mean in a Portuguese context the era of Vasco da Gama, but just as (within the novel) his creator, Pessoa, feels some (Bloomian) envy and anxiety towards his great poetic predecessor, Camões (pp. 351–2), so Reis blithely skips over this period of adventurous expansion, going back to an era now long dead, that of the classical gods in whom nobody no longer has any faith and whom even Camões openly acknowledged to be merely a literary device when writing over three hundred years before Reis' supposed sojourn in Lisbon.[32]

The major difference between Reis and the great sailors of Portuguese tradition is that the latter were able and willing to make their own way in the world, which he is not; as Cirlot writes, ironically first quoting the classical Pompey the Great:

> 'Living is not necessary, but navigation is.' By this he meant that existence is split up into two fundamental structures: living, which he understood as living for or in oneself, and sailing or navigation, by which he understood living in order to transcend.[33]

Reis fundamentally fails to make the transition from the former state to the latter: neither the travellers at the end of *Jangada* nor Reis know where their life's journey will take them, but the difference is that whereas Reis rejects the chance to take control of his own life, the surviving protagonists of the later novel at least have the opportunity to steer their own stone raft from now on. When they go to the same Hotel Bragança where he once stayed, the narrator speculates that even if the registration book from his time still exists, his record may have been erased by the passage of time (*Jangada*, p. 112), a process which is already seen to be underway when he can no longer read Herbert Quain's book on the last page of this text (*Ano*, p. 415).

Both of these novels close with the prospect of children being born from unions conceived during the course of the text; by the close of *Jangada*, it is still not clear whether José and Joaquim will be prepared to rise to the challenges of fatherhood, but Lídia's child will certainly be hers alone and denied the fruitful mixture of class and intellectual perspectives offered by having his/her biological father as well as a mother. Reis, whose only productive role in society is as a part-time doctor, somebody whose profession necessarily involves dealing with bodily fluids, ailments and odours, cannot bear the experience of being exposed to these gross corporeal realities, to the point that he attempts to avert perceiving these indicators of continuing human existence, as, for example in his accidental mingling with the crowds seeking charitable donations in the Rua do Século early in the novel, where he is appalled by the smell of the crowd (p. 69). Instead, Reis prefers to think of himself as being akin to a cloud, so that maybe his horror of his own bodily fluids leads him to effectively disown his own child and to present himself as alien from the material world which he so despises but which offers him the only context in which he could be genuinely said to be alive.

It is no surprise, therefore, that Reis should be almost oblivious to the existence of the lower classes: the society in which he has chosen to move has left them not only marginalized but almost invisible, with the dominant rhetoric of society acknowledging their existence only in the form of an undifferentiated mass, available for mobilization when it suits military leaders such as Mussolini (whose campaigns in Abyssinia are alluded to in a memorable appropriation of the poem by Pessoa's version of Reis, 'Ouvi contar que outrora na Pérsia'; pp. 300–2). Saramago's Reis thus prefers the safety of dry land, from the heights of the Calçada dos Caetanos (p. 70) to the potential uncertainties of the waters which he experienced on board the *Highland Brigade* on his return from Brazil.

Interestingly, elsewhere Saramago writes again of the relationship between present, past and future, and this time he uses the image of water to illustrate his point:

> I must admit that I have had some problems in understanding the reluctance of many people to accept that fundamentally they are their own past. They may be willing to accept this as individuals, albeit rather reluctantly, because to varying degrees they recognise that they are intimately connected to and inseparable from their past, but collectively they act as if at any given moment they were merely living the present time which each fleeting moment is, and as if the past consisted of a series of unconnected moments, each of them simply its own present time, beginning and ending in itself. In fact, we move forwards in time like an advancing flood: the water is followed by more water, that is why it moves, and that is what makes it move.[34]

Continuing with the water analogy, then, we can say that the advance of a flood is not fully predictable: there is some room for channelling the waters in a particular direction with forethought and advance preparation, and perhaps some random variation may be expected, even if the overall pattern of development may be a predictable one. The question, then, is how to ride the waves to best effect. Even the enigmatic *Todos* ends with some sort of reward for the initially mediocre Sr José, who discovers within himself some existential authenticity, some willingness to achieve more than what appears to be his lot, and whose own newly discovered sense of purpose in life is directly compared to that of a sea captain in search of an unknown island (*Todos,* p. 48). Similar imagery is also used in relation to Reis when Marcenda writes to him to tell him that she would prefer not to meet him again:

> Um homem recebe uma carta de prego ao largar do porto, abre-a no meio do oceano, só água e céu, e a tábua onde assenta os pés, e o que alguém escreveu na carta é que daí para diante não haverá mais portos aonde possa recolher-se, nem terras desconhecidas a encontrar, nem outro destino que o do Holandês Voador, não mais que navegar, içar e arrear as velas, dar à bomba, remendar e pontear, raspar a ferrugem, esperar (*Ano,* p. 296).

> [A man receives a sealed letter as his ship leaves port, and opens it in mid-ocean. There is nothing except sea and sky and the deck on which he is standing, and the letter says that from now on there will

> be no more ports of refuge for him, no more uncharted lands to discover, no destination, nothing left for him but to navigate like the Flying Dutchman, hoist and furl the sails, man the pump, mend and sew, scrape away the rust, and wait.] (*Year*, p. 254)

In spite of the use of the word 'navegar' here, the only option which Reis sees as still being open to him here comes closer to Pompey's sense of merely living, in that he merely drifts through the rest of his days on earth. Essentially, this means that the dilemma for Reis is that by the end of the novel he realizes that he can no longer be different from his proletarian compatriots in any essentialist sense, but equally he cannot bring himself to be the same as the vulgar hordes whom his aristocratic breeding has always taught him to scorn. He is willing, therefore, to travel on Marcenda's ship but not on Lídia's, which would require him to accept the humiliations imposed on him by a world transformed by its mass population. His entire life has been spent in simply being and not in doing; now, however, with Lisbon feeling the increasing closeness of events in Spain, he finds that, by contrast with the Persians in his famous ode, he can no longer sit back undistracted by the affairs of the world and concentrate on his private game of chess.

Feeling that by right he ought to be distinguished by what he is (a cultured aristocrat), he is forced to recognize instead that in his century of the common man and woman, he can achieve distinction only by action, which is alien to him. The time for choices has therefore come (at a political level, between participative democracy and monologic dictatorship, and, at an individual level, between negotiating coexistence with others and a life of splendid isolation), but Reis' problem is that the choice which he would rather make would be not to have to cope with the constraints of a mass urban society at all. That, however, is what the tides of history have created, and so, instead of suffering along with Lídia, who implicitly invites him to be his fellow traveller and whom he quite consciously abandons in her hour of greatest need (p. 415), he chooses instead to accompany Pessoa to the timeless (and appropriately named) cemetery of the Prazeres (in English, 'pleasures'), a setting more suited to this enjoyer of all things in moderation.

Reis' failing, therefore, is that while he cannot escape the massification of modern society, he misreads this as meaning the inevitable loss of the individual merit which he has to offer. Sadly, in spite of the promptings offered to him by Lídia and (the now deceased) Pessoa, he never makes that individuality evident to anyone else. Unlike the mysterious dead woman pursued by Sr. José in *Todos*, there appears to be nothing within him that can be extracted in order to exert a positive influence over the land of the living: he exercises the degree of choice which he does possess in trivial matters such as deciding where to have lunch or how best to engage in the vain pursuit of Marcenda, rather than engaging in the much more meaningful game of political chess going on around him in 1936.[35] Instead he, as an intellectual, who has the potential to be the king on the board ('Reis'), simply retires from the game and concedes victory to forces which offer the spectacle of being insurmountable: if death in *Intermitências* engages in a Bergman-type game of chess with her human victims (see *Intermitências*, p. 171), then Reis is all too willingly her partner. This is therefore an existential failure towards the self and a political failure towards his own country in equal measure.

3. Oh Death, Where is thy Sting?[36]

In view of Saramago's avowed atheism and the fact that the majority of the Portuguese population appear to be reasonably happy with the state of their country (certainly in comparison with the political climate which preceded the present one), one is tempted to wonder why this writer should disagree fundamentally with his own Ricardo Reis at all. After all, if death is inevitable and there is nothing to follow it, why disturb a reality in the here and now which appears to be at least a tolerably pleasant one? Thus, one could not fault Saramago logically if he were to follow the attitude expressed by Pessoa's Reis as he writes 'Não sei se é amor que tens, ou amor que finges,/ O que me dás. Dás-mo. Tanto me basta' ('I don't know if the love you give is love you have/ Or love you feign. You give it to me. Let that suffice').[37]

The reality, however, is that while real life may be pleasantly rewarding for an octogenarian novelist who has achieved commercial success, international acclaim and a lifestyle unimaginable for those who lived with him as a child in the village of Azinhaga in the Beira Interior of Portugal in the 1920s, for many others life is much more difficult: quite apart from the unpredictable ravages dealt to humanity by earthquakes, tsunamis, and other horsemen of the apocalypse of our own times, huge proportions of the world's population continue to suffer from underlying problems of poverty, poor healthcare provision, economic exploitation and underdevelopment, illiteracy, pollution, and corrupt government (and it should not be taken for granted that these negative conditions exist only in the so-called Third World). While global institutions and the governments of the privileged countries of Europe and North America have taken some actions to address such issues, their real effectiveness in resolving the challenges posed is debatable, especially (to a person of Saramago's political orientation) when the solutions recommended are too often developed from within the intellectual parameters of the same system which has contributed to the growth of the problems in the first place.

Seen in this light, the maintenance of a Reisian serenity cannot be regarded as anything other than an affront to the rest of the world, and, as has been observed in the preceding section, it cannot be said to be of much benefit to the poet himself either, who discovers his own need for real engagement with the other only when it is too late, when Daniel has been killed by Salazar's troops and Lídia has apparently given up on Reis as a lost cause. As Huici suggests, then, there is a deep-rooted recognition (owing much to Sartre) within Saramago's writing that the meaning of life can only be found in a functional coexistence with the outside world:[38] for all of Reis' elegant words, they become as dead as his classical gods if they do not place him into a systematic and ongoing relationship with a Lídia, who clearly sees herself as more than the silent woman to whom he addresses his poetry.

Love thus becomes central to the functioning of almost all of Saramago's work: most often this is expressed in the traditional sense of an adult relationship between a man and a woman (in *Manual, Memorial, Ano, Jangada, História, Evangelho* and *Caverna*), but it may also take some unusual and more interesting forms which contribute to an overall vision of the need for real commitment to the other in order for life to be at all satisfactory for all of us. In the case of *Cegueira,* for instance, the example set by the doctor's wife (who declares herself to be blind early on in the text in order not to have to abandon her husband to his solitary fate in the asylum; see *Cegueira,* p. 44) is ultimately seen to spread to others, as she thinks globally and acts locally by extending a helping hand to those around her and encouraging them to emerge from the isolationist mindset which has plagued the unknown city in its hour of need. Thus, when (in another positive example of language as meaningful action within the world) she declares all of the images in the church to have been blindfolded (pp. 301–2), the people taking shelter there flee the premises and set about constructing their own positive solutions to the crisis rather than waiting for a messianic saviour whom the author clearly sees as having no reality behind the form of His (overused) name.[39] Surprisingly, therefore, this constitutes an example of something very much like Christian charity in action.

It is, however, two other novels, both written in recent years, *Todos* and *Homem*, which perhaps provide the clearest indication of the way in which Saramago sees a mutual benefit to be derived from engagement with the other: in the latter of these texts, an undistinguished schoolteacher, Tertuliano Máximo Afonso, like other Saramaguian protagonists (H. in *Manual*, Raimundo Silva, and the anonymous cellist of *Intermitências* spring readily to mind) leads a routine existence with little stimulation, and either no love interest or one which is merely functional, until one day he is forced (in Sartrian terminology) to question the authenticity of his existence, when he discovers that he has an exact physical double in a relatively insignificant actor whom he sees on a rented videotape. The fact that his double is an actor, of course, only exacerbates the crisis, since his apparent identity with the other (who has a screen name, Daniel Santa-Clara, different from his real one, António Claro) thus implicitly requires him to ask himself if he is merely an imitation of an imitation of real life (precisely the status inherited by, but never transcended by, Saramago's reincarnation of the earlier invention of Ricardo Reis by Fernando Pessoa, who is also given fictional form within the text of *Ano*).

In the end, the crisis is resolved in what amounts to a showdown between Tertuliano's inauthentic identity (that of the actor) and the existential authenticity created by his own vigorous pursuit of a more meaningful purpose to his life: the actor, who has misled Tertuliano's long-term (but far from intimate) girlfriend Maria da Paz into accompanying him on a trip out of town, is killed (along with the girlfriend) on their way back home, when she discovers his false identity by recognizing the mark left on his finger by his wedding-ring and, in the course of the resulting argument between them, they are forced off the road and crash (*Homem*, p. 313). Tertuliano is then in a position to win over the actor's wife (in the best tradition of the mythological hero who has overcome his foe, or of the cowboy who has just cleaned the bad guys out of town[40]), as both his old inauthentic self and the unfulfilling relationship with Maria da Paz have now been relegated to memory, and the way is now clear for him to commit himself to the other in a manner which he has never done before.[41]

Nonetheless, the situation cannot be said to have been resolved entirely, for at the very end of the text Tertuliano receives a phone call from a man who has his own voice and who repeats the same words which he himself had earlier first used to the actor (p. 317); this leads him to set off to meet the man with a loaded gun, merely leaving a note for his new wife to tell her 'Voltarei' (p. 318) ('I'll be back'; *Double*, p. 292): the threat of inauthentic existence is one which therefore must be faced down constantly and which can never be regarded as being definitively resolved.

Todos is a much more complex novel than *Homem*, for the protagonist of this work, Sr José (who is never given a surname, in keeping with his essential status at the beginning of the work as a type of 'everyman' figure) finds his own fulfilment in discovering the significance to him of a woman whom he never meets and whom he will never come to know, for she kills herself during the course of the narrative. This develops into a quest, where (after the manner of Borges) Sr José has been described by Sans as being both detective and criminal, as well as a modern knight errant:[42] in this case he completes tasks comparable to those set to Hercules,[43] but, in spite of the total inaccessibility of his lady, the medieval *topos* of the spiritual ennoblement of the male is nonetheless achieved, as she leads him to discover new capacities within himself and new outlets for his energies.

At a symbolic level, it could, nonetheless, be suggested that it is actually Sr José who effectively kills the unknown woman: his work in the Central Registry of Births, Deaths and Marriages of an unnamed country requires him to treat her (and all other citizens) as a mere object, as a name on a piece of paper. Sr José's preoccupation with meticulously fulfilling his professional role of recording what might seem (to any outsider) to be the merely functional facts of other people's lives extends to a hobby which is, in effect, a recognition of his own essential lack of individual identity: for he regularly 'borrows' record cards and keeps newspaper cuttings relating to famous people in order to keep a private record of their lives and thus, vicariously, to be able to take possession of their achievements and pasts: 'provavelmente fazem-no por algo a que poderíamos chamar angústia metafísica, talvez por não conseguirem suportar a ideia do caos como regedor único do universo, por isso, [. . .] vão tentando pôr alguma ordem no mundo' (*Todos*, p. 23) ('perhaps because they cannot bear the idea of chaos being the one ruler of the universe, which is why [. . .] they attempt to impose some order on the world'; *Names*, p. 13). Indeed, he is also said (p. 32) to take a certain pleasure when his own investigations reveal facts about them which contradict the common-knowledge impression of them; in fact, this same perverse pleasure is merely a manifestation of the sense of dissatisfaction which leads him to new discoveries in his life later on.

In the process of 'borrowing' record cards from the Registry for this purpose, one day he accidentally removes from the files the record slip for the anonymous woman, who, unlike the celebrities, has no 'life' recorded in the press. In one sense, therefore, she is a blank canvas on to which he can paint whatever images of her that he pleases. In common with Raimundo Silva, however, he wishes to make this an authentic picture of her, but, with her death, it becomes apparent that any such approximation to her can be made only by also making use of the imagination.

Initially, however, his search is a merely factual one, and his aim is simply to track down the flesh-and-blood woman who bears her name. By treating her merely as a name, therefore, it is no surprise that her life should come to an end once he starts to pursue someone who is no more to him than that and who has no deeper reality lying behind that accident of ancestry, combined with the choice made on her behalf by her parents at her birth. The possibility that he bears some kind of mysterious responsibility for her death is suggested by his act of taking possession of a photograph of her from the old woman who actually knew her as a person (p. 66), followed by the strange incident where he wonders whether it is the unknown woman whom he sees on the bus going home (pp. 70–1).

The echoes in this incident of Pauline notions of seeing through a glass darkly (the bus journey is conducted on a wet evening) and of the vain (and eventually misguided) pursuit by Eça's Artur Corvelo of the Baronesa de Paradas in his *A Capital* suggest that the woman on the bus, in spite of being approximately the right age to be the person whom Sr José seeks, is almost certainly not her (p. 70). Nonetheless, the almost colonial gaze which he directs at her through the window of the bus when she gets off amounts once more to a reification of her:

> Ficaram assim até que o autocarro se pôs em andamento, continuaram assim enquanto puderam ver-se, o Sr. José esticando e virando o pescoço, a mulher seguindo-lhe de lá o movimento, ela porventura a perguntar-se, Quem será este, ele a responder-se, É ela. (pp. 70–1)

> [Both he and she stayed like that until the bus set off again, they stayed like that for as long as they could see each other, Senhor José craning and turning his neck, the woman following his movements from where she was standing, perhaps asking herself, I wonder who that is, he saying to himself, It's her.] (pp. 57–8)

Not only does Sr José possess the power to know her name (whoever she actually is), but she is on the outside in the rain, while he remains for the moment in the relative comfort of the bus. While, at a literal level, there are obvious practical reasons why his reply to her imagined question is actually made to himself and not to her, this fact does nonetheless represent the monological domination of the female other practised by Sr José. When he pieces together the date of death of his unknown beloved later in the text, it becomes evident that the other woman (the one of his search and not the one seen from the bus) died after this episode (pp. 179–80); his repeated act of possession of her has, therefore, effectively reduced her to the status of mere object, and, in terms of the nature of the relationships developed by Sr José with others at this stage in the narrative, it could be said that, in a figurative sense, he bears the responsibility for her death.

As Parra Bañón suggests, Sr José's house (attached to the Archive itself by a common wall and an unused door which connects the two spaces) is a liminal space, suspending him between life and death, and creating an illusion of security while all the time leaving him vulnerable to unknown and unimaginable threats;[44] this idea is further developed by Boulter[45] in terms of Freudian theories of the Archive as the physical space where human preoccupation with death in life mingles with desire, 'a desire for totality that cannot ever be achieved'.[46] The rest of the novel (after the discovery of the woman's death) may therefore be viewed not only as Sr José's voyage of self-discovery, but also (through his act of confession to the old woman on pp. 192–5) as his act of penitential expiation for his previous objectification of the other.[47] His journey from this point onwards therefore amounts to both a discovery of the self and a recovery of the woman whom he has lost/destroyed.

Responsibility for definition of the self lies beyond that name, with the individual and not with what one inherits from the past (a pattern already familiar in the author's earlier novels, such as *Memorial* and *Jangada*, both of which involve a trajectory of movement through physical space in order to represent the possibility of spiritual growth, in common with Camões and the Pessoa of *Mensagem*), although it is possible only to build up from the starting point where that past leaves the individual (*Levantado*, *História*). In this sense it is not important that Sr José (in common with Raimundo Silva before him) comes to relate to the other relatively late in life: the important point is that he does so at all, for his quest for the unknown woman leads him to discover something of her past and of the general relationships between life and death through conversations with the symbolic guardians of the route of access to her soul (her parents, pp. 256–9; the old woman who used to be her neighbour, pp. 52–66, 189–95 and 197–201; the staff of the cemetery where she is buried, pp. 221–4; the headmaster of the school where she worked, pp. 265–6; and, most enigmatic of all, the eccentric shepherd whom he meets inside the plot where her grave is, pp. 237–43), just as he gradually penetrates spaces ever more closely associated with her life (the block of flats where she once lived, the school which she attended as a pupil and where she worked as an adult, her parents' home, and finally the flat where she herself lived before her death).

Once again, these conversations raise the question of authentic existence, as much for the self as for the other, particularly those which Sr José has with the unknown woman's former neighbour, who in their first meeting confesses to having once had an affair with the woman's father (p. 62), before confronting him during their second encounter with the need for him to be similarly honest with her about the reasons for his questioning of her (pp. 194–5). Once he achieves this level of honesty and he then finally confronts the most fearsome figure of them all (the Registrar himself), he discovers that this apparently forbidding presence (who, in a less sinister echo of Big Brother's awareness of the activities of Winston Smith and Julia in Orwell's *1984*, has been casting a benevolent eye over all of his activities all along; p. 277) is actually not the ogre who he once imagined him to be. Instead the Registrar willingly takes up his suggestion that the sections of the Registry relating to the dead should be mixed with the records for the living (pp. 207–9), and the novel closes with him entrusting Sr José with the exploration of the underworld of the section of the dead and permitting him to invent a new life story for the dead woman in a similar way to Raimundo Silva's earlier reconstruction of Portugal's past (p. 278).

The major question to be resolved here is precisely what the distant figure of the Registrar represents: is he Death? Such an explanation has some plausibility, even if it would sit somewhat oddly alongside the representation of death as an attractive and chatty female figure in *Intermitências*: certainly, though, any figure who can effectively authorize the abolition of the distinction between life and death must be viewed as some kind of larger-than-life presence, and the Registrar is said somewhat ominously to know all the names, past and present, possible and actual (p. 62). Or is he perhaps Time? Certainly this archive of personal records effectively measures and records time in the same manner as the gravestones in the cemetery register bald facts of birth, name, and death for each person, but the effectiveness of these (and also, implicitly, of the Registry itself) is undermined by the shepherd's peculiar pastime of rearranging the gravestones in such a way that even he cannot remember which stone really corresponds to which corpse (p. 240). Or is he some satirical reflection of the modern police state, with its obsession with keeping records of all of its enemies, whether real or merely potential? One might make a case for such a sinister interpretation of the Registrar in view of the Portuguese experience of the PVDE under Salazar (and in *Ano* the PVDE agent who interviews Ricardo Reis is said to know many names; see *Ano*, p. 191), but this seems an unlikely option in view of Sr José's eventual discovery that the Registrar is actually a kindly figure who has ordered his assistants to check on the health and general well-being of his increasingly independent-minded employee (*Todos*, pp. 127–8 and 137–43).

Perhaps it is best (and most consistent with Saramago's later development of these questions in *Intermitências*), however, to view the Registrar less as something external to Sr José and more as something like his own awareness (and, of course, ours) of the passing of time and, with it, of our own (future) passing from this earth: for the Registry which he controls is effectively a database where each of us will have his/her record card completed in due course. Seen in this light, the Registrar in effect becomes a physical incarnation of the truth that only by recognizing our own non-essentiality can we make ourselves something more significant than the enigma which Ricardo Reis removes from the earth through his own suicide (*Ano*, p. 415); it is only through our awareness of the limitations of our time among others that we can make ourselves more than a spectral presence floating on the ocean (to adapt Pessoa's words to Reis; p. 361) and turn our raft into a boat which will guide us ashore where we want to go, just as Pedro Orce contemplates the stone boat in which Galician legend has it that the saints successfully traversed the ocean to bring their truth of Christianity to Iberia (*Jangada*, pp. 206–7);[48] and only through meaningful commitment to the other can the individual effect a worthwhile presence in this life.

In *Memorial*, Baltasar and Blimunda take their final leave of one another after an eerie episode amid a circle of static statues of saints destined to be placed on top of the Convent at Mafra (*Memorial*, pp. 329–30). The silent circle of the saints prompts Blimunda to comment with some pity on how they seem to have lost all personality and life which they may once have had:

> Devem ser infelizes os santos, assim como os fizeram, assim ficam, se isto é a santidade, que será a condenação, São apenas estátuas, Do que eu gostava era vê-las descer daquelas pedras e ser gente como nós, não se pode falar com estátuas. (p. 330)
>
> [The saints must be unhappy, as they were made, so they remain, and if this is sanctity, what must damnation be like, They're only statues, I'd like them to come down from those plinths and be human like us, for you can't hold a conversation with a statue.] (*Baltasar*, p. 317)

Unlike these saints, Baltasar and Blimunda refuse to accept meekly the silent place in history which is all that they would have had if it had not been for Saramago's 'recuperation' of them. Instead, Baltasar moves out of the circle and goes back to the flying machine, which has allowed him to transcend his allotted role in life; he ends up defeated in body when he is executed by the Inquisition, but at the very end of the text we learn that he achieves a victory of sorts in the reunion of his will with Blimunda at the last (p. 357). Blimunda may lose him after this encounter in a physical sense, but he has clearly at least taken to heart her mysterious words shortly before this:

> O pecado não existe, só há morte e vida, A vida está antes da morte, Enganas-te, Baltasar, a morte vem antes da vida, morreu quem fomos, nasce quem somos, por isso é que não morremos de vez, E quando vamos para debaixo da terra, e quando Francisco Marques fica esmagado sob o carro da pedra, não será isso morte sem recurso, Se estamos falando dele, nasce Francisco Marques, Mas ele não o sabe, Tal como nós não sabemos bastante quem somos, e, apesar disso, estamos vivos. (p. 331)
>
> [Sin doesn't exist, there is only death and life, Life comes before death, You're deceiving yourself, Baltasar, for death comes before life, who we were has died, who we are is being born, and that's why we do not die all at once, And when we go under the earth, and when Francisco Marques is crushed beneath the cart carrying the stone, is that not death without recourse, If we're talking about Francisco Marques, he is born, But he doesn't know it, Just as we don't really know who we are, yet we are alive.] (p. 318)

Sculpted figures of saints (and depictions of biblical scenes in church windows) were originally fashioned in order to convey moral or scriptural lessons to a largely illiterate population. In the context of *Memorial* they have now become merely decorative elements in a project designed to promote the selfish interests of a corrupt Church and a vainglorious monarch: on the one occasion in the text of the novel when a saint is declared to be active, it is merely in keeping a watchful eye over the theft of Church property (p. 20). The saints have thus (like the religious figures in the church towards the end of *Cegueira*; pp. 301–2) become meaningless to the very people for whose benefit they were originally designed, and, by implication, the stone used to form them would be better employed in a different design, as is hinted at in *Evangelho* when the stones in the desert are seen to be lying around awaiting some human hand to put them into meaningful shape (*Evangelho*, p. 110). Since in *Caverna* the consumer may become the object of consumption, it is incumbent on the individual to recover his or her full humanity and become more than a stone, an active part of the construction of a happier and better world, for themselves and for others. Grossegesse points out, in fact, that, even in biblical terms, stones may be seen as being more useful than they are in the scene discussed in *Memorial*, for the allusions to living stones in Revelation may be adapted to allow an interpretation of Saramago's great moving stone in *Jangada* as a recollection of the stone which rolled away from Christ's tomb at the Resurrection.[49]

Yet the statues also inspire positive reflection on the part of the prescient Blimunda, for they remind her (through the negative image of the crushing of Francisco Marques by the stone transported from Pêro Pinheiro) of the positive lessons about life which may be learned from the losses which she and Baltasar have suffered. The lesson which she draws from Francisco's death is, in its essence, merely a verbal counterpart to the visual pedagogical function which images of religious figures once had in the Church, but the content, instead of being the quietist message of static submission to a deadening concept of authority peddled by Church and State in eighteenth-century Portugal, is instead a potentially liberating and dynamic one, one which sees the individual in continual rebirth and growth, potentially even after physical death through the example which may be given to the living.

Blimunda does not know this at the time, but her mystical, spiritual comments relating to Francisco Marques will shortly also be applicable to her own beloved Baltasar: the memorial created by Saramago of this (invented, but plausible) figure from the past and the example which he, Francisco Marques, and others will give to the eccentric Blimunda will help to keep the world in its orbit, away from the control of those who would centralize all human life into their own reductive vision of how it ought to be, not just for themselves, but also for others. The obstinacy of figures such as Saramago's Lídia and Mary Magdalene, the imagination of his Raimundo Silva and the willingness to chronicle the dystopian nightmare demonstrated by the blind writer in *Cegueira* (see *Cegueira*, pp. 277–9): none of these are adequate to save us from death in any literal sense, but they convey the same radical message of the essence of the human spirit at its defiant best.[50]

Saramago's emergence from a society which prized conformity to a restrictive tradition dictated by authority leads him to communicate again and again the experience of discovering the free expression of mind and soul through the less formal nurturing which has so often been supplied within patriarchal structures by the subordinate gender, left to care informally for future generations out of the sight of the men who have dictated the patterns to which men and women alike must pay lip-service. Within the terms of this vision, the concept of men and women becomes removed from one of mere biological gender: as Saramago remarks in conversation with Berrini,[51] women are like another continent to him, but in this sense they surely function more as the expression of the unfamiliar (but rewarding) apprehension of reality by the other which is waiting to be discovered by the protagonist of *Conto* than they do as lovers in any literal sense.[52] For the truly enriching experience of life lies away from the claustrophobic centre, in the same, dynamic 'world on the move' (to echo the phrase used of the Portuguese period of expansion by the historian Russell-Wood) which the poet Landeg White detects as part of the greatness of Camões' epic poem: 'Nothing quite like this happened again until December 1968, when the Apollo 8 spacecraft showed us the first pictures of earth taken from space'.[53]

Giovanni Pontiero, Saramago's first English translator, once remarked that the beauty of the novelist's work for him was that 'every book is so totally new':[54] what would be even more enriching would be if each of us could find the inexhaustible seam of newness within the other, allowing the subaltern (as defined by class, race, gender, other categories, or, indeed, a mixture of these) to speak freely of his/her experience of the world, and allowing ourselves at the same time to be constantly enriched as individuals in this reciprocal process of constant discovery.

In his conversation with the administrative official at the graveyard in *Todos*, Sr José is told that the real justification for his search for the body of the missing woman is not so that he can be sure that she is dead, but so that he can be sure that she was once alive (*Todos*, p. 224), that is, that the benefit which he has derived from his search for her has some tangible reality. Just when he thinks he has found this, however, in the form of her grave, he meets the shepherd who makes it his pastime to switch the gravestones from one place to another, effectively ensuring that any such relationship with the past must be based on the signified (the real character and influence of those, like Francisco Marques, who have gone before us) and not merely on the signifier (the bare name, possessed in all its futile infinity by the Registrar). A meaningful growing relationship (as is illustrated by *Conto*, where the island sought is not a place but the protagonist's relationship with the cleaning woman who loves him) rests on continually searching for that other and the inexhaustible development which makes all of us individuals and not just names.

As the old woman remarks in *Todos*, if Sr José ever did locate the unknown woman of his quest, then it would have been necessary to recommence the search for her straight away (p. 198), for we are all constantly changing and growing, and a truly living human being cannot be reduced (as the Centre in *Caverna* would have it; see *Caverna*, p. 332) to a static object chained to a bench. The communication of individual, utopian dreams through the conversation of women (and men) is what Saramago visualizes as the most valuable contribution which we can make to the enrichment of our own lives and those of the others with whom we come into contact. It is, then, only by being constantly reminded (and reminding others) that 'tudo isto pode ser contado doutra maneira' ('all of this could be told in a different way'; *Levantado*, p. 14) that we can all become, and remain, fully alive.

NOTES

1 I gratefully acknowledge the advice offered to me by Adriana Martins, Mark Sabine, Rhian Atkin and Wendy Kolls in finalizing my ideas in this section of the text.

2 Quoted in Arias, pp. 80–1.

3 See Sabine, p. 246, and Daniel, p. 540.

4 If Saramago himself had died at the age of the character depicted here (fifty), the only novel which he would have left us would have been the undistinguished *Terra do Pecado*, written in his twenties and disowned by the author until its reappearance in a second edition issued by his contemporary publishers, Editorial Caminho, in 1997.

5 The motif of the delivery of the letters to announce imminent death is perhaps a morbidly humorous reflection on the contemporary phenomenon of unwanted junk mail, but it also bears some superficial similarities to the intimation of forthcoming death given to characters who watch a particular video in Hideo Nakata's 1998 film

Ringu (*The Ring*, remade in English by Gore Verbinski in 2002). Nonetheless, the development and contextualization of this motif are very different in this novel; in similar fashion, the anthropomorphization and love interest of the character of death later in the text bears some similarities to Martin Brest's 1998 film *Meet Joe Black*, which was itself a remake of Mitchell Leisen's *Death Takes a Holiday*, of 1934. Again, however, any speculation regarding possible influences here should recognize the fresh and independent twist given to these motifs by Saramago.

6 The text very pointedly rejects the use of the upper-case letter on her name 'morte'; I have therefore followed the same practice here myself with the English word 'death'.

7 This story is included in Borges, at pp. 143–58.

8 Comments made at the Seminar 'An Encounter with José Saramago', held at University College Dublin, 15 June 2006. The novelist did not expand on these remarks.

9 See Unamuno, *Del sentimiento trágico*, p. 128.

10 The apparent insinuation here that death allows her intended victim to achieve a level of immortality within the memory of others is perhaps reinforced by the fact that Saramago himself has stated that his choice of the name Blimunda for his most celebrated, most enigmatic and most philosophical fictional character constitutes a 'som desgarrador de violoncelo' ('a stray note from a cello'; see Saramago, 'Blimunda, Nome com Música'). The choice of a cellist as death's intended victim here, therefore, could be said to cross reference Blimunda's positive speculations on the nature of life and death towards the end of *Memorial* (see *Memorial*, p. 331 and *Baltasar*, p. 318). The potentially negative aspect of this association, however, is that the immortality to which Blimunda refers in the case of Francisco Marques is merely a provisional one, which will continue only for as long as those who knew him remain alive. In the context of *Intermitências*, then, the anonymous musician will have the pleasure of knowing that he has performed better than Rostropovitch for the sole benefit of the woman with whom he has fallen in love, but he remains unaware that this woman herself has the capacity to wipe out his very existence.

11 The Portuguese word *borboleta* used in the text is equivalent to both 'moth' and 'butterfly' in English; while the latter term clearly is more poetic and provides a better match for the associations with beauty and fragility evoked by Saramago in his use of this creature, this is technically a moth. See *http://www.museums.org.za/bio/insects/lepidoptera/sphingidae/acherontia_atropos.htm* (website consulted on 13 December 2005).

12 Álvaro de Campos, 'Todas as Cartas de Amor', in Galhoz (ed.), p. 265. The English translation is in Zenith, p. 211.

13 See Ricardo Reis, 'As rosas amo dos jardins de Adónis', in Galhoz (ed.), p. 203. The relevance of this allusion here is reinforced by a passage in the earlier *Manual*, where H. writes of 'aquela borboleta que não vive mais do que um dia, e desse mesmo dia não chega a

conhecer a noite' (*Manual*, p. 110) ('like that butterfly which survives for no longer than a day and has already perished by nightfall'; *Painting*, p. 58).

14 For a fuller account of the political situation in Europe in 1935–6 in relation to *Ano*, see Cerdeira da Silva, *José Saramago*, pp. 105–24.

15 Sapega, pp. 106–7.

16 See Sabine, p. 165, n. 1. The references to the apparent movements of Camões' statue are in *Ano*, pp. 257 and 351–2, while the stasis of the figure of D. Sebastião (ironically, in view of his fate in real life, also said to be 'miraculosamente incólume') is seen on p. 338 ('miraculously unharmed'; *The Year*, p. 292).

17 *Cadernos – III*, pp. 52–3 (entry for 24 February 1995).

18 See Carey, p. 20

19 From Álvaro de Campos, 'Lisbon Revisited (1926)', in Pessoa, *Selected Poems*, pp. 90–3.

20 The general atmosphere of the hotel in the opening chapter of the novel is one of darkness and resignation, mirroring the air of depression felt by Reis on his return to Portugal; this forms a clear contrast with the atmosphere of freshness with the open windows providing views to the river in Eça's depiction of the same hotel in the final chapter of *Os Maias* (see Eça de Queirós, p. 690). A further indication of national decline in the depiction of the Bragança in Saramago's text lies in the textual focus on the decorative doors to the hotel dining room, whose intricate patterns (which perhaps prefigure the sinister advertisement for Freire's engraving services later in the text) recall past Portuguese colonial expeditions in the tropics, 'assim dignificando as artes aplicadas o trivial ofício hoteleiro' (p. 24) ('bestow[ing] dignity on this otherwise modest hotel'; p. 13).

21 See Ornelas, '*A Jangada de Pedra* de José Saramago', p. 18.

22 Bakhtin, p. 16.

23 Carey, p. 21.

24 This advertisement appeared in the Portuguese press in the 1930s and is reproduced by Grossegesse in his *Saramago Lesen*, pp. 40–1.

25 The full account of this episode is in the *Metamorphoses*, VI, ll. 1–155. See Ovid, pp. 42–3.

26 See Schor, pp. 210–11, where he also identifies similar tendencies among the besiegers of Lisbon in Raimundo Silva's version of *História*.

27 *Metamorphoses*, VI, ll. 104–5 (see Ovid, pp. 42–3).

28 The bullring, of course, is a motif exploited elsewhere in Saramago's writing, generally associated with the suppression of legitimate individual rights. It is in the bullring in Lisbon that Reis observes a fascist rally (*Ano*, pp. 394–7), in the course of which ordinary workers from several countries voluntarily renounce their own individuality to the *Führerprinzip* favoured by Salazar, Mussolini and Hitler. In the passage relating to the slaughter at Badajoz, the related motif of the Minotaur (in Greek mythology, the beast which was half human and half

animal and which was believed to consume all of those who succeeded in penetrating the labyrinth) is explicitly mentioned, but with the added irony that this image is used as an expression of fascist paranoia towards the threat posed to its hegemony by the republicans, while the real all-consuming monster is the Francoist movement itself (p. 391). Even in *Levantado,* when João is summoned to the anti-communist rally in the bullring at Évora, he is given his 'invitation' by an anonymous agent of power, who is described as having 'duas pernas e nome de homem, mas é bicho de morder' ('two legs and the name of a human being, but in reality he is a beast who will bite'; *Levantado,* p. 91): this man therefore functions as a reincarnation of the Minotaur. For a brief summary of the symbolic associations of bulls with human death in the origins of the Iberian bullfight, see, for example, Josephs and Caballero, 'Andalucía: tema y visión', in Lorca, pp. 19–54, especially pp. 30–4.

29 See Carey, p. 83.

30 See Carey, pp. 21 and 86.

31 This is the title listed for *Jangada* as a text in preparation in the sixth edition of *Ano,* published in 1985 (*Ano,* p. 4).

32 See Camões, *Os Lusíadas,* Canto X, Stanza 82 (p. 335).

33 Cirlot, pp. 280–1.

34 *Cadernos – III,* pp. 172–3 (entry for 7 October 1995).

35 It could, of course, be suggested that Reis' decision to leave Portugal for Rio de Janeiro eight years before the start of the text forms an implicit parallel to the decision of the Portuguese court of Queen Maria I and her consort Pedro III to flee to Brazil in the face of invading French troops in 1808. Such a parallel would permit the conclusion that the Reis of 1936 is unable to emerge from the (essentially cowardly) script written for him by some of his own privileged predecessors.

36 1 Corinthians 15:55.

37 From Ricardo Reis, 'Não sei se é amor que tens, ou amor que finges', in Galhoz (ed.), p. 220. The English version is in Zenith, p. 132.

38 See Huici, p. 461.

39 In Saramago's *In Nomine Dei,* the character Heinrich Gresbeck declares 'Talvez Deus não seja católico, talvez não seja protestante, talvez não seja senão o nome que tem' ('Maybe God is not Catholic or Protestant, maybe he is no more than his own name'; *In Nomine Dei,* p. 138).

40 This Western motif is, of course, developed at length to represent the downfall of Salazar in the short story 'Cadeira', included in the much earlier *Objecto.*

41 While the achievement of Tertuliano's new identity here is accomplished at the expense of the lives of both the actor and Maria da Paz (the latter being entirely innocent in the whole process), this need not be viewed as an indication of the expendability of the woman as such, as a similar plot could easily be developed with the gender-roles reversed: in the purely fictional context, it is therefore important to view Maria da Paz in a functional sense rather than as a character of

equal importance to Tertuliano himself. Similarly, it would be inappropriate to make negative moral judgements on Tertuliano's effective deception of Helena (the actor's wife) into believing him to be her husband, for he effectively becomes both actor and more fully himself by overcoming his shadow.

42 The same critic also sees the novel as possessing elements of the *Bildungsroman*; see Sans, p. 441.

43 See Huici, p. 454.

44 See Parra Bañón, pp. 87–9.

45 See Boulter, pp. 117–8. Parra Bañón makes a contrast between the archive (as a place for keeping records stored and away from sight) and the home, where memories continue to live; see Parra Bañón, p. 48.

46 Boulter, p. 118, n. 5. Such interpretations of the Archive in Saramago are, in fact, reinforced by means of reference to *Intermitências*, where death herself keeps an archive of the living which mysteriously updates itself through time, increasing the age of people as they celebrate birthdays and indicating other major life events (see *Intermitências*, p. 147); the description of this database effectively alludes to the earlier novel, by suggesting that it would be even more useful if it could have continually changing photographs of the people represented (p. 157), a function which Sr José recognizes as existing in the annually updated records of the school which he burgles in search of the mysterious woman's past, unlike the Registry, which uses only names (*Todos*, p. 112).

47 In this respect, Sr José's (relatively minor) misdeeds in this novel are, nonetheless, identical in their nature (if not in degree) to the general indifference to the other which forms the crux of the dystopian vision of *Cegueira*. For further development of this point, see Frier, 'Righting Wrongs', pp. 106–7.

48 For further discussion of the mythological backdrop to *A Jangada*, see Frier, 'José Saramago's Stone Boat', and Sabine, pp. 249–50.

49 The reference to living stones is less straightforward in its biblical context than Grossegesse suggests: the chapters of Revelation to which he makes reference (21 and 22) concern the physical construction of the City of God over an area with an outer wall measurement of 144 cubits (Revelation 21:17). However, in view of the clearly allegorical nature of the image of Heaven projected here, this figure could be seen to be a representation of the 144,000 saved from the tribes of Israel alluded to earlier (Revelation 7:4). The relevance to Saramago's notions of utopia and dystopia surely lies in the idyllic vision of life within the City of God, by way of contrast with the nightmare beyond its walls: 'Blessed are they that do his commandments, that they may have the right to the tree of life, and may enter in through the gates into the city. For without are dogs, and sorcerers, and whoremongers, and murderers, and idolaters, and whosoever loveth and maketh a lie' (Revelation 22:14–15). Clearly, the parallel is not to be seen in a transcendental sense in relation to Saramago; at a purely spiritual level, however, the imagery used is

striking in its similarities to the nightmare experienced inside and outside the asylum in *Cegueira*, thus reinforcing the implicit parallel with the living stones of the Bible. For Grossegesse's comments, see his *Saramago Lesen*, p. 20.

50 The summing up of his experiences given by the blind writer in *Cegueira* is precisely one of the recognition of his non-essentiality: 'Estou de passagem' (*Cegueira*, pp. 278–9; 'I am only passing through', *Blindness*, p. 277).

51 'Entrevista com José Saramago', in Berrini, pp. 227–44, p. 240. It should be noted, however, that in the same passage the writer also emphasizes that all other men are like different countries to him; the point is, therefore, surely that the experience of the other must always, by definition, be alien to the self, but that gender differences create an extra element of difference to be overcome.

52 Sabine devotes some considerable space to discussing whether the apparent idealization of women within Saramago's fiction (and, indeed, in the rhetoric used in relation to women in some interviews, including that given to Berrini; see Berrini, pp. 239–40) is actually productive or merely 'a particularly new and shiny bowling ball with which to knock down the capitalist skittles, while inadvertently reducing the presentation of female characters to a potentially oppressive stereotyping' (see Sabine, pp. 157–9, and pp. 158–9, n. 102; the quotation given is from p. 158). His conclusion is firmly that the example given by Blimunda not only challenges women's traditional passivity, but also that it encourages men to transcend their traditional gender roles as well (see Sabine, p. 159). Such arguments are backed up in general terms (although with some degree of caution) by Ferreira in her study of Saramago's fiction throughout the 1980s (see Ferreira, pp. 232–4). I would suggest that her hesitancy (with reference to *História*) over 'the implications of a textual model of affirmative negativity that suspends in bliss the continued siege' (Ferreira, p. 234) is answered by the clearly proactive role attributed to the doctor's wife in *Cegueira*, who is obliged to take on the role of 'o cordeiro que tirará o pecado do mundo' (*Memorial*, p. 354) ('the lamb that will take away the sins of the world'; *Baltasar*, p. 340), not because she is a woman, but because for large parts of the narrative she is the only true human being left in the city of the blind. If it is more difficult to sustain such arguments in relation to some more recent female characters created by the writer, then this is largely because Saramago's recent work has tended to focus on individual (male) protagonists, with the result that the female characters become functional in terms of the plot rather than fully developed individuals (see, for example, *Todos*, *Caverna* and *Homem*).

53 White, 'Introduction', in Camões, *The Lusiads*, ix–xxii, p. xi.

54 Quoted in Winder.

Bibliography

1. Literary Works by José Saramago (including English translations)

The following are the editions of works by José Saramago used in the preparation of the present volume. Where the edition used of a work by Saramago is not the first edition, the original date of publication has been indicated immediately after the title of the work in question.

All the Names, translated by Margaret Jull Costa (London: Harvill, 1999).

O Ano da Morte de Ricardo Reis (1984), sixth edition (Lisbon: Editorial Caminho, 1985).

O Ano de 1993 (1975), second edition (Lisbon: Editorial Caminho, 1987).

Os Apontamentos (1976), second edition (Lisbon: Editorial Caminho, 1990).[1]

A Bagagem do Viajante (1973), third edition (Lisbon: Editorial Caminho, 1988).

Baltasar and Blimunda, translated by Giovanni Pontiero (London: Harvill, 1998).

Blindness, translated by Giovanni Pontiero (London: Harvill, 1997).

'The Bureaucratic Tale of the Harbor Master and the Collector of Customs', translated by George Monteiro, in Klobucka (ed.), pp. 239–43.

Cadernos de Lanzarote: Diário, 5 vols (Lisbon: Editorial Caminho, 1994–8).

The Cave, translated by Margaret Jull Costa (New York: Harcourt, 2002).

A Caverna, first edition (Lisbon: Editorial Caminho, 2000).

'The Centaur' (from *Objecto Quase*), translated by Giovanni Pontiero, in Mike Gerrard and Thomas McCarthy (eds), *Passport to Portugal* (Huntingdon, Camb.: Passport, 1994), pp. 5–19.

'The Chair' (from *Objecto Quase*), translated by Giovanni Pontiero, in Gerrard and McCarthy (eds), pp. 136–51.

'O Conto Burocrático do Capitão do Porto e do Director da Alfândega', in *O Escritor*, No. 7 (1996), 81–4.

O Conto da Ilha Desconhecida (Lisbon: Editorial Caminho, 1999).

'O conto do diabo e das pedras', in *Quaderni Portoghesi*, Nos 15–24 (1984–8), 149–54.

Deste Mundo e do Outro (1971), third edition (Lisbon: Editorial Caminho, 1985).
Don Giovanni, ou o Dissoluto Absolvido (Lisbon: Editorial Caminho, 2005).
The Double, translated by Margaret Jull Costa (London: Harvill, 2004).
'Embargo' (from *Objecto Quase*), translated by Giovanni Pontiero, in *Cimarron Review*, 110 (January 1995), 10–18.
Ensaio sobre a Cegueira, first edition (Lisbon: Editorial Caminho, 1995).
Ensaio sobre a Lucidez, first edition (Lisbon: Editorial Caminho, 2004).
O Evangelho Segundo Jesus Cristo, first edition (Lisbon: Editorial Caminho, 1991).
Folhas Políticas: 1976–1998 (1999), second edition (Lisbon: Editorial Caminho, 1999).
The Gospel According to Jesus Christ, translated by Giovanni Pontiero (London: Harvill, 1993).
História do Cerco de Lisboa, first edition (Lisbon: Editorial Caminho, 1989).
The History of the Siege of Lisbon, translated by Giovanni Pontiero (London: Harvill, 1996).
O Homem Duplicado, first edition (Lisbon: Editorial Caminho, 2002).
As Intermitências da Morte, first edition (Lisbon: Editorial Caminho, 2005).
In Nomine Dei (1993), second edition (Lisbon: Editorial Caminho, 1993).
A Jangada de Pedra, first edition (Lisbon: Editorial Caminho, 1986).
Journey to Portugal, translated by Amanda Hopkinson and Nick Caistor (London: Harvill, 2000).
Levantado do Chão (1980), eighth edition (Lisbon: Editorial Caminho, 1988).
Manual de Pintura e Caligrafia (1977), fifth edition (Lisbon: Caminho, 1998).
Manual of Painting and Calligraphy, translated by Giovanni Pontiero (Manchester: Carcanet Press Ltd., 1994).
Memorial do Convento (1982), nineteenth edition (Lisbon: Editorial Caminho, 1989).
'Natal' (1946–1947), in Seixo (ed.), pp. 249–66.
A Noite (1979), second edition (Lisbon: Editorial Caminho, 1987).
Objecto Quase (1978), second edition (Lisbon: Editorial Caminho, 1984).
'O Ouvido', in Ana Hatherly, Augusto Abelaira, Isabel da Nóbrega, José Saramago, Maria Velho da Costa and Nuno Bragança, *Poética dos Cinco Sentidos: La Dame à la Licorne* (Lisbon: Livraria Bertrand, 1979), pp. 21–6.
Os Poemas Possíveis (1966), second edition (Lisbon: Editorial Caminho, 1982).
Provavelmente Alegria (1970), third edition (Lisbon: Editorial Caminho, 1982).
Que Farei com Este Livro? (1980), second edition (Lisbon: Editorial Caminho, 1980).
'Reflux' (from *Objecto Quase*), translated by Giovanni Pontiero, in *Frontiers (Leopard III)* (London: Harvill, 1994), pp. 293–304.
'Revenge' (from *Objecto Quase*), translated by Giovanni Pontiero, in *Frontiers (Leopard III)* (London: Harvill, 1994), pp. 305–7.

A Segunda Vida de Francisco de Assis (1980), second edition (Lisbon: Editorial Caminho, 1987).
The Stone Raft, translated by Giovanni Pontiero (London: Harvill, 1994).
The Tale of the Unknown Island, translated by Margaret Jull Costa (New York: Harcourt Brace, 1999).
Terra do Pecado (1947), second edition (Lisbon: Caminho, 1997).
'Things' (from *Objecto Quase*), translated by Giovanni Pontiero, in Pilar Orero and Juan C. Sager (eds), *The Translator's Dialogue: Giovanni Pontiero* (Amsterdam: John Benjamins Publishing Company, 1997), pp. 189–243.
Todos os Nomes, first edition (Lisbon: Editorial Caminho, 1997).
Viagem a Portugal (1981), tenth edition (Lisbon: Editorial Caminho, 1995).
The Year of the Death of Ricardo Reis, translated by Giovanni Pontiero (London: Harvill, 1992).

2. Interviews with or Essays by José Saramago

Arias, Juan, *José Saramago: el amor posible* (Barcelona: Planeta, 1998).
Baptista Bastos, Armando, *José Saramago: Aproximação a um Retrato* (Lisbon: Dom Quixote, 1996).
Cristóbal, Ramiro, 'Tengo poca confianza en la condición humana' (interview with José Saramago), in *Cambio 16* (24 July 2000), pp. 58–9.
Jorge, Maria, Transcript of Saramago's notebook for the composition of *A Jangada de Pedra*, reproduced and transcribed in Seixo (ed.), n.p.
Reis, Carlos, *Diálogos com José Saramago* (Lisbon: Editorial Caminho, 1998).
Saramago, José, 'Blimunda, Nome com Música', in *Jornal de Letras* (15 May 1990), p. 29.
Saramago, José, 'Cheguei até aqui', *http://www.midiaindependente.org/pt/blue//2003/04/252911.shtml* (website consulted on 30 November 2003).
Saramago, José, 'De las piedras de David a los tanques de Goliat', in *El País* (21 April 2002); available online at *http://www.elpais.es/archivo/buscador.html* (website consulted on 30 November 2003).
Saramago, José, 'O escritor vidente' (Interview with Maria Leonor Nunes), in *Jornal de Letras* (25 October 1995), pp. 15–17.
Saramago, José, 'Europa sim, Europa não', in *Jornal de Letras* (10 January 1989), p. 32.
Saramago, José, 'La explanada del absurdo', in *El País* (24 March 2002); available online at *http://www.elpais.es/archivo/buscador.html* (website consulted on 8 February 2006).
Saramago, José, 'Fantástico é apenas aquilo que não se sabe', in *A Capital* (12 November 1986), p. 9.

Saramago, José, Interview with César Antonio Molina, in *Sobre el iberismo, y otros escritos de literatura portuguesa* (Madrid: Ediciones Akal, 1990), pp. 47–75.

Saramago, José, Interview with Ivone Pereira, in *Quadrant*, No. 10 (1993), 215–19.

Saramago, José, 'La isla ibérica' (interview with Jordi Costa), in *Quimera*, 59 (1986), 50–57.

Saramago, José, 'José Saramago: Todos os Pecados do Mundo' (interview with Clara Ferreira Alves), in *Expresso Revista* (28 October 1995), pp. 81–5.

Saramago, José, 'Mi Iberismo', in Molina, César Antonio, *Sobre el iberismo, y otros escritos de literatura portuguesa* (Madrid: Ediciones Akal, 1990), pp. 5–9.

Saramago, José, 'A Península Ibérica entre a Europa e a América Latina', in *Vértice* (2nd series), 47 (March–April 1992), 5–11.

Saramago, José, preface to Sebastião Salgado, *Terra: The Struggle of the Landless* (London: Phaidon Books, 1997), pp. 9–13.

Saramago, José, 'Quieren la guerra, pero no les vamos a dejar en paz', *El País* (16 March 2003); available online at *http://www.elpais.es/archivo/buscador.html* (website consulted on 8 February 2006).

Saramago, José, 'Situação do Romance Português' (unpublished text of a lecture given in 1972–3), reproduced in Seixo (ed.), pp. 219–26.

Saramago, José, 'Sobre literatura, compromiso y transformación social', in *Quimera*, 119 (March–April 1993), 12–15.

3. Studies on José Saramago

Arnaut, Ana Paula, *'Memorial do Convento': História, Ficção e Ideologia* (Coimbra: Fora do Texto, 1996).

Arnaut, Ana Paula, *Post-Modernismo no Romance Português Contemporâneo: Fios de Ariadne – Máscaras de Proteu* (Coimbra: Livraria Almedina, 2002).

Arnaut, Ana Paula, 'Viagem ao Centro da Escrita: da Subversão à Irreverência da(s) História(s)', in Seixo (ed.), pp. 325–34.

Berrini, Beatriz, *Ler Saramago: O Romance* (Lisbon: Editorial Caminho, 1998).

Boulter, Jonathan, 'The Melancholy Archive: José Saramago's *All the Names*', in *Genre*, Vol. XXXVIII (Spring–Summer 2005), 115–43.

Cavaliere, Mauro, *As Coordenadas da Viagem no Tempo: Uma Contribuição Para a Teoria da Ficção Histórica Baseada em Alguns Textos Portugueses dos Séculos XVI, XIX e XX* (Stockholm: Stockholms Universitet – Institution för Spanska, Portugisiska och Latinamerikastudier, 2002).

Ceccucci, Piero, 'L'utopia saramaghiana como progetto della storia umana', in Giovanni Battista de Cesare and Silvana Serafin (eds), *El Girador: Studi di letterature iberiche e ibero-americane offerti a Giuseppe Bellini*, 2 vols (Rome: Consiglio Nazionale delle Ricerche and Bulzoni Editore, 1993), I, pp. 209–15.

Ceccucci, Piero (ed.), *Viaggio intorno al convento di Mafra: Dal 'Memoriale del Convento' di José Saramago alla 'Blimunda' di Azio Corghi. Atti del Seminario Italo-Portoghese. Milano, 17–18 Maggio 1990* (Milan: Guerini Studio, 1991).

Costa, Horácio, 'A Construcção da Personagem de Ficção em Saramago: da *Terra do Pecado* ao *Memorial do Convento*', in Seixo (ed.), pp. 205–17; reprinted in English in Klobucka (ed.), pp. 33–48.

Costa, Horácio, *José Saramago: O Período Formativo* (Lisbon: Caminho, 1997).

Daniel, Mary L., 'Symbolism and synchronicity: José Saramago's *Jangada de Pedra*', in *Hispania*, Vol. 74 (September 1991), 536–41.

Fernandes, Ceres Costa, *O Narrador Plural na Obra de José Saramago* (São Luís, Maranhão: Universidade Federal do Maranhão, 1990).

Ferreira, Ana Paula, 'Cruising Gender in the 80s (from *Levantado do Chão* to *The History of the Siege of Lisbon*)', in Klobucka (ed.), pp. 221–38.

Filho, Linhares, 'Uma leitura de *Memorial do Convento*', in Beatriz Berrini (ed.), *José Saramago: Uma Homenagem* (São Paulo: EDUC, 1999), 169–91.

Frier, David G., 'Agouros e Oportunidades: *A Jangada de Pedra* de José Saramago e o País Desconhecido', in T. F. Earle (ed.), *Actas do Quinto Congresso da Associação Internacional de Lusitanistas (Universidade de Oxford, 1 a 8 de Setembro de 1996)*, 3 vols (Oxford and Coimbra: Associação Internacional de Lusitanistas, 1998), II, pp. 713–20.

Frier, David G., 'Ascent and Consent: Hierarchy and Popular Emancipation in the Novels of José Saramago', *Bulletin of Hispanic Studies*, Vol. LXXI, 1 (January 1994), 125–38.

Frier, David G., '"In the Beginning Was the Word": Text and Meaning in Two Dramas by José Saramago', in *Portuguese Studies*, Vol. 14 (1998), 215–26.

Frier, David G., 'José Saramago's Stone Boat: Celtic Analogues and Popular Mythology', in *Portuguese Studies*, Vol. XV (1999), 194–206.

Frier, David G., 'José Saramago's *O Evangelho Segundo Jesus Cristo*: Outline of a Newer Testament', in *Modern Language Review*, Vol. 100, 2 (April 2005), 367–82.

Frier, David G., 'Padre Bartolomeu Lourenço de Gusmão: Inspiration for *Memorial do Convento*?', in *Romance Quarterly*, Vol. 50, 1 (Winter 2003), 56–68.

Frier, David G., 'Righting Wrongs, Re-Writing Meaning and Reclaiming the City in Saramago's *Blindness* and *All the Names*', in Klobucka (ed.), pp. 97–122.

Frier, David G., 'Viagem Para as Ilhas do Sul: Uma Leitura de *A Caverna* de José Saramago', in *Veredas: Revista da Associação Internacional de Lusitanistas*, 5 (2003), 41–53.

Gomes, Cordeiro Renato, 'A Alquímia do Sangue e do Resgate em *Levantado do Chão*, de José Saramago', in *Estudos Portugueses e Africanos* (Campinas), Vol. 13 (January–June 1989), 19–27.

Grossegesse, Orlando, 'Das "Deutsche" und das "Europäische" im Werk von José Saramago', in Marília dos Santos Lopes, Ulrich Knefelkamp and Peter Hanenberg (eds), *Portugal und Deutschland auf dem Weg nach Europa* (Pfaffenweiler: Centaurus–Verlagsgesellschaft, 1995), pp. 221–31.

Grossegesse, Orlando, 'José Saramago: *O Evangelho Segundo Jesus Cristo* (1991)', in Rainer Hess (ed.), *Portugiesische Romane der Gegenwart: Neue Interpretationen* (Frankfurt-am-Main: TFM–Domus Editoria Europaea, 1993), pp. 123–39.

Grossegesse, Orlando, 'Journey to the Iberian God: Antonio Machado revisited by Saramago', in Klobucka (ed.), pp. 167–84.

Grossegesse, Orlando, 'José Saramago, *Memorial do Convento*', in Rainer Hess (ed.), *Portugiesische Romane der Gegenwart* (Frankfurt-am-Main: Vervuert, 1992), pp. 137–50.

Grossegesse, Orlando, 'Messianismo Telúrico em *Levantado do Chão* de José Saramago', in A. M. Brito, Isabel Pires de Lima *et al.* (eds), *'Sentido Que a Vida Faz' – Estudos Para Óscar Lopes* (Oporto: Campo das Letras, 1997), pp. 207–15.

Grossegesse, Orlando, *Saramago Lesen: Werk, Leben, Bibliographie* (Berlin: Edition Tranvía, 1999).

Huici, Adrián, 'Perdidos en el laberinto: el camino del héroe en *Todos los nombres*', in Seixo (ed.), pp. 453–62.

Júlio, Maria Joaquina Nobre, '*Memorial do Convento' de José Saramago: Subsídios para uma Leitura* (Lisbon: Editora Replicação, Ltda., 1999).

Klobucka, Anna (ed.), *Portuguese Literary and Cultural Studies,* 6 (*On Saramago*) (Spring 2001).

Lanciani, Giulia (ed.), *José Saramago: Il Bagaglio dello Scrittore* (Rome: Bulzoni Editore, 1996).

Lepecki, Maria Lúcia, 'José Saramago: *Levantado do Chão*', in *Sobre-impressões: Estudos de Literatura Portuguesa e Africana* (Lisbon: Caminho, 1988), pp. 83–112.

Letizia, Marie-Eve, 'O lugar da mulher dentro do espaço e o processo da sua conscientização através da narrativa *Levantado do Chão* de José Saramago', in *Taíra,* 3 (1991), 157–76.

Lima, Mirella Márcia Longo Vieira, 'Notas sobre José Saramago e sua máquina de fazer voar', in *Estudos Portugueses e Africanos,* 16 (July–December 1990), 39–56.

Lopes, Óscar, '*Memorial do Convento*', in *Os Sinais e os Sentidos – Literatura Portuguesa no Século XX,* pp. 201–8.

Losada, Basilio, 'Figuras de mujer: presencias femininas en la narrativa de José Saramago', in *Quimera,* 150 (September 1996), 36–7.

Lourenço, António Apolinário, 'José Saramago, A Falácia do Romance Histórico', in *Jornal de Letras* (26 February 1990), p. 10.

Lourenço, António Apolinário, 'História, ficção e ideologia: representação ideológica e pluridiscursividade em *Memorial do Convento*', in *Vértice* (2nd series), 42 (September 1991), 69–78.

MacNab, Gregory, 'A interface história-intervenção em três romances de José Saramago', in *Revista de Letras* (Curitiba), Vol. 38 (1989), 134–42.

Madruga, Conceição, *A Paixão Segundo José Saramago* (Oporto: Campo das Letras, 1998).

Maia, Armandina, 'Stregoneria e Inquisizione nel *Memorial*: una Storia al Femminile', in Ceccucci (ed.), pp. 53–63.

Moniz, António, *Para uma Leitura de 'Memorial do Convento' de José Saramago: uma Proposta de Leitura Crítico-Didáctica* (Lisbon: Editorial Presença, 1995).

Nunes, Ângela Pereira, *Vergangenheitsbewältigung im Interkulturellen Transfer* (Frankfurt-am-Main: Peter Lang, 2003).

Oliveira Filho, Odil José de, *Carnaval no Convento: Intertextualidade e Paródia em José Saramago* (São Paulo: Editora UNESP, 1993).

Ornelas, José N., '*A Jangada de Pedra* de José Saramago: A auto-reflexão e a consciencialização do processo de produção literária', in *Literatura de Vanguardia Luso-brasileira*, 4 (1989), 10–22.

Ornelas, José, 'Resistência, Espaço e Utopia em *Memorial do Convento* de José Saramago', in *Discursos: Estudos de Língua e Cultura Portuguesa*, 13 (October 1996), 115–33.

Parra Bañón, José Joaquín, *Pensamento Arquitectónico na Obra de José Saramago*, translated by Margarita Correia (Lisbon: Editorial Caminho, 2004).

Picchio, Luciana Stegagno, 'El discurso oral de José Saramago: un estilo como ideología', in *Espacio Escrito/ Espaço Escrito*, 9–10 (Winter 1993–4), 135–40.

Presedo, Elvira S. 'O romance de intervençom nas literaturas portuguesa e galega actuais: a propósito de *Memorial do Convento*, de José Saramago', in *Vértice*, Vol. XLIV, 461 (July–August 1984), 32–43.

Presedo, Elvira Souto, 'Saramago e o Mito', in *Lenguaje y Textos*, 1 (1991), 85–90.

Ramos, Ana Maria, *'Memorial do Convento' – da Leitura à Análise* (Lisbon: Asa, 1999).

Real, Miguel, *Narração, Maravilhoso, Trágico e Sagrado em 'Memorial do Convento' de José Saramago* (Lisbon: Caminho, 1995).

Rebelo, Luís de Sousa, 'A Consciência da História na Ficção de José Saramago', in *Vértice* (2nd series), 52 (January–February 1993), 29–38.

Reis, Carlos, '*Memorial do Convento* ou a Emergência da História', in *Revista Crítica de Ciências Sociais*, 18–20 (February 1986), 91–103.

Rouanet, Maria Helena, '"Em pedaços de encaixar": Leitura de *Memorial do Convento* de José Saramago', in *Colóquio: Letras*, 101 (January–February 1988), 55–63.

Sabine, Mark J., 'Form and Ideology in the Novels of José Saramago' (unpublished Ph.D. thesis, University of Manchester, 2001).

Sans, Ana Monner, 'De aventuras, azares, amores y taumaturgías: la subversión genérica como estrategia narrativa en *Todos los nombres*', in Seixo (ed.), pp. 441–52.

Sapega, Ellen W., 'Memória pública e discurso oficial: visões da época salazarista na obra de Irene Lisboa, José Saramago e Mário Cláudio', in *Discursos: Estudos de Língua e Cultura Portuguesa*, 13 (October 1996), 99–114.

Schor, Andreas, *José Saramago: Schreiben Gegen Mythen* (Bern: Peter Lang, 1997).

Seixo, Maria Alzira, 'Os espelhos virados para dentro: configurações narrativas do espaço e do imaginário em *Ensaio sobre a Cegueira*', in Lanciani (ed.), pp. 191–210.

Seixo, Maria Alzira (ed.), *José Saramago: O Ano de 1998* (special number of *Colóquio: Letras*), Nos 151–2 (January–June 1999).

Silva, Teresa Cristina Cerdeira da, *O Avesso do Bordado* (Lisbon: Editorial Caminho, 2000).

Silva, Teresa Cristina Cerdeira da, 'Do Labirinto Textual ou da Escrita como Lugar da Memória', in Seixo (ed.), pp. 249–66; reprinted (in English) in Klobucka (ed.), pp. 49–72.

Silva, Teresa Cristina Cerdeira da, *José Saramago. Entre a História e a Ficção: uma Saga de Portugueses* (Lisbon: Publicações Dom Quixote, 1989).

Silva, Teresa Cristina Cerdeira da, 'O *Memorial do Convento* ou a Repressão da Utopia', in Roberto Reis (ed.), *Towards Socio-criticism. Selected Proceedings of the Conference on Luso-Brazilian Literatures: A Socio-critical Approach* (Tempe, Arizona: Center for Latin-American Studies, 1991), pp. 115–24.

Silva, Teresa Cristina Cerdeira da, 'Mulheres e Revolução: A Cultura Marialva Posta em Questão', in *O Avesso do Bordado*, pp. 213–24.

Silva, Teresa Cristina Cerdeira da, 'No Paraíso da Memória, Um Outro Valor da Terra se Alevanta', in *O Avesso do Bordado*, pp. 260–9.

Silva, Teresa Cristina Cerdeira da, 'Saramago e Redol: referência e reverência', in Lanciani (ed.), pp. 37–47.

Tesser, Carmen Chaves (ed.), 'A Tribute to José Saramago, 1998 Nobel Literature Laureate', in *Hispania*, Vol. 82 (March 1999), 1–28.

Venâncio, Fernando, '*Memorial do Convento*: um ano de crítica', in Lanciani (ed.), pp. 109–19.

Viçoso, Vítor, '*Levantado do Chão* e o Romance Neo-realista', in Seixo (ed.), pp. 239–48.

Winder, Robert, 'Adventures in humility', in *The Independent* (Weekend) (17 July 1993), p. 28.

4. General and Miscellaneous

Andrade, Carlos Drummond de, *Antologia Poética*, thirteenth edition (Rio de Janeiro: Livraria José Olympio Editora, 1979).

Bakhtin, Mikhail, *Problems of Dostoevsky's Poetics*, edited and translated by Caryl Emerson, with an introduction by Wayne C. Booth (Eighth Printing, Minneapolis: University of Minnesota Press, 1999).

Belard, Francisco, 'Meio Século de Livros', in *Expresso Revista* (17 October 1998), pp. 68–71.

Birmingham, David, *A Concise History of Portugal*, second edition (Cambridge: Cambridge University Press, 2003).

Borges, Jorge Luis, *Ficciones* (Barcelona: Editorial Planeta, S.A., 1971).

Camões, Luís de, *Os Lusíadas*, edited by Emanuel Paulo Ramos (Oporto: Porto Editora, n/d).

Camões, Luís de, *The Lusiads*, translated by Landeg White (Oxford: Oxford University Press, 1997).

Camões, Luís de, *Versos e Alguma Prosa de Luís de Camões*, edited by Eugénio de Andrade (Lisbon: Fundação Calouste Gulbenkian, in collaboration with Moraes Editores, 1977).

Carey, John, *The Intellectuals and the Masses: Pride and Prejudice among the Literary Intelligentsia 1880–1939* (London: Faber and Faber, 1992).

Carpentier, Alejo, *Baroque Concerto*, translated by Asa Zatz (London: André Deutsch Limited, 1998).

Carpentier, Alejo, *Concierto Barroco*, in *Obras Completas de Alejo Carpentier*, Vol. 4 (México, DF: Siglo Veintiuno Editores, SA, 1983), pp. 145–213.

Cervantes Saavedra, Miguel de, *Don Quijote de la Mancha*, 2 vols (Barcelona: Editorial Juventud, 1955).

Cirlot, J. E., *A Dictionary of Symbols*, translated from the Spanish by Jack Sage, with a foreword by Herbert Read (London: Routledge and Kegan Paul, 1962).

Eagleton, Terry, *Ideology: an Introduction* (London: Verso, 1991).

Forster, E. M., *Aspects of the Novel* (New York: Harcourt Brace, 1927).

Galhoz, Maria Aliete (ed.), *Fernando Pessoa* (Lisbon: Editorial Presença, 1985).

Garrett, Almeida, *Frei Luís de Sousa* (Mem Martins: Publicações Europa-América, 1971).

Gramsci, Antonio, *Selections from the Prison Notebooks of Antonio Gramsci*, edited and translated by Quintin Hoare and Geoffrey Nowell Smith (New York: International Publishers, 1987).

Griffiths, Richard, 'Fascist or Conservative? Portugal, Spain and the French connection', in *Portuguese Studies*, Vol. 14 (1998), 138–51.

The Holy Bible, Authorized (King James) version (Cleveland, OH: The World Publishing Company, n.d.).

Homer, *The Odyssey*, translated by E. V. Rieu (London: Methuen, 1952).

Kaufman, Helena and Anna Klobucka (eds), *After the Revolution: Twenty Years of Portuguese Literature, 1974–1994* (Lewisburg: Bucknell University Press and London: Associated University Presses).

Lisboa, M. M., 'You Can't Go Home Again', in T. F. Earle and Nigel Griffin (eds), *Portuguese, Brazilian, and African Studies: Studies Presented to Clive Willis on his Retirement* (Warminster: Aris & Phillips, 1995), pp. 345–57.

Lorca, Federico García, *Poema del cante jondo y Romancero gitano*, edited by Allen Josephs y Juan Caballero, second edition (Madrid: Cátedra, 1978).

Lourenço, Eduardo, *O Labirinto da Saudade*, fourth edition (Lisbon: Dom Quixote, 1991).

Machado, Antonio, *Campos de Castilla*, edited by José Luis Cano (Madrid: Ediciones Cátedra, 1974).

Nunes, João Paulo Avelãs, 'O conceito de "fascismo" na história recente de Portugal', in *Vértice* (2nd series), 52 (January–February 1993), 53–65.

Ovid, *The Metamorphoses* (Books V–VIII), edited with translation and notes by D. E. Hill (Warminster: Aris and Phillips, Ltd, 1992).

Owen, Hilary, *Portuguese Women's Writing, 1972 to 1986: Reincarnations of a Revolution* (Lewiston, N.Y.: Edwin Mellen Press, 2000).

Pessoa, Fernando, *Mensagem*, eleventh edition (Lisbon: Edições Ática, n/d).

Pessoa, Fernando, *Poesias Inéditas (1930–1935)* (Lisbon: Edições Ática, 1967).

Pessoa, Fernando, *O Rosto e as Máscaras*, edited by David Mourão-Ferreira, second edition (Lisbon: Edições Ática, n/d).

Pessoa, Fernando, *Selected Poems*, bilingual edition with translations by Peter Rickard (Edinburgh: Edinburgh University Press, 1971).

Pires, José Cardoso, *Jogos de Azar*, fifth edition (Lisbon: Edições *O Jornal*, 1985).

Queirós, Eça de, *Os Maias*, fixação do texto e notas de Helena Cidade Moura (Lisbon: Livros do Brasil, n/d).

Raby, D. L., *Fascism and Resistance in Portugal: Communists, Liberals and Military Dissidents in the Opposition to Salazar, 1941–1974* (Manchester: Manchester University Press, 1988).

Ransome, Paul, *Antonio Gramsci: A New Introduction* (Hemel Hempstead: Harvester Wheatsheaf, 1992).

Ribeiro, Bernardim, *Menina e Moça* (Lisbon: Editorial Verbo, 1972).

Russell-Wood, A. J. R., *A World on the Move: the Portuguese in Africa, Asia, and America, 1415–1808* (New York: St Martin's Press, 1993).

Salazar, Dr António Oliveira de, *Doctrine and Action: Internal and Foreign Policy of the New Portugal, 1928–1939*, translated by Robert Edgar Broughton (London: Faber and Faber Limited, 1939).

Saraiva, Arnaldo and Lopes, Óscar, *História de Literatura Portuguesa,* sixth edition (Oporto: Porto Editora, 1969).

Sena, Jorge de, *O Físico Prodigioso*, second edition (Lisbon: Edições 70, 1979).

Serrão, Joaquim, *História de Portugal: A Restauração e a Monarquia Absoluta (1640–1750)*, second edition (Lisbon: Verbo, 1982).

Serrão, Joel (ed.), *Dicionário de História de Portugal*, 6 vols (Oporto: Iniciativas Editoriais, 1979).

Silva, Lígia, '(Re)telling History: Lídia Jorge's *O Dia dos Prodígios*', in Claudia Pazos-Alonso (ed.), *Portuguese Literary and Cultural Studies*, 2 (*Lídia Jorge: In Other Words/ Por Outras Palavras*) (Spring 1999), pp. 19–32.

Strabo, *España y los españoles hace dos mil años, según la geografía de Strábon*, edited by Antonio García y Bellido (Madrid: Espasa-Calpe, SA, 1945).

Thompson, Stith, *Motif-Index of Folk-Literature: a Classification of Narrative Elements in Folktales, Ballads, Myths, Fables, Mediaeval Romances, Exempla, Fabliaux, Jest-Books and Local Legends*, 6 vols, revised and enlarged edition (Copenhagen: Rosenkilde and Bagger, 1955–8).

Unamuno, Miguel de, *Del sentimiento trágico de la vida en los hombres y en los pueblos* (Madrid: Espasa-Calpe, SA, 1982).

Unamuno, Miguel de, *Por tierras de Portugal y de España,* third edition (Buenos Aires: Espasa-Calpe Argentina, SA, 1946).

Verde, Cesário, *Obra Completa de Cesário Verde,* edited by Joel Serrão, third edition (Lisbon: Portugália, n/d).

Wilhelm, Balthasar, *Die Anfänge der Luftfahrt: Lana-Gusmão* (Hamm in Westfalen: Breer & Thiemann, 1909).

Zenith, Richard, *Fernando Pessoa & Co.: Selected Poems by Fernando Pessoa* (New York: Grove Press, 1998).

NOTES

1 This second edition incorporates also the texts from the work *As Opiniões Que o 'DL' Teve,* which was originally published under separate cover in 1974.

Index

A Caverna SEE *Caverna*
A Jangada de Pedra SEE *Jangada*
Alentejo region 3–4
Ano
  politics, concern with 31
  spirit of rebellion 112
  writing style 6–7
As Intermitências da Morte SEE *Intermitências*
Brazil
  Landless Peasant Movement 9
Camões 18–19
Caverna
  negative flight 151
  politics, concern with 31–32
Ceguira
  politics, concern with 31
  spirit of rebellion 112
Centripetal and centrifugal forces 111–174
Chiapas 9
Cuba
  capital punishment 10
Death 175–208
  association of eroticism with 181–182
  atheism, and 197–197
  granting of conscience to 180
  moth, as 181–183
  personalized system 178
  reality of 175
  Ricardo Reis, and 183–196
    accommodation 186
    association of *eros* with *thanatos* 190–191
    children, prospect of birth 193
    choices, time for 195
    confused state of mind 191–192
    distaste for world 188
    existential failure towards self 196
    historical events, and 188
    intellectual's sense of superiority to masses 189
    lack of fulfilment in life 192
    lower classes, and 193–194
    malaise of early twentieth-century intellectual 185
    political failure towards own country 196
    popular culture, and 187
    Portuguese sailors, and 192
    relationship 191
    serenity, maintenance of 197
    stability and passivity 184
    statues, and 184
    suffering of 187–188
    water analogy, and 194–195
Dictatorship
  realities of 17
  ultimate injustice 175–208

Ensaio sobre a Cegueira SEE *Cegueira*
Ensaio sobre a Lucidez SEE *Lucidez*
Evangelho
challenging established hierarchies 114
erasure of self 114–115
God, nature of 127
resistance to authority 113
Jesus 114, 115
Jesus' ultimate conflict with God 125–126
pessimistic ending 116
Temple 123–124, 125, 127
Female characters 155
catalysts for change, as 161–164
fertility, presentation of 165
oppression of 161–162
romanticized idealization 165–166
Gramsci, Antonio
analysis of functioning of cultural hegemony 159–160
conception of Revolution 155
contract between organic and traditional intellectuals 155
cultural hegemony 155
Gramscian-based interpretation of Saramango's work 156
intellectuals, on 156–157, 158
'organic intellectual' 157
specialization, on 158
transformation of Portugal, and 152–166
valorization of all forms of experience 158–159
História do Cerco de Lisboa
Drummond de Andrade 119–120
erasure of self 114–115
Fernando Pessoa 116–117
flight of seagulls 118–119
historical accuracy 132
link of historical motif to personal concerns 131
Lisbon, seizure of 122
Marxist reality 32
mystery of writing 117
north and south winds 121
resistance to authority 113
revolutionary potential of mass organisations 129
rewriting of Portuguese history 128
siege of Lisbon 114
truth, conceptions of 127–128
mutual benefit from engagement 198–199
Ideological commitment 31–32
Intermitências
association of eroticism with death 181–182
black comedy 177–178
circular structure 176
conversations with death 178–179
death as type of moth 181–183
death, question of 175–176
granting of conscience to death 180–181
incompleteness 180
irrelevance of traditional pillars of society 177
'personalized' system of death 178
society without death 177
Israel 9
criticism of 9
Jangada
allusions to Portugal's maritime past 147
breach in Pyrenees 142
collision with Azores 141
continuity, spirit of 137
dog Constante/Ardent 146
European identity 140

exploration of national history 138
focus on peripheral regions of Portugal and Spain 140
intellectual maze 144
labyrinth, image of 144
Marxist reading 32
mass pregnancy 149
natural expression of people 150
negative flight 151
personal relationships 138–139
political controversy, and 21
scepticism 148–150
Trojan War 145
uncertainty in interpretation of events 146–147
utopian nature of 139
Levantado do Chão 3
abuse of powers 50
alienation 52–68
animal imagery 64–68
Antonio Mau-Tempo 44–48
ants as witnesses to torture 51–52
ants, significance of 64–65
awareness of people's own circumstances 49
brutality, forms of 50
'cabeca' 47
Christ's passion, allusions to 46
Church, role of 43
comically rhyming names 79
contract between rich and poor 32
decline of family 44–48
differences of class, power and privilege 43
disregard for natural cycles 63
dogs, significance of 65–66
dominant social order 81
Domingos 44–48
emphasis on material resources 42–43
enforcement of authority 48–52
experimental techniques 90
exploration, notion of 83–84
freedom, concept of 61–62
functioning of patterns of alienation 58–59
future acts of defiance 47–48
hierarchies of power 68–77
illusion of permanence 78–90
industrialization 85
João 44–48
landowners, interests of 78
Lisbon, nature of 61
machismo 45–46
military virtues 86–87
names of landowners 79
natural processes 52–68
path to 1974 Revolution 86
permanence of land 80
policy of keeping workers ignorant 78–79
potential for change 78–90
potential of Portuguese people 88–89
prison conditions 51
privileged classes, representation of 74
references to historical events 59–60
reflection of hierarchies of power 76–77
religious panacea 84–85
renewal of Revolution 89–90
resistance of workers 63–64
Revolution of 1974 45
ridicule of negative figures 68
Russian Revolution 60
sea, importance of 81–83
social and economic relations 32–43
social progress 76
solidarity, importance of 77
spitefulness of landowners 47
style 3

suppression of resistance 48–52
underprivileged, representation of 74–76
unseen forces 68
victory of ordinary Portuguese men or women 49
workers acting against own interests 62
workers as part of production process 62–63

Literary, political and cultural context of Saramago's novels 16–24
democracy, and 22
dictatorship, and 19–20
hope, note of 24

Lourenço, Eduardo
totalitarianism, on 21–22

Love 175–208
centrality of 197
mutual benefit 198
ultimate injustice 175–208

Lucidez
politics, concern with 31–32

Manual
importance of 17–18

Marxism
relevance of 134
usefulness of 136

Marxist readings 32

Memorial do Convento 31–109
alienated labour 53
alienation 52–68
border between Iberian states 87
Church as institution 42
Church, position of 56
Church, role of 40–41
contrast between rich and poor 32
Crown, extravagance of 34–35
decorative elements of Church 205–206
'decrowning' of the King 37
division between ruling classes and oppressed 87–88
enforcement of authority 48–52
exploitation of workers 53
expressive potential of *Passarola* 54–55
female Don Quixote 153–154, 164
força bruta 33
Francisco Margues, death of 55–56
hierarchies of power 68–77
illusion of permanence 78–90
João Elvas 57–58
Julião Mau-Tempo 56–57
keeping world up in orbit 111
King and queen, role of 70–71
life and death 204–250
Lisbon, impressions of 54
manipulation of events for effect 42
megalomania of King 40
natural processes 52–68
Pasarola 137
potential for change 78–90
potential of Portuguese people 88–89
princess, status of 71–73
Rabelaisian tone 36
ridicule of negative figures 68
rounded and flat figures 73
sacrifices required of ordinary people 39
social and economic relations 32–43
suppression of resistance 48–52
wealth of Crown 38–39

Neo-Realist movement 16–17
unsuitability of 17–18

New State 15, 16

Nobel Prize
award of 1

O Ano da Morte de Ricardo Reis SEE *Ano*

O Evangelho Segundo Jesus Cristo SEE *Evangelho*
Objecto Quase
  link between love and establishing appropriate social order 131–132
Os Lusíadas 18–19
Pessoa, Fernando
  Mensagem 20
  Jogos de Azar 133–134
Police for Vigilance and Defence of the State 15
Politics 9–11
Pontiero, Giovanni
  beauty of Saramago's work, on 207
Portuguese Communist party 9–10
Portuguese cultural history
  Revolution of 1974, and 135
Portuguese history and tradition 11–16
  'civilizing' mission overseas 14
  Empire, and 12–13
  European expansion in fifteenth and sixteenth centuries 12
  maritime heritage 13–14
  pluralist vision of modern society 14–15
Privilege and exclusion 31–109
Revolution of the Carnations 11, 15
Ricardo Reis
  death, and SEE Death
Roman Catholic Church
  grim depiction of 16–17
  influence of 9, 11
Salazar regime 14, 15
Saramago, José
  dictatorship, and 1
  dismissal of 3
  early life 1–2
  early writing 2
  European single currency, on 22
  journalism 2
  literary prizes awarded to 1
  Nobel Laureate 1–9
  oral narrator, as 7–8
  poetry 2
  rustic language 5–6
  writing style 3–9
Sebastianism 13
Serra, João Domingos
  letter from 5–6
Soviet Union 10–11
  criticism of 10
Terra do Pecado 2
Theme-rheme sentence construction 7
Third Way
  denunciation of 135–136
Todos os Nomes
  authentic existence, question of 202–203
  death, representation of 203–204
  illusion of security 201–202
  responsibility for definition of self 202
  seeing through a glass darkly 200–201
  spiritual ennoblement of male 199–200
Translation
  effect 7–8
Viagem a Portugal
  travel, metaphor of 23